Blueprints *for* Awakening

Blueprints for Awakening

Published by Open Sky Press Ltd.
483 Green Lanes, London N13 4BS
office@openskypress.com

First edition

ISBN 978-0-9555730-4-0

Cover design by Devi.
Photographs from Sri Ramana Maharshi Ashram: cover, front flap.
All other photographs from Open Sky House archive.

Printed in Hong Kong

OPEN SKY PRESS
www.openskypress.com

Acknowledgements

I owe an enormous debt of gratitude to my two direct Masters, Osho and H.W.L. Poonja. Without my twenty years sitting at their feet, this book could not exist. Sri Ramana Maharshi came into my life quietly and invisibly, gradually becoming my main inspiration and guide.

My gratitude also goes to all the exceptional Masters who gave their time to meet me and later to proof read their *Blueprints for Awakening* interview. Their availability to meet so many people as part of the annual Arunachala Pilgrimage Retreat gave the opportunity to collect more footage for the film, *Blueprints for Awakening – Wisdom of the Masters*, and the series of sixteen films, *Blueprints for Awakening – Meeting the Master*, the companion films to this book.

An interview is a spontaneous and unique conversation. My thanks to Kali Devi for her sensitive editing of the interview transcripts, accurately produced by Aruna and Meenakshi from the original recordings. To Kali Devi and Jyoti for patiently proof reading the manuscript over and over again! To Mahima and Saraswati who, while translating this book into German, added the final touches.

I should like to thank Sri V.S. Ramanan, the president of Sri Ramana Ashram, for permission to use photographs of Sri Ramana Maharshi and the text from *Who Am I?* Also Kali Devi, Jyoti and Darshana who have taken the majority of the photos that have not been taken from the films as stills. Swamini Pramananda, who, besides being one of the Masters interviewed for the book, gave her expert advice on compiling the *Sanskrit* glossary. Swami Suddhananda stepped in at the last minute and produced a foreword which greatly adds background to the teachings revealed in the interviews. Thank you.

Thanks go to Arjuna for creating the Video Website, allowing so many short videos extracts from the interviews to be available, to Devi and Parvati for the graphic design of the numerous art pages and to Shivananda for his fine graphic advice and support with the cover design.

Thank you to Darshana for her great work on *Blueprints for Awakening – Wisdom of the Masters*, the book's companion film, and the series of sixteen films, *Blueprints for Awakening – Meeting the Master*. In addition, for her translation and proof reading skills and for always being ready to give aesthetic advice.

My heartfelt thanks to all the residents of the Open Sky House Community for giving such loving, energetic support, creating a space for all those working actively on the book and films, and to Shanti Devi for feeding our team of eight people during our two months on the beach polishing and finishing up the book.

Finally my deep thanks and appreciation to Parvati and Kali Devi, the directors of Open Sky Press, for their painstakingly careful work and consistent support in every facet of this project. Parvati formatted the book and supervised our printer in a style that has produced such a fine quality. She has truly been invaluable.

Premananda 2008

Bhagavan Sri

Ramana Maharshi

I dedicate this book to
Bhagavan Sri Ramana Maharshi,
the sage of Arunachala. He came into my life
quietly, imperceptibly, through a photograph
twenty years ago, and has become a central
inspiration in my life.

Thank you for the exemplary life you led
and for the simplicity and clarity with which
you guide us. The question, 'Who am I?' has
provided a golden key to all who wish to know
their essential nature.

Interview Questions

These questions are designed to unfold and explain the teachings of Bhagavan Sri Ramana Maharshi, as set out in his original booklets *Who Am I?** and *Self-Enquiry*. I believe these teachings reflect the ancient Indian wisdom.

1. Sri Ramana proposed the fundamental question, '**Who am I?**'* Who are you?
2. Many Western seekers come to India looking for enlightenment as if it is an experience. What is enlightenment?
3. Are there any qualifications for enlightenment? Is *sadhana* (spiritual practice) necessary? If yes, what form do you advise?
4. Sri Ramana said that Self-enquiry is the most direct route to realising the Self. What do you say about Self-enquiry? How to conduct Self-enquiry?
5. When Sri Ramana was asked, '**When will the realisation of the Self be gained?**' he replied, '**When the world which is what-is-seen has been removed, there will be realisation of the Self which is the seer.**'* What is the true understanding of the world? How to remove the world?
6. It has been suggested that the mind must be destroyed for liberation to occur. Do you have a mind? Sri Ramana used the term *manonasha* to describe the state of liberation, meaning destroyed mind. How to destroy the mind?
7. What about *vasanas*, the tendencies of the mind? Must these be removed before Self-realisation can become permanent? Is it enough to achieve a *sattvic* (calm and peaceful) state of mind and to know one's *vasanas* so that they no longer bind? How to remove the *vasanas*?
8. At the end of his book, *Self-Enquiry*, Sri Ramana says, '**He who is thus endowed with a mind that has become subtle, and who has the experience of the Self is called a *jivanmukta*.**' Is this the state that can be called Self-realised?

   He goes on, '**And when one is immersed in the ocean of bliss and has become one with it without any differentiated existence, one is called a *videhamukta*. It is the state of *videhamukti* that is referred to as the transcendent *turiya* (state). This is the final goal.**' Is this the state that can be called enlightenment?
9. It appears essential to meet a *guru* and stay with that *guru*. Who is the *guru*? What is the *guru's* role? How to recognise a true *guru*?
10. Sri Ramana's devotees had tremendous devotion to him, and he to Arunachala. Please say something about *bhakti*, devotion, in the pursuit of awakening.
11. Seekers often have curious ideas about the enlightened state. Please describe your typical day and how you perceive the world.
12. You have given us a profound discourse on awakening. When you meet someone with a passion for awakening, what would your short advice be?

* Original text *Who Am I?* at the end of this book.

Contents

Introduction

Blueprints for Awakening is for everyone who has an inner passion to know who they are and what they are doing here as a human being. It is for all who ask the question 'Who am I?' and for those who are looking for guidance on the teaching of Bhagavan Sri Ramana Maharshi to 'be as you are'. It covers the main issues that arise on a spiritual seeker's journey to awakening to their essential nature, to Truth. It delves into the fascinating depths of the Indian spiritual tradition, and, in that sense, it follows in the footsteps of the famous book by Paul Brunton, *A Search in Secret India*.

Twelve questions have been asked of sixteen Indian Masters who have crossed my path in the last five years. I did not approach them as a seeker, but rather as a teacher wishing to clarify my own understanding and to offer a platform for each Master to give his or her blueprint to be put out into the world, a world in great need, and, hopefully, a world where these teachings will find a receptive audience. The questions are referenced to Sri Ramana Maharshi's teachings, even though the intention is for each Master to express his or her own teaching blueprint. Naturally, there is no actual blueprint as each person's spiritual journey is unique.

My own Master was Papaji, who met his Master, Sri Ramana Maharshi, in the 1940s. Sri Ramana came into my life through an original Welling portrait that I found in a pile of debris in a room I had rented in the years before I met Papaji. During my five years with Papaji he greeted a photograph of Sri Ramana every morning, and on occasion said that he spoke as a channel for him. In the last ten years many Western *Advaita* teachers have begun teaching in the world. Sri Ramana Maharshi is the spiritual inspiration for most of them.

During the last years of Sri Ramana's life, a small number of Westerners made it to his *ashram*, most attracted by Paul Brunton's book:

> *There are moments when I feel this power of his so greatly that I know that he has only to issue the most disturbing command and I will readily obey it. But the Maharshi is the last person in the world to place his followers in the chain of servile obedience, and allows everyone the utmost freedom of action. In this respect he is quite refreshingly different from most of the teachers and* yogis *I have met in India.*

Maurice Frydman, the editor of *I am That*, the teachings of Nisargadatta Maharaj, visited Sri Ramana in 1943. He was clearly impressed:

> *It was the immense privilege of the writer to meet a few gigantic spiritual men, but nobody ever produced on him a deeper impression than Ramana Maharshi. In him the sublime majesty of the divine life stood and moved in all simplicity. The ultimate had revealed itself as the immediate, and the undreamt had become the actual.*

The idea for this book, and particularly the films, came to me in 1993, while living in Lucknow, North India, in the *sangha* (spiritual community) of my Master, Papaji. One day I received an inner message or vision telling me to go and catch the great Indian Masters on film before they were lost to the world. I was deeply touched, but had no idea how to carry out such a task. Ten years later, after five years living in Australia, I was on my way to Europe. In between I took a personal retreat of one year in southern India, in Tiruvannamalai, at the holy mountain, Arunachala.

During my stay I made a series of interviews with David Godman, the well-known editor of Sri Ramana Maharshi's teachings published as *Be As You Are*, and author of other important books on Indian *gurus*. The interviews were about the life, teachings and devotees of Bhagavan Sri Ramana Maharshi. These interviews will be published by Open Sky Press in 2008 as *Arunachala Shiva*. During our dialogues, David insisted that Ramana's greatness came from the fact that his mind had been destroyed (*manonasha*), and that he spoke from the Self, like a wireless. While being sympathetic to this notion I had doubts about whether it was possible to be alive and have a destroyed mind. This short excerpt from David Godman in *Arunachala Shiva* sparked my curiosity and was the seed from which this book grew. My question to him was:

> **You say that in realisation the mind is dead, but wouldn't such a person be a zombie?**
> *This is a misconception that many people have because they can't imagine how anyone can function, take decisions, speak, and so on, without a mind. You do all these things with your mind, or at least you think you do, so when you see a sage behaving normally in the world, you automatically assume that he too is coordinating all his activities through an entity called 'mind'. In his written works, Bhagavan uses the term* manonasha *to describe the state of liberation. It means, quite unequivocally, 'destroyed mind'.*

As this notion is also believed by many of the world's seekers, such as Buddhist monks searching for no-mind, I had the idea to approach different Masters and ask them what they thought about this issue. D.B. Gangolli sums up the response of most of the Masters:

> *The mind cannot exist apart from the Self. It is a projection. But at the same time it is a misconception, a false appearance. So there is no question of destruction of the mind. Many people, including Ramana Maharshi, talk about this* manonasha, *but it is not the correct word.* Manonigra *can be used.* Manonigra *means you give up the identification with the mind.*

This is supported by Swami Dayananda Saraswati:

> Manonasha *is the isolation and destruction of this I that alienates you from everything else. The mind is reduced to I, and that I alienates you from everything else. When they say 'no-mind', what do they mean? They mean 'thought-free mind'. A 'thought-free mind' is an empty mind.*

And by Ramesh Balsekar:

> *Mind is something which any person requires to live in this world. What the sages mean when they say the ego has to be destroyed – but for some reason don't bother to make clear – is that doership in the ego has to be destroyed.*

With this issue as a basic question, I met with sixteen Masters, several of them already well-known in the world, Hans Raj Maharaj, Ramesh Balsekar and Swami Dayananda Saraswati. Others are hardly known, Sri Brahmam and Ma Souris. Others, like Ganesan and Radha Ma, would be surprised to hear themselves referred to as Masters. Several run large *ashrams*, Swami Dayananda Saraswati, Swami Satchidananda and Swami Suddhananda. Thuli Baba and Sri Nannagaru choose to be available mainly for Indian seekers. Since the interviews, Ajja, Kiran, D.B. Gangolli and Ma Souris have left their bodies. It is lovely that there are three women, Ma Souris, Radha Ma and Swamini Pramananda. Several of the Masters have become dear friends who have graciously allowed me to introduce many people to them during my annual Arunachala Pilgrimage Retreat. Additional material gathered at these later meetings has been included with the original interviews.

The basic structure of each interview uses the same twelve questions (see Interview Questions in front of book). However, being with an Indian Master is very different from asking a professor to explain his teaching. In each interview there was the strong energy of the Master's presence and often he or she was surrounded by a large group of devotees. In the very first interviews, the questions were not yet firmly set. Later, questions were added and further questions were asked spontaneously to illuminate an answer, leading to many exceptions to the basic twelve-question structure.

The Master's presence was always felt to add an extra, vital dimension to the interview and I searched for a way to include this presence in the book. Hence you will find a DVD Sampler in the back of this book. It contains part of a Video Website, www.blueprintsforawakening.org, a set of Masters' Portraits and a trailer for *Blueprints for Awakening – Wisdom of the Masters*, the companion film of this book. This film includes selections from all sixteen interviews and sets out important aspects of the teachings presented in this book. A series of sixteen separate films, *Blueprints for Awakening – Meeting the Master*, showing each Master's complete interview as well as material filmed during subsequent visits, will also be available. This set of seventeen films and the Video Website create a unique archive for those wishing to taste the Indian spiritual tradition through the grace of these Masters.

Many of the Masters come from the ancient tradition of *Vedanta*, a metaphysical Indian philosophy derived from the *Upanishads*, and from *Advaita Vedanta*, a non-dual school of *Vedanta* philosophy, whose chief spokesman was *Adi Shankara*, teaching the Oneness of God, soul and the universe. The exceptions are Kiran and Samdarshi, whose Master was Osho; Swami Satchidananda, who served both Papa Ramdas and Mother Krishnabai; and Ramesh Balsekar, who was with Nisargadatta Maharaj but also had a strong connection with Sri Ramana Maharshi.

All the Masters, particularly the *Vedanta* Masters, Swami Dayananda Saraswati, D.B. Gangolli, Swamini Pramananda and Swami Suddhananda, use *Sanskrit* terms. *Sanskrit*, the ancient language of *Vedic* philosophy, with its unparalleled richness of expression, has been considered the language of the gods. You will find an English explanation with each *Sanskrit* word the first time it appears in each chapter. The comprehensive glossary gives a more detailed explanation of the italicised *Sanskrit* words.

While writing this introduction, I recognise the depth of the spiritual wisdom contained in this book, the films and the Video Website. It is a valuable archive and I am pleased that I have been able to manifest the original vision that came to me fifteen years ago. It was a timely call to action as four of the Masters have since left their bodies. This archive directly concerns Indian Masters, but, as Maharaj says, spirituality is One. With this understanding, I have sought out Western Masters and will publish their wisdom in a second volume in 2009. This is the ancient wisdom of humanity passed down through generations of Masters and their disciples.

Premananda 2008

Foreword
Swami Suddhananda

Writing about Bhagavan Sri Ramana Maharshi, or any great sage, is like celebrating the magnificent embodiment of the eternal, formless, absolute existence. They are such beautiful icons, where nature or God seems to have excelled its own excellence. When a majestic mountain range or a vast expanse of blue ocean can throw us back into ourselves without our knowledge, the great sages, with their living, their action, their speech and their every movement, can consciously take us to the same place.

One such sage in recent times was Bhagavan Sri Ramana Maharshi. As time passes, many great sages become legendary, almost to the point of becoming mythological, as the average man cannot even comprehend the possibility of the infinite wisdom they lived and loved as their own true nature. Slowly and steadily, Ramana Maharshi too shall be part of that legend, but at this moment in history he is still fresh in the minds of many as he was alive and well fifty-eight years ago, to be exact! There are still some people, children in those days, to whom Bhagavan appeared as a loving grandfather figure. They enjoyed the whole atmosphere around Sri Ramana without realising the mighty presence that he was, is and shall always be!

Though attempts have been made to present Sri Ramana as a very exclusive phenomenon, everything about him showed the possibility of every person understanding the Truth that he realised as a tender teenager. He was ever ordinary, commonplace, simple and innocent, which is a natural expression of an extra-ordinary yet commonplace existence! Whether in the caves, in the solitary confinement of the temple premises, in the *ashram*, in the kitchen, interacting with the cowherds, playing with children, playing with cow Laxmi, feeding the monkeys, or discoursing with very learned and orthodox minds or secular people, he was always himself – the unhurried, the ever restful, the quiet, overwhelming presence.

That is why the memories and memoirs are full of such lovingly tender human anecdotes where Sri Ramana never made any attempt to make himself exclusive or dismissed anything frivolously. Never was there an attempt on his part to erase any part of his life or to whitewash everything as pure and sacred. He was a child from a faraway village in Tamil Nadu, growing up in a town called Madurai, exposed to the timeless traditions of *sanatana dharma* (Hinduism) in the temple celebrations and in his loving family.

Curious to know about death, the innocent youngster puts himself into physical stillness, leading ultimately to a stillness within, where everything appears to subside, yet a Presence continues without any movement at the level of thought and the body. The incident had an unforgettable impact on the innocent youngster who held and maintained it. It was only later he found the description of that state in the lives and the writings of great saints.

The immediate family, and the great tradition which talks about renunciation, vision, realisation, wisdom, the sages and the exploits of gods in all names and forms, drew the youngster to Arunachala mountain in Tiruvannamalai. As they say, the rest is history. Spending days, months and years in solitude, he found the reflections of his understanding in the writings of many sages, gloriously described in rich Tamil and *Sanskrit* literature.

Later on, with the little formal education that he had before undertaking this great pilgrimage, Sri Ramana went on to master many languages to express his vision, the Self that he was, is and shall always be. His modes of expression in different languages were shaped not only by the great Tamil saints but also by the writings of *Adi Shankara*. He was already aware of the Truth before learning to express it in any language.

In the great teaching tradition of the *Upanishads* (ancient Indian scriptures), the scriptures and teachers just 'point out' the Truth, the knowledge, the experience that every person always 'is', but is never aware of. The greatness and the blessing Bhagavan Ramana had as a youngster was to hold onto and maintain that something that everybody 'is' all the time but never gives any importance to. When somebody finds 'it', it is not even 'near' as it is one's own Self. When somebody looks for 'it', it is always far away as one is denying it as one's own Self by looking for it. One who does not look for it never finds it either.

Bhagavan Ramana himself would never have opened his mouth to speak, or attempted to write, had he supported the idea that no teacher, teaching, realising or thinking is needed to appreciate one's own Self. He himself was an exceptional young man to be in touch with himself accidentally, and to maintain this, but he was supremely ordinary enough to acknowledge the human need to be taught, and therefore was a compassionate teacher in his living, speaking and writing. In his day-to-day dialogue he was always hitting the bull's eye, directly moving into the 'I'. He has taken extraordinary care in his writings to deal with problems faced by the average man in the relative world. He was indeed a great blossom in the living tradition of teaching.

The beauty of the timeless tradition of the ancient wisdom, still alive in India, is that no teacher or *guru* considers himself or herself in any way exclusive. The Truth is eternal and nobody 'creates' it. Since the Truth is timeless, and therefore exiting at all times, in all places, in and through everything, it is the nature of every existing object, sentient and insentient. Hence, nobody can 'give' it to another. It is already the nature of everything and everybody.

But not many are aware of this. Everybody can grasp that they are ignorant about the world, but not many can grasp that there is ignorance about one's own Self. We question the perceptions or experiences but never question the perceiver or the experiencer. If questioning or challenging the perceptions marks the beginning of science, then challenging 'the perceiver', the 'I', marks the beginning of real thinking where the thinker himself is challenged. There are millions of people who never question their perceptions, but there are billions who never question the perceiver, the thoughts or the thinker. As a result, the vast majority of human beings live under the spell of ignorance.

This ignorance is of two kinds – ignorance about the relative, the objective world, and ignorance about the subject, the absolute. It is easier to grasp the first kind of ignorance as everybody encounters the objective world everyday. Though we 'experience' objects directly through our senses, still we do not 'know' those objects. The experience may be effortless – one may see a tree, a mountain, an ocean or a person, but unless it is named, nobody 'knows' which tree, mountain, ocean or person one experienced. The more creation is explored and named, the more aware a person becomes of his ignorance about many things.

In our generation, we feel so strongly about our ignorance of the relative world that we forget the most important, second type of ignorance: the ignorance about our own Selves. Not many of us are aware that we are ignorant about our true nature – the Self, the 'I'! Until something is 'named' we do not even know that we are ignorant about that something.

If we are asked: Do you know yourself, the 'I'? there shall be answers at various levels. I am continuously using and experiencing my sense of 'being' without a name, the nameless being, yet the name 'I' will throw anybody out of gear with a sudden awakening to ignorance, as nobody can give 'a' specific meaning to the word 'I'. The word 'I' is peculiar in that it has two levels of meaning – the relative and the absolute.

There are many answers to the question, 'Who am I?' Everybody will begin with the same word in any language. In English we begin with 'I am…' and then we fill the gap with some object or relative identity. The 'I' and the 'amness' are one and the same.

The subject 'I', the universal first name, is the same for all. But the object, the relative identities, the second names, are just countless. I am rich, poor, young, old, Hindu, Muslim, Christian, a socialist, a monarchist. Thus, there can be thousands of relative identities. Long before we pick up any secular or religious identity, we already exist. Our sense of 'being', the existence itself, is not a matter of belief or disbelief to be picked up sometime later in life. Nor does it need the name 'I' for its existence. The existence of anything is independent of a name, and in the same way, who I am, the being, the 'I', is a nameless existence, independent of a name.

Not only is it ever-existent, but also it is a continuing 'experience' as all experiences at the level of the senses, and even thoughts of all kinds, are experienced in its absolute presence. A sound, a touch, a sight, a taste or a smell is 'experienced' through corresponding sense organs to invoke sensations at the level of the body and impressions at the level of the thoughts. But 'the Experience', the Self, the awareness, is ever an experience, even before it is named as 'I'. That or this nameless being which is always 'the subject', and is never available for objectification, is an eternal Experience that everybody or everything 'is'!

The *Vedas* (ancient Indian *Sanskrit* texts), the *Upanishads*, the most ancient literature, the common heritage of mankind, reveal this Truth with many words, ever aware of the limitation of the words. Even though every person is always in that experience, nobody knows about that, just as we forget the planet Earth while living in our village, city, country or continent. While listening to the sound we forget our ears, while enjoying the sights we forget our ever-present eyes behind the sights, or we forget the ever-present tongue that processes the taste while enjoying various taste sensations.

Similarly, we seem to forget the ever-present Experience, the eternal awareness Existence, while losing ourselves in the sensations of various physical experiences and the feeling experiences of many thoughts and emotions. We always use our 'being', 'the Experience', long before we experience the experience of a sound, touch, taste, sight, smell, thoughts or emotions. Long before we see the word 'I' in any relative identity, we are already 'being' ourselves.

The knowledge of the Self is like the man sitting on the donkey looking for the donkey. The moment he searches for the donkey, he denies that he is the owner of the donkey. If he does not search, he does not find the donkey either. Similarly, in the search for happiness, the Self, the Infinite, the God, the Truth, one denies that one is That, and if one stops searching one does not find That either.

This is the point where the need for a *guru* comes in. The *guru* dispels the darkness or ignorance about one's own nature. The geography book does not 'create' the country or the landscape it talks about, and the *Upanishads* or the *Vedas* do not 'produce' the Truth that they reveal. The Truth, the Self, the God, does not exist because of the *Upanishads*; because That is, the book talks about it. Similarly, I am the Infinite, the Absolute, not because the *guru* says so; because I am That, the *guru* reveals it. Thus no book or *guru* becomes the authority.

But the knowledge, the *jnana*, must be freed from both doubt and error. Often we have doubt-free knowledge, but it can be erroneous. We may have no doubt that the earth is flat, but it is erroneous as the earth is round. Science begins with the doubting of perceptions. If we take for granted that the earth is flat, stationary, or the center of the solar system, then we shall continue to remain under the spell of ignorance.

Similarly, the knowledge about one's own Self. We may have no doubt that 'I am the body', but it is erroneous as 'I' goes on shifting from 'I am the body' to 'I am the mind', 'I am the father, mother, professional', 'I am sick, healthy…' Thus this shifting 'I' is to be understood.

When the individual starts doubting the 'I' that takes so many roles, it marks the beginning of true knowledge about the Self. The *guru* takes into account the ever-changing roles and the changeless constant that is the 'I', to prove the immortality of one's 'being'. Logic is used to establish that long before the name was attributed, the nameless universe was already existing. That goes to prove that long before the universal first name, 'I', was used, the nameless being pervaded it all.

Somebody is always needed to challenge the perceptions, thoughts and individuality as most people take all these aspects for granted and never question them. When this false knowledge is given a religious sanction, in the long march of time the error is hardened as the true knowledge, and the followers become fanatical. Nobody must hide behind the infallibility of a past declaration, as that will prevent every chance of opening up to immortality from mortality, absolute peak from misery, and light of knowledge from the darkness of ignorance.

The *Upanishads* challenge the individual 'I', as that is the focal point where all identity happens. That the body is changing or ageing is natural, but 'I am changing' is an error. The teaching and the teacher facilitate the understanding of the 'I' to its true, absolute identity, and then the person learns to live and to manage with all the changes. When the knowledge of the objective world helps us to learn to use the creation more efficiently, the knowledge of the subject, the 'I', helps us to deal with all thoughts, including the 'I' thought, and the emotions, very effectively.

The Self-knowledge, the awareness of one's own true nature, does not impose any type of identity, but reveals 'the actor', the immortal, the absolute peace, who infuses every role with the touch of absolute bliss. The *guru* reveals it. A teacher or *guru* is absolutely essential. The scriptures point it out and then drop out of one's life for the person to live out his wisdom in perfect harmony with creation. It is like the driving instructor teaching driving then dropping out of one's car for the learner to drive around to his own destinations.

The relative world can ever remain a domain of constant exploration and discovery, but the absolute identity of man is known once and for all. This is '*Vedanta*', the end of all knowledge. There is nothing to know 'beyond' the Infinite, as the Infinite is all that ever 'is'! But the finite world can always be explored and the horizon of the relative knowledge shall be an ever-expanding realm!

Vedanta, the *Upanishads*, the most ancient literature, begins with the 'i', the individual, to end in 'I', the Infinite. The true teachers in the tradition reveal that Infinite to be the 'I', the individual, and to be all inclusive, where nothing or nobody stands apart. Such teachers will have no conflict with anybody or any idea whereas the ones who believe in one relative idea or identity as the Absolute shall inevitably end up in conflict. One pays a huge price by remaining sheltered, unquestioned and unchallenged in one's own unverified and unverifiable convictions.

Most of the thinkers, theologies or belief systems are busy explaining the creation or the creator, but not many begin with the 'I', the individual whose presence makes the creation and the creator a mystery. As the world shrinks with globalised communication, few can stand apart in isolation. The time has come for the world to open up, and teachers of all persuasions must be open enough to challenge and be challenged, taking into account all shades of human experiences, and never hiding behind an idea, a person, a book or anything that is beyond questioning or analysis! Absolute openness is the name of the teaching, learning and living. We can be grateful in having Bhagavan Ramana as an ever-present reminder.

Swami Suddhananda 2008

Sri

Hans Raj Maharaj

You try to purify yourself by the grace of guru but you can't purify yourself; you have to take help from a guru. If you have the utmost demand for realisation you will get a guru. Until you have extreme demand for realisation you will not get a guru.

If you have extreme desire to realise, your guru will come.

Sri Hans Raj Maharaj

Sri Hans Raj Maharaj

Sacha Dham, Holy Place of Truth, is the *ashram* of Sri Hans Raj Maharaj. It is located in the tiny village of Laxman Jhulla, near Rishikesh, North India, on the banks of the rushing waters of the sacred Ganges river. It is a small and simple place, providing a home for Maharajji, his Indian disciples and their families. It's a very traditional Indian *ashram*.

I visited Maharaj in 2000 with a group of students from Australia. We glimpsed him over several days going to and fro to take **darshan** ***(being in the presence of a saint) at the shrine of his master. There was a strong attraction and we were granted the rare honour of sitting with him in his room for some twenty minutes. He answered one question, briefly, and it clearly sets out his Blueprint for Awakening. We were all deeply touched by his enormous presence.***

We're living in Sydney, Australia. It's a very beautiful city, but it is very materialistic. Is there something you would like to say to the people of Sydney? Is there a message we could take to them?

I have only one message – spirituality. That is called peace. Love is not in the mind and thoughts. Love is in the heart, and that is universal. Maybe in Sydney, maybe in France, maybe in England, maybe another country – spirituality is not particular to any country.

Spirituality is the universal point. Whether it's Christ's way, Mohammed's way, Ram or Krishna's way, everybody understand one thing – love is God. Christ also said this. Mohammed also said this.

When the seer becomes one with the seen, when the seer becomes the seeing, then you lose your false identity.

Ajja

Ajja

Ajja, born Ramachandra Bhat in Nettar, India, was a modest farmer and family man until he underwent a spontaneous and dramatic awakening aged thirty-six. From that day on, he declared himself 'dead', no longer the owner of his own body. He came to Puttur, Karnataka, in 1970 and started sharing his views with like-minded persons. He lived at Ananda Kuteera in the village of Kemmai. He stuck to his famous buzzline, 'This body is not mine,' to the end. Ajja left the body on March 12th 2007, at the age of ninety-one.

Visiting Ananda Kuteera over the last five years I was always struck with the loving atmosphere amongst the residents and the playful, non-serious nature of their beloved Ajja. Over a four-year period I had the good fortune of bringing many people to meet Ajja as part of the Arunachala Pilgrimage Retreat. He always gave us a wonderful welcome, full of his wisdom and laughter. We sang, danced and made music together. All were touched by his aliveness and presence and his simply stated wisdom.

These questions are designed to unfold the ancient wisdom of India.

It's not only India, it's for universal love. It's not come only from India. So, I want to use the whole world, and beyond that also. (all laugh)

Sri Ramana proposed the fundamental question, 'Who am I?' Who are you?

Is it the fundamental question? (all laugh) Who am I? That is the second step. I want the more fundamental one, which should come from you.

I see. I think you will have to tell us.

That question, 'Who are you?' is also my question to you. If I answer that it will become a discourse. My style is not of discourse. You should ponder on it and then ask me this question. Looking at all of you people, it's as if we met earlier. So, I know you people. Do you know me?

Yes. We know you. We are all one friendship.

We are beyond that. We are not confined to the circle, we are beyond that.

We are part of the whole.

Maybe.

No separation.

That's the final stage – we are all One. The first step is we are all One; the last step is we are all One. There is something which is in between. That is 'I'. If that 'I' goes, it's the first step and the last step. Everything is. 'I', 'you'; we are all tied to this between, and if we just cross beyond that there is nothing like 'I' and 'you'. We have to go to that final stage. The first stage and the final stage are One. We have to cross the between stage.

What is that first stage? Can you grasp it? The first stage and the final stage are One, but we want to know – and we have to know – what is that first stage? The first stage is the beginning. The beginning of the *jivatman* (individual soul); beginning of the Self. The beginning of the Self is itself the end of the final stage of Self. That is Self-realisation. Formerly, in the beginning or in the initial stage, it was so pure, but in between there came impurity. Because of the impurity we say that 'I' am doing this, 'I' am doing that. Initially we were pure and after realisation we will be pure. That is all.

Are you saying this impurity is our wrong idea about 'I'?

It has already come so why do you want to think about the past or the future? Think about the present. How we view now – that is the secret.

And how is that?

If you are really pure in all ways – in talk, in work, in thinking – then it is okay. We are all here to become pure; but how to become a pure soul? That we want to know; that is the in-between. If a person is one hundred percent pure there is nothing to worry about.

We are speaking about the present and by present I mean action – what are your present actions? How are your actions? I want to know the way you are living, your actions now.

Many Western seekers come to India looking for enlightenment as if it is an experience. What is enlightenment?

Enlightenment, in the beginning, is to know oneself; that's the first step – when you want to know about yourself, then the knower, the known and the process of knowing are the same. If all these things blend together they become One, then silence begins.

Enlightenment, Self-realisation, is a two-stage process. First is the transformation, next is evolution. First we have to transform the 'I'. The present 'I' is there and that should be transformed into 'thy': you, he – or father. Now I am the son and after a few years I will be the father, if there is a young man to be the son. The second stage, evolution, can only come after the first stage. So now you want to know about the first and the second stages.

Yes, I would like you to talk about both stages.

To whom should I say this?

You could say it to everybody who is seeking enlightenment.

It should be the heart speaking to heart. So, to whom should I say this?

To everybody. We are One heart.

You say that in presence you are One. But in presence, if I look right now, everybody is appearing differently and the bodies are all different. In the original stage it's the One, in the final stage it's the One, but in the middle part, the present part, everybody is looking different. So what do you say to this?

The bodies are different, the forms are different, but the spirit is One; the Self is One.

Do you want to speak about the spirit or beyond the spirit?

You can speak about beyond the spirit.

To go out of the spirit, first you have to speak from within the spirit. (laughs) Do you all know that you have come to this life? Have you realised that you have taken birth?

Yes. We have taken birth.

Do you believe that you are born?

The body is born, the form of the body is born, but the essential nature is never changing.

Do you mean to say that there is something different from the body? You said that the body has taken birth, so you mean to say that there is something different from the body? I want to ask a question to all of you (talks to audience): Do all of you believe that you are the body or are you something other than the body?

Audience member: I am not the body.

So you believe you are not the body. Then who are you? If you are not the body, who are you?

Audience member: I am the one who is aware of the body.

Who is that 'I' who is knowing that body? What is that 'I' referring to? The person who is not realised, says, 'I don't know anything,' but the person who has attained realisation, he also says, 'I don't have the identity so there is nothing left.' He is beyond identity; there is no identity existing.

Are there any qualifications for enlightenment? Is* sadhana *(spiritual practice) necessary?

It is not a question of *sadhana* but rather inquisitiveness, searching, *shodhana*. *Sadhana* means you are trying to see something which is not there, but searching, *shodhana*, means you search for what is there. You see the thing which is there, present. That is the finest.

If you are searching then you are seeing something in the present – you are trying to be aware of it – and there is the action which is seen, the seer, and then the object which is to be seen. When all these things blend and become One, then it becomes spirituality. That is the Oneness which you have to attain. When the seer becomes one with the seen, when the seer becomes the seeing, then you lose your false identity.

Usually in India is is said that meditation is necessary. Do you agree?

Meditation; you call it *sadhana*. What happens in meditation? In meditation the 'I' becomes the identity. The finest is searching for the known, which is there. (passing a small booklet of Ajja's teaching) You can read this, and then based on this you can ask questions.

***(Reading from the booklet) 'The individual soul loses his individualised existence through right action and wisdom. He then becomes independent. He alone is liberated while alive:* jivanmukta.'**

It says, 'Oh God, lead me from darkness towards light.'

Your questions are tricky. (all laugh)

Usually we say that we are human beings, but actually I say that it is not correct. We are in a human body. The body which you have is from your parents. But you, that 'I' which is there inside, it doesn't have any parents. That is the *omkara* (sound of universal consciousness). You are the final spirit.

Everybody should do *karma*. True *karma* (*karma yoga*) means action, and through action you transform. After *karma* comes true *jnana*, which means knowledge. Knowledge leads you to blossoming. So you have to ponder on that 'I'. You are not the body, you are the Universal Spirit; you are that *omkara*. But we do not realise this. We do not know it by experience. That is the difference. We know it through books or teachings, but we do not know it by experience. That is what we want to know again. In the initial stage, that is the real quest.

This is what we call Self-enquiry.

Self-enquiry is through the question, 'Who am I?' When we ask this question we should see the present and when the seer becomes one with the seen, then the identity loosens. If you ask the question, 'Who am I right now?' then it usually leads to this body. Right? You are going to ask the question to this body. But if you go inside and then ask the question it might lead you to somewhere else. So being an introvert is the main requirement. If you go inside, then you find *prakasha* (clarity). It is the Self-illumination; it is the *shakti* (female creative force).

Is that the final state?

No, it is the beginning. We are from the light and again becoming light. That is the process. We do not know what we were but now we are finding it. That is the path. At present in the world, when you become introverted and try to search for yourself, you always see the unreal, and then darkness and then death. This is what we are seeing now. But with transformation the false transforms into the Truth, the darkness transforms into light, and death transforms into life. Truth, light and life; all these are the basic qualities of life.

When will the realisation of the Self be gained?'

The answer to this is to understand the world; before that you need to understand yourself. So first, try to know about yourself, the 'I'. Afterwards you can think about the world.

So the answer lies in knowing oneself. How to remove the world?

Just by removing our 'bodies'. The Self is covered with 'bodies'; that is why we have lost our real identity. So first, let us dissolve from this bondage and the whole world will be anew. Not only the world. So removing the world means you have to first follow the path of *karma*, action. When the action starts, and when that transforms you, it makes you blossom. Evolve. The answer lies here.

Reading from your booklet you say: 'A man gains the bliss that is his original nature when he enquires – Who am I? What is the secret of my birth? – and engages in his duties. Upon finding out answers to these questions, his very nature then becomes bliss.' Is that right?

Yes. But before that I say all these things should be done: repeating the chanting of God's name, selfless action, believing in Truth. All these things have to be passed through. First through the path of action, secondly through the path of knowledge. Usually people start to think about knowledge only. This is a small problem.

Let's move to the next question.

When you ask a question is it for the benefit of yourself, or is it for the benefit of the whole of mankind?

For the benefit of mankind. Your eyes don't need any translation. (all laugh) (Ajja sings a song) I think now I need a translation. (all laugh)

I sang that beautiful song right now. It meant that there are not two races, there is just one race, one *dharma* (teaching of the Truth), one *atman* (individual aspect of the Self). I am for the individual and I am for the whole of mankind. But for this one race there are so many *dharmas*. Caste, colour and creed are One only. There is only one religion.

You are the beginning. You are the end. In the middle, I am here. I am giving a message for mankind, that we are One. We have to remove from our minds that we are from different religions. There is only one race, that is the human race; then there is only one religion, only one *atman*. Whatever I say is for the entire humanity. (all laugh as Ajja moves his hands)

Your hands need no translation!

If you make the enquiry 'Who am I?' The immediate answer would be 'I am this body.' But that is not what I am talking about. I am talking about the primordial 'I', the first 'I'. You have to go to that bliss which I call *nithyanandam paramanandam*. When you go to that state, the world will not be seen. This is how the world is removed.

You have to go to that supreme state of bliss. Only then is this life worthy. You are not the ones who are born out of the womb of your parents. You are Self-illuminating. The state without a state. Stateless. There is no state at all, no identity at all. That is the real bliss, the real light.

We do not belong to this world, we do not belong to this body. You said, 'When I see your eyes, Ajja, I am happy and there is no need for translation.' But who is the one who is seeing? When the seer is melted in the identity he is identity-less. So, who are you seeing? What do you mean by seeing? Who is the seer?

In these moments, there is just light.

Yes, the light is seen here. (all laugh) Just because the light is there, everything is seen; visible.

You are a bit naughty, because that's a bit tricky. (all laugh)

What's the price of your finest radio?

About 2000 rupees. (all laugh)

What is the price of this radio? (pointing to his body)

Priceless.

It is not priceless, but there is no price at all for this because an unseen power is using this body as a medium to put forth words. I am comparing this body to a radio.

Do you have a mind?

Who is the one who is questioning? Who is the one who is asking?

Now you're being tricky again.

No, it's not. This is the way it has to be.

Are you saying that these words are like a radio coming from the source? So my question is: Do you have a mind?

This is something which is beyond the mind and the intellect, which the mind and intellect cannot accept.

Can we use the word **manonasha,** ***destroyed mind?***

Nobody is there to say even that, so it is left to you to decide. You have to cross beyond the barriers of the mind and the intellect. You will understand when you go beyond the mind and the intellect. You will understand that state.

Can you say something about* vasanas, *the tendencies of the mind?

(Ajja sings a song) Ajja sang a beautiful song right now. It means the answer should come; I cannot say just like that. If it comes, it comes. That's all. It has to come out naturally, then you can pick out something and then write it down. It cannot be forced.

I am asking about tendencies within the mind; these are old patterns in our psychology which repeat and they're called* vasanas. *Can you say something about this?

Please read that in the booklet. (Ajja's small teaching booklet) The mind is presently out-turned; it is extroverted. The answer is found within you. I am only a witness. I only try to bring out the answer from you. When there's a question there should be an answer also. This mere witnessing can sprout the answer within you. Where there is a question, the answer is also in you.

The 'I' which is seeing right now, it should be taken inside. The sight which is being seen, it should be taken inside. The mind is there. The sight should go inside now. Sight is seeing outside; let it find the origin.

I am giving an analogy: the sun has a lot of rays. When they are all focused at one point, at the core of the sun, there will be a big bang. When all the thoughts are focused inside, then there will be a big bang; an expansion. It's called *vikasa,* the illumination. Likewise in our heart, when all the thoughts are focused at the centre of the heart, then there will be expansion – there will be a bang.

Are you suggesting that this will be a moment of Self-realisation? Like, Aha!?

At that time there'll be no *vasanas*; when the person who feels this *vasana* is not there, the *vasana* is also not there. Then, everything is melted and all becomes One. This is real death. I am talking about the non-dual life beyond death, and death does not mean the death of the body.

The mind is travelling everywhere. We are all searching for peace; we need peace. But who is it that needs this peace? From the falseness we have to go towards the Truth. That is what is called *Satsang* (meeting in Truth). *Satsang* is the companionship of the good ones, the true ones.

I am not speaking about the death of this body, but there is some source, the energy, the root energy, which has come from the origin. So that has to be placed into the heart. At that time there will be a bang. It means a loss of identity. That is death. The death of that which is born, this energy which has come out. It is illuminating the Self. So the energy which is born has to lose its identity. Then the life starts. Which life? Life after death. That is the real life. There you can enjoy the bliss.

I agree.

The mind seeks peace.

Audience question: Please tell us how to do it?

The question was how to take the mind inwards, but the mind is already inside. So the best thing you can do is not to let it go outside. That's all. There are no steps for taking it inside. It is already inside. Just see it; be aware of it. You can do *dhyana* (meditation), with open eyes. Do the *dhyana* keeping your mind inside. Do not let it wander outside.

We can do this with Self-enquiry.

Yes, that's what I meant by Self-enquiry.

Self-enquiry is bringing us to the source.

The mind going to the heart, resting in the heart region, that is not Self-realisation. Once the mind goes and rests in the heart, subsequently what happens is *shodhana*, searching for what is really there, or *vichara,* enquiry. That would eventually lead to Self-realisation, which means losing this individuality completely.

I talk about two things. One is the path of action and the other is the path of wisdom (knowledge) or enquiry. Through the path of action the *jivatman*, the individual soul, gets transformed. Subsequently, through the path of wisdom he evolves. Evolution means he loses his individuality completely.

Audience question: Swamiji, you mentioned concentration of the mind. For example, at this moment I am feeling hunger; hunger is arising. So mind is already thinking of food – the future. It is very difficult to keep it in the present. There are obstacles. So what is the best way?

That we sleep in the waking state. During sleep the mind is visible. Let that state be in the waking state also.

Let us go and have lunch. (all laugh) That is the first step.

We are not so hungry actually. We are hungry for your wisdom, not for your food.

First, let us fill this. (patting his stomach) How to awaken? Awakening is very important. We are asleep, actually. That is why we do not know who we are. When we awake, that knowledge will come automatically, within.

On the spiritual path awakening is different from what we think it will be. First we have to try for that awakened state. What is awakening? How to awake from this sleep? If once we are awake, it is forever. Real awakening is only once. No sleep afterwards.

(Interview continues after lunch) Ajja, you have told us many wonderful things.

That you only know. I don't remember anything.

***It appears essential to met a* guru *and stay with a* guru. *Who is the* guru?**

You are *guru* to yourself. There is no other *guru* apart from you. If you are a *guru* to yourself then you can also see a *guru* on the outside. Otherwise you can never meet a *guru*. The *guru* can be manifest or unmanifest. He can come in any form. He need not come in a physical body; it is not necessary. But it can happen only when we are in an awakened state, not in a sleep state as we are now. When we are in a sleeping state we can't know the awakened state, but in the awakened state we can know the awakened state and the sleeping state. Your daily life, your daily transactions and activities, become spiritual.

This mind can know a lot of things outside. That is science. But when you go beyond that, at the same time you can see this as well as that – both at the same time. Later on, there is no such thing as this and that. It is One. Right now, we are all different. But once we have reached there, then we can say, very rightfully, that we are One. Because we are not awakened we can only say we are all One internally, but externally we are different.

And we need the* guru *to bring light and awaken us.

Yes, that is what I am saying. This question is very important because each and every person should have a *guru*. We can understand and know who is a true *guru* only when we awaken. Until then we can search in different places for a *guru*.

What is the* guru's *role?

If you can tell us something about the role of yourself, then we can speak about the role of the *guru*. First find out what your role is. Subsequently you will know what the role of the *guru* is.

***For example, today we are coming to you as the one who can bring the light. This is the* guru.**

I can give that light when there is no light in you. When already it is there…

… we don't need a **guru.**

Ah, there is no need of one. What you want to know is there but it is covered with ignorance. If you just remove that ignorance you can understand and gain the knowledge of what it is and what I am. It is only because of this ignorance that you do not understand.

I need some help to take off this ignorance so I come to the **guru** ***because he is a wise man.***

The *guru* is only guiding.

Dusting; taking off the dust.

Guiding towards the goal. Just removing that ignorance. When the mind is extroverted we tend to see the outer things, but when the mind is introverted then it tries to see the light. When there is no seer, when the sight itself has become one with it, then the inner Self expands and then it becomes the light. There is no such thing as seer or sight. They merge together and then there is just light. You are your own Self-*guru* and there is nothing to give light. It is already there in you. You just see.

The light is within. But there is a veil that covers this light. That is ignorance or darkness. Then this same mind, which is extroverted, is made introverted and it merges in that ignorance and veiling and explodes. What would remain is light. Once that happens, there is no one to say that there is only light – there is no individuality, there is no seer. As long as the veil is there, there is individuality. Once the veil is taken off there is no individuality; there is just light.

Does it take the help of the **guru** ***to take off this dust?***

Yes, it can happen.

The* guru *is a kind of housewife taking the dust off.

There are many kinds of *guru*. First, the disciple should be so fine that he can find a good *guru*. Before searching for a *guru*, our mind should become introverted and find the source of the energy. That power within us leads us towards the *guru*.

And how to tell a true* guru*?

Guru is the one who cannot be put into words. He is beyond any explanation. If he is a real *guru* he comes into your inner Self and then works on you. You can never find him, he finds you. If your subconscious mind is awakened, then you can see the *guru*. You can find him and you can see who he is. He'll remove that dust and ignorance. Everything will be his responsibility. The *guru* will take the entire responsibility.

The *guru* works from within. With this external mind we cannot analyse the *guru*, cannot trust the *guru* at all. A *guru* can only come when the mind is introverted and the subconscious mind is awakened.

What do you exactly mean by awakened? Because if I am really awakened I don't need a* guru *any more. The* guru *is to help me take off the dust.

I am talking about the awakening of the subconscious mind. This is an external mind. The awakening which you are talking about is the final state. That is not what I am talking about presently. I am talking about the mind which has become introverted.

So you are saying that when I realise I am asleep and I need help to awaken, you can say then I have a kind of awakening mind that's looking for somebody to help me with my ignorance.

Yes. Once the subconscious mind is awakened, when you awaken from the sleeping state to the subconscious state, then there can be a *guru* who will come and help you, who will work on you.

So, in the moment that you are available, the* guru *is there.

That is the preparation that we have to do. That has to happen. You are your own *guru*, actually. To speak about a *guru* our mind should be empty, all the desires should be completed. Then you can speak about *guru*. It should be empty, totally empty. Desireless. Where do you go in search of him when all the desires completely dissolve? Then, you can feel that the *guru* is working on you.

We all fold our palms like this and pray, 'Oh God, You are in heaven.' But why do you need a God who is in heaven? He is already inside your heart; God is residing in you. Be an introvert. Let us not fight for God who is somewhere in heaven. Let us pray for one who is within ourselves, within this body itself. The one who resides in that 'I'. Let us pray to Him. We want that One. Where do we go in search of that God who is in heaven?

In oneself there is a *jivatman*, an individual soul. That *jivatman* has to be transformed, and then he becomes an *atman*, the Self-illuminating One, the light. Then you do not speak or think about all these things.

We are the creation and the Creator is there, but in this transformation we know that we are the Creator Himself. He is there inside. We are the Creator. I am the God. That transformation will take place but that is also an ignorance because God is also not permanent. He also has an identity that should cease. Who is this 'I', the new 'I', the new one who says that 'I am the God'? That is also ignorance and should cease. Only then will it be light. That is the evolution, the final state, the transformation.

Are you saying that there are two levels of awakening?

Two stages. Usually people do not understand it. (Interpreter: It is the speciality of Ajja. You can take it as you want.)

Can you explain a little bit more about these two stages?

We know we are nothing but God. That is the first stage. That is called transformation. Then we will try to say I am such a man. We will also say that I am God. I can do miracles. Usually such an ego will come when we transform. But that ego, that ignorance, should also go. That's the second stage. In that second stage the evolution takes place. For that, total meditation is the only secret. We should search and question again and again: 'Who is this I who is telling that I am God?' Only you can get the answer and remove that ignorance. It's not real transformation; it's transcending, it's the second stage.

Then there is a statement – *aham brahmasmi*. *Aham* is the feeling of 'I am the one residing in the body'. *Brahmasmi* is the feeling of 'I am God, I am *Brahma* (the Creator)'. Both these things should go. What should remain is *Brahma* only. There is no *aham*, no *asmi*, just *Brahma*. Only this, only *jyoti*, only light. There is no identity at all.

We always struggle, you know, like we have *sadhana* or spirituality, we struggle with that ego – *aham*. Or else we say we have transformed something – *aham brahmasmi* – I am the one who is residing in the body. That is like God. Both these things are distracting. So both should go and then only one should remain, that is *Brahma*. That is bliss. Only then can we be like a radio. There is nobody there. Nothing is there. Only words come, that is all.

We have been here for several hours today and you shared a lot of wisdom and understanding. When I look at your disciples I feel your heart. There is a lot of* bhakti*, devotion, here. Can you say something about the role of devotion in finding Truth?

Faith! Not the faith outside, the faith within oneself. You should feel it. Right now we are not trusting the one who is residing inside us. We are trying to find trust in the world outside but we must trust the one who is residing inside us. One has to trust oneself. We are going on searching: Who is God? But before that let us first search and understand: Who am I?

There are about ten people living in this ashram *and they give themselves to Ajja as the* guru. *But they also give themselves to the community, to the* ashram, *with selfless work and this is what I am calling* bhakti. *So my question is, how important is that giving of yourself, selflessly, in the spiritual life?*

We are doing our duties as human beings. If you want you can call it *bhakti*. If the people of this *ashram* are interested in spiritual points, Ajja is here to help them, if they are in need of food it is our duty to give them food.

My question is what is the effect of this duty for the person?

Purification. The effect is purification. Before saying anything about spirituality you have to complete your *karma*, action. You have to complete your path of work – selfless action. Unless you have done the action and the *karma* part is over, you cannot go to spirituality. So all these things which you saw are a part of completing that *karma*. The secret is to forget about what you were yesterday and from today to act with selfless motives. From today, if we undertake unselfish duties without selfish action and selfish motives, it may help us in this path towards progress.

Bhakti *is a part of everyday life in India, but in Western countries it is a little unusual. It's more rare. It seems that devotion is a very important part of the spiritual life.*

Devotion should be inward. We should be devoted to God or *guru* inwardly. Outwards means absolutely nothing. So even in the West you can do devotion. These actions are only the vehicles. Only if an action is done without the thought of 'I' can it be called a selfless action. I know how to cook, but when I cook I have some feeling, some thought. This cannot be called a selfless action. With selfless action there should be no ego there. Only those actions which are bare of the sense of 'I' and 'my' can become selfless actions.

Are you saying that* bhakti *is a way of achieving this 'no ego' state by giving selfless service? You are, in a way, giving up this 'I' who is doing something?

'I am giving up myself.' Even that I should not be there. It cannot be called selfless action. When we have done some good work we feel that we have done it without profit for ourselves. But even that is not selfless.

Seekers often have curious ideas about the enlightened state. Can you describe your typical day and how you perceive the world?

Whatever the answer I give, people think it is Ajja who is giving it, but it is not Ajja who is speaking. It is the Self-Illuminating One. There are no rules for me. No rules, nothing, no bounds. I am not bound by anything.

If you people, all of you, stay here right now, can anyone of us say that this place is mine? Is this yours? Is it not yours? Does this *ashram* belong to you? Does this *ashram* belong to everyone else who is present here? Anyone? This *ashram* is not mine, this *mandir* (temple) is not mine. Just like you, it does not belong to me. I am here as a witness. Your own body itself does not belong to you. When I am saying that this body is not me, not mine, then how can I say that this place is mine? How can we say, 'I am a *guru*, my *ashram*'? This thought will never arise in the mind. So there is no *guru* and no disciples and no *mandir*.

There is a difference between* guru *and disciple because when we come here we have to wash our feet. When Ajja comes in he doesn't wash his feet. This is the difference. It's a joke. Now it's my turn to be tricky!

You are speaking about washing the feet. I have not taken a bath for so many days. Even if I do take a bath it is by the force of somebody else. I never take a bath. If I don't take a bath I don't care. I don't care because the body is not mine. I am not the body. So the complete conviction that I'm not the body is there. So whether it is the feet or the body doesn't matter for me. I am not the body. This shirt I am wearing is not mine, this *dhoti* (lenght of cotton cloth worn around the waist) is not mine. Anybody can have this understanding.

There is a message to give: we have not taken birth for ourselves, but for the entire universe. There is a fruit in it. The fruit is not there for itself. It is there for others. It is to be distributed among all people. If you have a knowledge or a treasure, it has to be distributed.

When the *jivatman*, the individual soul, loses its individuality completely through the path of action and the path of wisdom, he becomes independent, he becomes free. He is called a *jivanmukta*. It can happen to anyone.

One who has taken birth has to die while still in this body; then he becomes free. If not, he has not really died and, if you believe in reincarnation, that soul comes back again. If it comes back it has not died. If it is really dead it cannot come back again. So the one who has come to birth, not this body, should die. Until this happens the principle of incarnation goes on until the death of that who was born. Once the real death takes places then he is liberated.

You have given us a profound discourse on awakening. When you meet someone with a passion for awakening, what would your short advice be?

Everything is in the hands of the people. Whatever you people want from me you can take. How should you take it? It depends on each individual. You can take from one who is empty in himself, empty inside. It's up to us you to pick what you want. To have the grace of God we should be free from our desires, not to let a single desire stain us. The desires are related to the mind, but what I am speaking about is beyond the mind.

Only to one who has resigned from the feelings of 'I' and 'my', only to that person, what remains is That. There is a state where action is there, but the feeling of not having done the action is also there. Action is not action, meaning though you act it is not really action. It doesn't bind. You have already come here. Since you have come here nothing is needed. You have come here with all the preparations for your return trip; you are well prepared. Is it not so?

We are very well prepared.

Similarly, why do we have to make all these problems, all these questions, all these meditations? We have been born and now it is our duty to think about how to go back. We have to go. There is no other way. Our tickets are already reserved, so we are just waiting; waiting for the right time. That waiting process is called meditation. Meditate and wait.

All of you have come here and then ask something for yourself or for the whole of mankind. But you have to go back to your place and contemplate and ponder on what I have said and then something will come out of you. That will be the right answer for you. The answer lies in contemplation and it is waiting for you.

Thank you. I am happy you have such a strong energy.

I cannot always speak like this. The energy is given by people. It depends on the people's interest.

So we will come again next year!

When you want to come next time, stay where you are, then come.

Only the bus came. We are already here, but the bus came, slowly.

Do you want the telephone number?

Definitely!

The number is One! Stay where you are, dial that number One and then you get the answer that's inside you; One.

In the Buddha's last moments he said, 'Be a light unto yourself.'

Be a *guru* to yourself, be a light unto yourself. Today's student is tomorrow's teacher. You are *guru* to yourself. You are a disciple, then you will become a *guru*. When you become a *guru* then your *guru* comes and meets you. The disciple has to turn into a *guru*, then a *guru* comes and says 'Hi'.

Sing a song or a *bhajan* (devotional song) now in your language. Whether it is French, Australian or English. Sing a song. (The interview ends in a riot of singing.)

Ramesh Balsekar

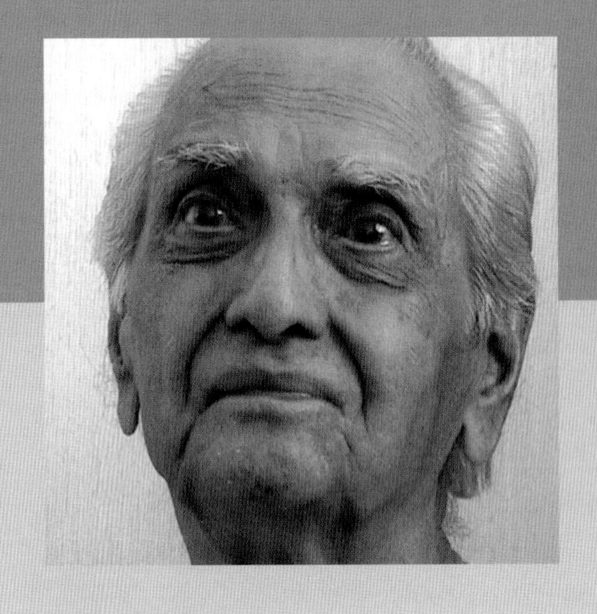

What the sages mean when they say the ego has to be destroyed – but for some reason don't bother to make clear – is that doership in the ego has to be destroyed. The ego cannot be destroyed. Similarly, the mind cannot be destroyed.

RAMESH BALSEKAR

Living means, from moment to moment, never knowing whether the next moment is going to bring peace, pleasure or pain.

Ramesh Balsekar

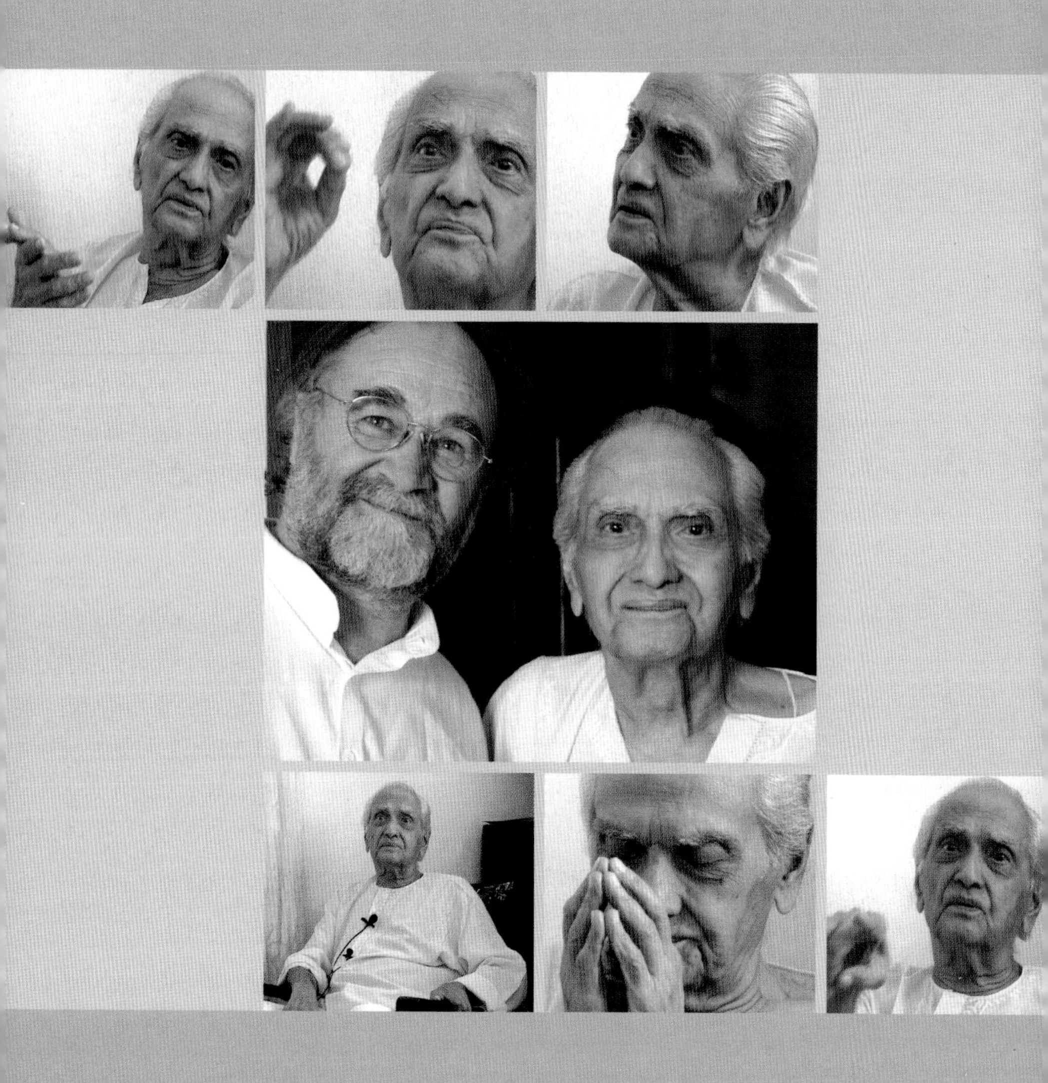

Ramesh Balsekar

Ramesh Balsekar lived his life as a householder, raising a family and having a career in the Bank of India where he rose to become president. After retirement he became Nisargadatta Maharaj's translator and later began to teach. Ramesh has written many books on both his master's and his own teachings. Several of his disciples now teach in their own right. *Satsang* is held every morning at Ramesh's residence in Mumbai from nine to ten-thirty.

My first meeting with Ramesh was in 1992. In the following years I enjoyed sitting in his apartment, which he rarely leaves, while he spoke to us as non-doers, explaining that everything happens in our life according to destiny. He has maintained his morning meetings for more than twenty years and even now, at the age of ninety, these continue. His master was Nisargadatta Maharaj but he has always displayed a deep connection to Sri Ramana Maharshi.

I have twelve questions to ask you. I've approached sixteen Indian teachers and asked each the same set of questions.

You see the extent of the madness? (both laugh) Sixteen people!

Sri Ramana proposed the fundamental question 'Who am I?' Who are you?

Are you asking me 'Who am I?'

Yes.

I would change the question to 'Who am I who thinks he is the doer of his actions as separate from the other who is a doer of his actions?' This investigation leads me to the conclusion that neither I am the doer nor the other is a doer. In fact, there is no doing, as such. All there really is, is a happening of a happening. In the world, what happens is a happening according to the cosmic law. Ramana Maharshi called it Self-enquiry. I call it Self-investigation.

Are you saying that Ramesh is a manifestation of the source?

Ramesh is a name given to a three-dimensional object, which, together with billions of other three-dimensional objects, constitute the totality of manifestation. Ramesh is a three-dimensional object from a specific species. The regular species are, according to my concept, a stone, a growing plant, an animal and a human being. In other words, the human being is an animal with senses like an animal but with the additional sense of personal doership and the dubious gift of mind-intellect which makes him tense and frustrated. But basically a three-dimensional object.

Many Western seekers come to India looking for enlightenment as if it is an experience. What is enlightenment?

Enlightenment is a happening. For a happening to happen, a three-dimensional object, a human being, is necessary, living its life as a separate entity.

So it's definitely not an experience?

Enlightenment is not an experience. An experience is what I call a free sample of what enlightenment truly means.

Like a glimpse, a* satori*?

Yes, a glimpse.

Do many of the people that come to your* Satsang *(meeting in Truth) have such a glimpse?

Who has the experience depends on the person's destiny. But there is a danger in such an experience. When an experience like this happens, the individual seeker may then consider himself a special person who has been offered this experience. Thereafter, instead of seeking enlightenment as he was doing before, the seeker mistakenly now seeks that experience, which to my mind is an obstruction. Whether the person gets involved in the experience or not is his destiny, but there is that danger of mistaking a sample for the real thing.

Is there a way of telling what is the real thing and what is the experience?

It is an experience, there's no question about it. The question is how much importance I give to that experience. If I have the wisdom to realise that an experience is an experience, a free sample, that is one thing, but if I consider that 'this is it! I'm enlightened!' then I go after more experiences. The real thing is there for all time.

Are there any qualifications for enlightenment? Is* sadhana *(spiritual practice) necessary?

Who does the *sadhana*? Someone is supposed to do the *sadhana*. So someone does the *sadhana*. Someone, some separate entity doing the *sadhana*, sees other separate entities not able to do that *sadhana*. He considers himself a special person who deserves enlightenment and to me that is a big obstruction. So if you are able to do the *sadhana* and realise that *sadhana* is just what is supposed to happen through that body-mind organism and that there is no doer of any *sadhana*, that is excellent.

Would you say that some kind of practice is a prerequisite to prepare this mind-body organism for understanding to happen?

The understanding happening is a happening. Whether that understanding happens or not is ultimately the destiny of that particular entity, according to the cosmic law. So if enlightenment is to happen, it will happen. If enlightenment is to happen without any *sadhana*, enlightenment will happen without any *sadhana*. I do not think *sadhana* is a prerequisite. In fact, that is the whole point about Ramana Maharshi; he said he was never a seeker, he didn't do any *sadhana* and the final understanding happened.

In his case it happened when he was rather young, about sixteen years old. But I guess that's a fairly rare case.

Indeed!

In the majority of cases it seems to happen more to people who spend many years in some kind of practice such as chanting or meditation.

If the final understanding is to happen without too much *sadhana*, then too much *sadhana* is not necessary, but if it is the destiny of a particular separate entity for considerable hard *sadhana* to be done, then that will happen. Nothing can happen unless it is supposed to happen according to the cosmic law and the destiny of the person concerned. That is the ultimate acceptance. There cannot be any hard and fast rule that certain things need to be done for you to get enlightenment, or that any *sadhana* will necessarily produce the result.

The ancient Indian wisdom of **Vedanta** ***(*****Vedic** ***philosophy) sets out a programme for somebody who would aspire to awaken which involves many years of practice. Do you see any benefit in this ancient wisdom?***

That's an ancient practice. It is not ancient wisdom. For me, the ancient wisdom is all said in one sentence that the Buddha said twenty-five hundred years ago, ancient enough for me. 'Events happen, deeds are done, consequences happen, but there is no individual doer of any deed.' That is enlightenment.

Enlightenment is taken as a goal. It is not a goal. What do I expect to get out of enlightenment or Self-realisation for the rest of my life that I didn't have before? Why am I asking? Who is seeking enlightenment? I am. I, Ramesh, a separate entity is looking for enlightenment. So, having got enlightened, the separate entity must ask himself: What will I have for the rest of my life that I didn't have before? Unfortunately, that is the question the seeker usually doesn't go into. Enlightenment – that's what is seen as the goal.

Would you like to go into it now?

Sure. The answer has been given by the Buddha. Enlightenment means the end of suffering. Straight. No problem, no confusion. What is enlightenment? Events happen, deeds are done, consequences happen, but there is no individual doer of any deed. That is the final understanding: enlightenment. Then I have to find out what the Buddha meant by the word 'suffering'. Usually suffering would be understood as the pain in the moment. Living means, from moment to moment, never knowing whether the next moment is going to bring peace, pleasure or pain; that is life and living. What does the human being want? Pleasure all the time, no pain. So most people, when they understand that enlightenment means the end of suffering, they say, 'Yes, yes! That's what I've been looking for. No more pain in the moment, no more pain in the future, no more physical pain, no more psychological pain, no grief, no financial pain.' No more pain.

But Buddha was no fool. Buddha knew that the basis of life means living from moment to moment, never knowing whether the next moment is going to bring pain or pleasure. In fact, alternating pain and pleasure is the very basis of life and living. How can you remove it? The Buddha could not possibly have promised the end of pain in the moment. Therefore, what could the Buddha have meant by suffering? When I asked myself this question I came to the understanding that obviously enlightenment means accepting that I'm not the doer. So that ends the suffering which I have created for myself in my life because of my sense of personal doership, for me and the other. I came to the conclusion that this suffering is obvious: my carrying a load of guilt and shame for what I thought were my stupid and bad actions, and a load of hatred and malice, jealousy and envy towards the other for his actions. That is the suffering which I have been carrying because of my sense of personal doership for me and the other.

Once I'm able to accept totally that no one is a doer, that is enlightenment according to the Buddha – which I wholly accept. Then I no longer have to carry the load of guilt and suffering for my actions, hatred and malice, jealousy and envy about the other's actions. I go through life necessarily without choice, having to accept the pain or pleasure of the moment, but me, Ramesh, the ego, is always clean and pure without the impurity of guilt and shame, hatred and malice towards the other. According to me, the basis of happiness and suffering is my relationship with the other, and the ego being clean and pure in life means peace with myself and harmony with the other. For me, life means not what is happening around the universe. Life for me means what is happening in me, in my relationship with the other, whomever the other is. From morning till night there's always a relationship: at home with my wife and children, with my neighbours; when I go to the office, with my business colleagues; if I am in business, with my customers; or with a total stranger. Unless my relationship with the other is harmonious I cannot ever dream of any happiness. That is simple and clear.

So am I happy now? No. Why? Because obviously my relationship with the other is not harmonious. Why is my relationship not harmonious? Because my entire conditioning, ever since my birth, at home, in school, in society, has been that the other is a potential rival. Life means competition, life means struggle – struggle against the other. Therefore, the basis of life and living is competing with the other. With this kind of conditioning every human being has been trained to regard the other as a potential rival. How can the relationship between me and the other ever become harmonious? Only if I'm able to totally accept a revolutionary concept contrary to all previous conditioning: that if I'm not supposed to be hurt – according to my destiny, God's will or cosmic law – no power on Earth can hurt me. If it is not my destiny to be hurt and no power on Earth can hurt me, why should I regard the other as a potential danger? And if it is my destiny to be hurt, then through which body-mind organism something happens which hurts me is irrelevant, and I cannot see the whole world as a potential danger. So it is with the understanding that the other is helpless to do anything but God's will that everything is happening. How that happening affects whom is the destiny of that particular individual. I shall only be hurt if it is in my destiny to be hurt by some happening. The other is just not concerned.

If I'm able to totally accept this revolutionary concept then I have a real basis for accepting the other, but only if I'm able to accept totally that 'I' as a separate entity and the other as a separate entity are both only uniquely programmed instruments through which life happens, according to the cosmic law. Then there is no reason for me not to have a harmonious relationship with the other. We find universal brotherhood as helpless instruments. Only with this total acceptance can I get rid of the thousands of years of conditioning regarding the other as a source of potential danger.

The absolute basis of the acceptance, Premananda, is this: everything is a happening. Who is affected by this happening, and how, will depend on his destiny. Therefore, there is no question of my blaming and condemning anyone for any happening, neither me nor the other. Not blaming myself means not carrying a load of guilt and shame. Not blaming the other means not carrying a load of hatred and malice. Then there is harmony with the other and peace with myself. And what is left is precisely what the seeker can hope to have if enlightenment happens. That is all. In fact, I would tell the seeker this is all you're going to get; if you want something more, like the power to walk on water, you're not going to get it with this understanding; so be sure of what you want. Anything can happen in the world, but it will not be the result of this understanding, not the result of this enlightenment.

The Buddha was well known for spending many years doing very hard* sadhana. *Now his followers are doing much* sadhana *in monasteries. What will Ramesh's followers be doing?

I don't have the faintest idea, Premananda! I don't know who my followers are. I don't know what they'll be following.

They'll have no* sadhana *to do?

Since you mention that, let me be clear. A certain amount of *sadhana* I do recommend. The understanding that everything is a happening means acceptance of non-doership, and the acceptance of non-doership has to be total.

Would you call this surrender?

Yes, but the point I'm making is that the basic understanding is: everything is a happening, nobody does anything. Now, intellectually, who will be unable to accept it? It's easy to accept intellectually, a beautiful, lovely concept of non-doership. It relieves me from blaming myself and feeling guilty. It relieves me from blaming the other and making an enemy of them.

But for the concept to work the acceptance has to be total. What then arises is that I know it is only intellectual, I know it is not total. What do I have to do to make the intellectual acceptance total acceptance? The moment I think about it I realise the foolishness in the question. What do I have to do to be able to accept totally and be absolutely certain that I'm not the doer? Obviously nothing. There's nothing I can do, I'm not the doer! It can only happen if it's supposed to happen according to God's will, cosmic law and my destiny. Clear? It can only happen.

I accept that I have to wait until something happens, but while I'm waiting for something to happen or not to happen, is there not something I can do to pass the time? Because the doership is still there, that's the whole point. For that my answer is yes, and this is the only *sadhana* I recommend. It is very basic, it is what I call Self-investigation. I'm not asking you to drop any other *sadhana* you may be doing. If you are doing a *sadhana* you like to do, go ahead. Why should you deprive yourself of the pleasure of doing something? This is what I recommend. At the end of the day take twenty minutes off, sit quietly, be comfortable. If you like your usual glass of beer, take it. This is not a discipline. Then do some very, very simple Self-investigation. From the many activities of the day, select one action which you are certain is your action. Then do some simple investigation to find out whether it is truly your action.

The question is, 'If I consider this my action, did I decide to do this action at any time?' You will find, 'No, I didn't.' 'How did the action happen?' Then your investigation tells you, 'I happened to have a thought and that thought led to what I now call my action. If the thought had not happened then the action would not have happened; I had no control over the happening of that thought at that time and place. How can I call it my action?'

As simple as that. Then, having convinced yourself that the action which you were so sure was your action turns out not to be your action, take another action, and another. I tell you with great confidence that you may investigate any number of actions, and every single time the action which you're convinced is your action would not have happened unless something else had happened first. If I had not happened to be at a certain place and time, and seen something, or heard something, or smelled something, or tasted something, or touched something, my action would not have happened and I truly had no control over the happening. Every single time, without exception, you come to the conclusion that the action which you thought was your action turns out not to be your action.

This *sadhana* makes the understanding go deeper every time you do the investigation; at some point it is more than likely that a flash of total acceptance will happen. 'I simply cannot be the doer of any action, and if I cannot be the doer of any action no one else can be the doer of an action either.' Only when this flash happens is there likely to be total removal of doubt.

Sri Ramana said that Self-enquiry is the most direct route to realising the Self. What do you say about Self-enquiry? How to conduct Self-enquiry?

I'm turning Self-enquiry into Self-investigation, and you'll find that Ramana says in plenty of places that the basis of the ego is doership. Sri Ramana Maharshi obviously knew that the ego has to be there. He knew full well that he, himself, until the moment of his death, had an ego. He called it the sage's ego, 'remnants of a burnt rope'; helpless. You can't tie the rope which is burnt; it couldn't tie anybody. Therefore, you see the sage's ego is helpless. The sage does have an ego and the ordinary person has an ego. The sage responds to his name being called, the ordinary person responds to his name being called. Where is the difference? The difference is that the ordinary person believes he is the doer and the other is a doer, whereas the sage has been able to accept totally that neither he is a doer nor the other is a doer. Therefore, in the sage's case the ego has been purified of the taint of doership. That is all.

My understanding of Self-enquiry is that Sri Ramana was suggesting that people would ask themselves who is the doer of whatever is happening. For example, 'Who is washing the dishes?' And the answer is, 'I am washing the dishes.' Then you ask, 'Who is this I?' The effect of asking this is to take attention from out there – the hands washing dishes – inside to the source. From what I understand of Self-investigation, it has exactly the same effect. Is that a correct understanding of Self-investigation?

Self-investigation is more focussed. For an ordinary person it is much easier than general Self-enquiry.

When Sri Ramana was asked, 'When will the realisation of the Self be gained?' he replied, 'When the world which is what-is-seen has been removed, there will be realisation of the Self which is the seer.' What is the true understanding of the world? How to remove the world?

The world cannot be removed. The world is there. My relationship with the other is the basis of my life in this world. When I come to the conclusion that neither I am a doer nor the other is a doer, neither of us can be blamed for anything that happens in the world. The immediate result is that I don't blame anyone. I'm free of guilt and shame for myself and hatred and malice for the other. The ultimate understanding is that there has never been a creation. But we're talking about the illusory individual living his illusory life.

It has been suggested that the mind must be destroyed for liberation to occur. Do you have a mind?

Obviously I have a mind, since I'm not an idiot. My understanding is that the mind cannot be destroyed. Ramana Maharshi's understanding is the same as mine. Mind is something which any person requires to live in this world. Without the brain and the mind a person would not be able to live the rest of their life as a separate entity, yet sages talk about destroying the mind. Sages talk about destroying the ego. My point is you have to go behind what the sages say and work out what they mean. Ego cannot be destroyed, as I have explained; that is clear. We need the ego to live. Indeed, it is the ego who does the individual living.

What the sages mean when they say the ego has to be destroyed – but for some reason have not bothered to make clear – is that doership in the ego has to be destroyed. The ego cannot be destroyed. Similarly, the mind cannot be destroyed. Some aspect of the mind has to be destroyed. What aspect? Very simple: the mind has two aspects, the working mind and the thinking mind. The working mind has to be there even for a sage to live his life. For the simplest action to be done, when some planning has to be done, the working mind has to be there. In the case of a sage, the doership in the ego has been destroyed. In the mind, the thinking aspect has been destroyed, but the working mind always functions.

The working mind is always doing its job in the present moment, whereas the thinking mind is never in the present moment. The thinking mind is always either worrying and thinking about what has passed, or projecting into the future. The thinking mind creates problems, imaginary, illusory problems about what might happen, which is what causes unhappiness. In the case of a sage, he's only concerned with what happens in the moment and is not concerned with what happens in the future. Why? Because the total acceptance of 'everything is a happening' means that whatever happens in the future, no one is to blame. Therefore, the sage does not keep thinking of the future. The future has already been determined. Whatever is to happen is going to happen according to God's will, cosmic law. So it is the thinking mind aspect which is removed in the case of a sage, just as the sense of doership is removed from the ego of the sage.

***My understanding is that Sri Ramana used the word* manonasha.**

Mano is mind, *nasha* is destruction; *manonasha*. What is to be destroyed? Not the working mind. You won't be able to live without it. Therefore, the *manonasha* is the destruction of the thinking mind.

That's very good, very clear. There is a great deal of misunderstanding about that.

Indeed!

Many of the people who sit in Buddhist monasteries for years are trying to destroy the mind.

Yes, yes.

What about* vasanas, *the tendencies of the mind?

Now, what is generally meant by *vasana* I refer to as conditioning. Your eyes see something, your ears hear something; promptly there is a reaction in the body-mind organism. Your eyes see something. My eyes see the same thing, but the reaction in the two bodies can be different. See what I mean? Therefore, the reaction which happens in the body-mind organism depends on what I call the programming. My concept is that we have no control over being born to particular parents, therefore we have no control over the genes in this human object. As you know, research is now bringing out the fact that more and more of what we think are our actions turn out to be a natural result of our genes.

Increasingly, research says that the genes have a greater impact than previously thought on many things that happen. You have no control over being born to particular parents, in a particular geographical environment, in a particular social status in that environment. And in that geographical and social environment you've had conditioning from day one. Conditioning at home, conditioning in society, conditioning at school, at the social level, conditioning in church or temple, continuous bombardment of conditioning. 'This is good, that is bad. You must do this. You must never do that.' It is happening continuously, and therefore my concept is that whatever you think in every moment depends on your genes, over which you have no control, and your conditioning over which you also have no control. That is why I say no action is your action. Whatever I think and do at any moment is based entirely on my genes and conditioning, which God created. Therefore, does it not simply mean that whatever I think and do at any moment is precisely what God wants me to think and do? With this understanding, I firmly believe that whatever I do is precisely what God wants me to do, therefore the consequences are also what God expects me to accept.

Vasanas are tendencies based on what? Based on, they say, your past. I say there is no past. *Vasanas* are tendencies based on my genes and my conditioning, which God created.

And must these tendencies be removed before Self-realisation can become permanent?

Vasanas cannot be removed totally. If *vasanas* could be removed then you could expect a sage to be a perfect human being. If all the *vasanas* were removed, if Self-realisation does this, you would never find a sage getting angry; no anger, no fear, only total compassion all the time. Is that how you find the sage? Nisargadatta Maharaj would become angry very quickly, and fear would also arise. When he had to go to a dentist he said, 'Will it hurt?' Fear. Anger could arise, fear could arise, compassion could arise. All these can arise in the body-mind organism over which no ego has any control.

When Sri Ramana Maharshi was asked about some of his disciples who had spent many years, maybe twenty or thirty years, sitting with him but not awakened, he said that if the* vasanas *are too strong then the person won't become realised in this lifetime, and also that if somebody does become realised he can become unrealised if the* vasanas *are very strong. In other words, they can pull you out of awakening. Is that your understanding?

No. For me realisation happens, then one cannot be pulled out of it. Realisation, ultimate understanding, cannot be unrealised. If something is a strong obstruction, realisation will not happen. Once realisation happens, there can not be unrealisation.

But I would guess that many of the people who sit regularly in your* Satsang *are still very awakened one hour after, but maybe four or five hours later they're not anymore.

Then that is their destiny, to be awake only for two hours, three hours, four hours. Basically, what happens when people listen to me is their respective destiny according God's will, cosmic law: temporary reaction or total transformation.

But isn't it their* vasanas *that take them away from that after four or five hours?

Maybe; only if that is their destiny. Their *vasanas* are removed only if they're supposed to be removed according to their destiny.

At the end of his book,* Self-Enquiry, *Sri Ramana says, 'He who is thus endowed with a mind that has become subtle, and who has the experience of the Self is called a* jivanmukta.*' Is this the state that can be called Self-realised?

Yes, sure.

He goes on, 'And when one is immersed in the ocean of bliss and has become one with it without any differentiated existence, one is called a* videhamukta. *It is the state of* videhamukta *that is referred to as the transcendent* turiya *(state). This is the final goal.' Is this the state that can be called enlightenment?

No. *Jivanmukta* is the sage who lives his life according to my concept – totally without the sense of personal doership. Also that is *videhamukta*. *Videhamukta* means free from the doership of the body. He cannot be free of the body until the last breath.

There's no question of Self-realisation and enlightenment as two different states? Shivananda, for example, talks about seven stages of enlightenment.

That's his concept.

I would like you to make it clear that there is only one understanding and that Self-realisation and enlightenment are in fact the same thing.

Self-realisation, enlightenment, means one with God. You can have half a dozen synonyms. The only question is, what do I mean by enlightenment? Enlightenment for me means the total acceptance that there is only one source, the one unmanifest source that has become the many in this phenomenal manifestation. And in the functioning of manifestation, which we call life, ego is the separate entity. Without the ego inter-human relationships wouldn't happen, and without inter-human relationships the functioning of manifestation, life as we call it, would not have happened. Therefore, the one consciousness identified itself with the many sentient objects and created separate entities, which each identified consciousness as the separate ego. Because of this, inter-human relationships happen and life happens.

***It appears essential to meet a* guru *and stay with that* guru. *Who is the* guru?**

First and foremost there is no pure *guru*. There are many *gurus*. To which *guru* you will go depends on your destiny. Whether you go to a genuine *guru* or whether you go to a false *guru* is your destiny, and if your destiny is to go to a false *guru* for five, ten, fifteen, twenty years, you will do it. There may not be a clear distinction between false *guru* and a genuine *guru*. There may be a *guru* where the enlightenment is not total, but still teaching can happen through him.

So someone goes to a *guru* for twenty-five, thirty years. Deep down there is a frustration. There is a specific case I know. For thirty years this man was a remarkably honest and sincere *sadhaka*, spiritual seeker, but at the end of it there was a certain amount of frustration. Something made him come to me, and after two or three years he had the final understanding. Three months after he had the final understanding he was dead. He had blood cancer, leukaemia. In his own words he said, 'Ramesh, the report was practically a death sentence: galloping leukaemia. When I read it, I had never felt better in my life.' That was his destiny.

And what is the* guru's *role?

If you ask me, the *guru's* role is first to tell his disciples that whatever he says is a concept. It is not the Truth. And all that a concept can do for you is to bring you peace and harmony in life. So if the concept from the *guru* leads you to this peace and harmony, that is your destiny. The *guru* can only give his concepts. Whether the disciple will be able to accept the concepts and whether the concepts will do the disciple any good is his destiny. According to me, the duty of the *guru* is to tell the disciple it's just a concept, and also to make his own concept as clear as he possibly can so that no confusion remains in the mind of the disciple.

***Is there any way a seeker can tell who is a true* guru?**

If the seeker knows that in the presence of a *guru* he has come home, that's his *guru.*

Sri Ramana's devotees had tremendous devotion to him and he to Arunachala. Please say something about* bhakti, *devotion, in the pursuit of awakening.

Whether devotion happens in a particular body-mind organism is part of his destiny, but even *bhakti* must ultimately lead to the one conclusion, according to my concept, and that is that no one is a doer. Everything happens according to the will of God or according to the cosmic law, whichever way you go.

I will tell you the story of Tukaram. He's a very famous saint from Maharastra, a total *bhakta* (devotee). He was an uneducated man who wrote more than five thousand verses. In the original story he addresses his *guru*, Vitala, the temple *Vitobha*, a representative of *Krishna* and *Vishnu*. He tells him, 'Lord, the *jnani* (one who knows) can see you as formless, but for me, please show yourself in a form which I can enjoy and pursue, which I can pray to, for life after life.' Life after life he lived in rebirth, in devotion. See what I mean? *Bhakti*. Then when the final understanding had happened the same *bhakta*, Tukaram, goes to the temple and tells *Vitobha*, '*Vitobha*! You are a cheat! I myself didn't know that you and I are ultimately the source, but you knew and yet you extracted so many years of worship from me. You are a cheat!' The *Bhakta* suddenly becomes a *jnani.*

The *bhakta* says, *Tvameva bhakta, tvameva karta.* 'You are the doer, you are the enjoyer.' Then he says, 'You are the speaker and you are the listener. You are all there is, therefore how can the speaker be anything other than you?' Which means it may seem as if I'm speaking and Premananda is listening, or Premananda is speaking and Ramesh is listening, but the *bhakta* says it only appears like that. What is really happening is it is God functioning through both body-mind instruments, speaking through one, listening through the other. That is the difference; the *jnani* says, 'I am not the doer,' and the *bhakta* says, 'You do the speaking and you do the listening and you do the enjoying.'

Basically, it's the same thing. I'm not saying that there are two different paths to reach the same goal. The words are different, but they mean the same thing. You are the only doer. You do the speaking. You begin as a *bhakta*, end as a *jnani*, or you begin as a seeking *jnani* and end as a *bhakta*.

Seekers often have curious ideas about the enlightened state. Please describe your typical day and how you perceive the world.

Now how do I live my life? The basic answer is, in any given situation, what is life? Daily, one situation after another situation. I live my life as if I have total free will, with the total understanding that I'm not the doer. Therefore, for practical purposes, I do exactly as I think I should do as if I have free will. Having done it I know that the results have never been in my control. In any given situation I decide what I want, I put in my best efforts. I do this with a total acceptance that what results has never been in my control. I don't keep thinking of the results, wishing particular things; therefore I'm not frustrated. Basically, that's what life is, isn't it? I always do what I think I should do and accept the consequences, whether they're good, bad or indifferent, as my destiny.

The last question.

Oh! Very well planned.

Yes. It must be destiny at work.

Sure.

You have given us a profound discourse on awakening. When you meet someone with a passion for awakening, what would your short advice be?

In any given situation do whatever you think you should do and never expect any result. If you keep expecting some result you'll be frustrated;

the results have never been in your control. Therefore, at any moment do whatever you think you should do as if you are the doer. Total free will. I do whatever I think I should do to get what I want, but, having done it, I forget about the results which have never been in my control. Therefore there is no frustration. Finally, I do not condemn anyone for anything – neither myself nor the other.

Thank you.

Sri

Brahmam

When you have tendencies, impressions, desires, habits, and in that moment you ask the question, 'Who am I?' it is just another thought. When we have many thoughts this question is of no use. It is only for ripe, mature people. When there is peace inside then naturally, heartfully, comes the question, 'Who am I?'

Whoever is seeking enlightenment must disappear.

Sri Brahmam

Sri Brahmam

Sri Brahmam was born in 1944. Since childhood he always questioned the purpose of life, knowing that everybody will eventually die. When he was about six years old, a *mantra, Om Nama Shivaya,* arose naturally and repeated spontaneously inside him at all times. During a visit to the Sri Ramana Ashram he had a spontaneous awakening while still a young man. He worked for many years as a school teacher and in the last years, since his retirement, has made himself available to seekers.

I met Sri Brahmam through some friends whom I could see had been changed by their time with him. He could often be found in the Sri Ramana Ashram and I came to know how he had awakened within the **ashram.** ***We met only once to conduct this interview. I was impressed by the clear way in which he expressed Sri Ramana's teachings.***

Sri Ramana proposed the fundamental question, 'Who am I?' Who are you?

(Silence)

When you have tendencies, impressions, desires, habits, and in that moment you ask the question, 'Who am I?' it is just another thought. When we have many thoughts this question is of no use, it is just another thought. To ask this question requires peace and purity inside. It is only for ripe, mature people. When there is peace inside then naturally, heartfully, comes the question, 'Who am I?'

If you have any impressions or desires, don't enquire, because if this question does not enter deeply into the heart it will merge into your mind and become another thought. So, first, you need peace. Peace is Self, peace is grace. Without grace, without peace, the perfect answer to the enquiry 'Who am I?' cannot arise. The answer is that all thoughts should disappear. You are questioning, 'Who am I?' If any thought arises, that is 'I'. Thought only arises with the help of 'I'. So, how can you enquire into that 'I'? Only without thoughts, otherwise the false 'I' will remain.

Here at Arunachala, by the grace of *Arunachaleswara* and Bhagavan Sri Ramana Maharshi, everyone has Self-experience. But the work cannot be completed. Why? Because there are so many tendencies, so many habits, so many activities. In these moments it is not possible to enquire, 'Who am I?' This enquiry is a deep search inside. If any thought arises, enquiry has stopped. If any light, any experience, any god, any vision arises, if you know anything, that is the false 'I' only – it is not real, and that 'I' has become one of the thoughts. You're far away from the Self.

A very deep level of enquiry is necessary. There should be full consciousness. If you lose your consciousness, sleep will come, or thoughts will arise. If you lose that 'I' thought, if you don't observe it, it will produce so many thoughts. If you forget it, you go to sleep, deep sleep. Deep sleep is not helpful for realisation. Thought is a waste; sleep also is a waste.

You must be fully conscious. In consciousness there are no thoughts, no deep sleep, no sleep, no body, no world, nothing. In full consciousness, the 'I' thought merges into the Self and will disappear. Nothing to know, nothing to achieve, nothing to see. In Self-realisation, the 'I' thought disappears. Then that consciousness of Self will remain. When you reach the source of Self it is very easy to observe the rising of thought. If you observe the rising of thought very easily, then you have no problems about death, about life, about anything, because you know very clearly that the 'I' thought is an illusion. All thoughts are created by, through, this 'I'. You are always in Self, and always, when anything rises within you, you see: 'This is illusion, this is all illusion.' You don't have any problems in your life. From that experience onwards you always find the source of the 'I' thought. The Self doesn't change.

But for full consciousness, awareness is needed, then there is no chance to power thoughts.

But here, again, there is the false 'I'. You already have Self-experience, you have consciousness, awareness inside. But there is the false 'I'. The Self-grace, Self-power, removes the 'I' thought. The 'I' thought will escape the awareness, and again it will arise. But this consciousness is never lost, so the 'I' thought has no power. Why? It must be born from the Self. You are the Self. How could it be born from Self? There is no chance for the 'I'. It has created so many births and now it is going to die – it cannot be still, it is trying to get strength. But there is awareness, there is grace, there is power of Self.

When the 'I' thought is going to die, automatically thoughts have no power. All your tendencies, all your habits, all your life incidents are going to die. When the false 'I' is completely dead then there is no mind, no body, no world – only Self remains. That was the case with Bhagavan Sri Ramana Maharshi. Bhagavan said, 'I am trying, I am trying so much but no thoughts.'

There was no 'I'. Bhagavan killed the 'I' permanently, with no chance for it to rise again. So, no thoughts for him, no 'I' for him. That is the enquiry. That is 'Who am I?' Observe your 'I' thought without escaping, without forgetting. Observe steadily till that thought disappears, then immediately you may reach the source of thought. But how to observe the 'I' thought? Where is it? You don't know the 'I' thought; you call it ego.

Every thought is 'I', every thought is ego. How do you know: this is ego, this is the 'I' thought? When you are in meditation all thoughts disappear. You are seeing emptiness. But the emptiness is seen by the 'I' thought, and you are having an experience, 'Oh, no thoughts. I feel good. I have peace.' That experiencer is 'I'. Who is observing the emptiness? That is 'I'. So Bhagavan said, 'See the seer.' The mind is seeing from inside. From inside there is a seer; see the seer, then the problem will dissolve. There is a seer inside so there is much activity, many thoughts. If there is no seer? Then also, no thoughts; there is the feeling, 'Oh.'

Focus your keen observation directly on that seer, on that experiencer. If that experiencer falls down, your breath will stop suddenly, your mind will smash immediately. Then you are not able to control it. Then so much fear will arise, it is not easy to control. Every moment we must die. After death it is very easy to get Self-realisation because death means losing the 'I' thought. If the 'I' thought dies it is equal to death because we are dying with the 'I' thought. So, observe that 'I' thought. In emptiness there is the seer – catch him, see him and you will experience nothing inside. That is the original 'I' which remains. Focus your full strength and keen observation on that experiencer. Don't lose that keen observation. If you lose it, then thoughts will arise. So this is the process of enquiring, 'Who am I?'

When Sri Ramana was asked, 'When will the realisation of the Self be gained?' he replied, 'When the world which is what-is-seen has been removed, there will be realisation of the Self which is the seer.' What is the true understanding of the world? How to remove the world?

If you remove the 'I' thought, without thoughts, you never see the world. In deep sleep, when the 'I' thought is absent, it is not possible to see the world. Thoughts will be absent, then there is no world. It is difficult to understand because all holy persons move around in this world: 'Oh, if there is no world, how do they do their activities?' That doubt will arise in us. It is impossible for the mind to understand. Mind itself is an illusion because it is moving, it is changing, it is coming, it is going, it is absent in deep sleep. The world is seen by this mind. Mind itself is an illusion. So what about the world? It is also an illusion.

Every Self-realised person sees only the Self. They have no illusions. They all see the same as Bhagavan: they see no difference between men and women; they don't know the world. The Self-realised person has no false 'I', he has no thoughts, he has no illusion. So there is only Self-experience. Everywhere there is the Self. Bhagavan said, 'I have no thoughts. There is only the Self everywhere. I am also the Self. I know nothing.'

There is form, that is an illusion created by the false 'I'. There are attractions – are they real? They were created by the illusion of the mind. So, remove all your illusions, remove your false 'I'; then there is nothing in the world. At this superior level you are seeing the world only as

Self. If you see any person, anywhere, they appear only as the Self. Real understanding of the world is possible only without the 'I' thought, the ego.

It has been suggested that the mind must be destroyed for liberation to occur. Do you have a mind? Sri Ramana used the term* manonasha *to describe the state of liberation, meaning destroyed mind. How to destroy the mind?

'Destroy the mind' means destroy the 'I' thought only. This is the *manonasha*. If you try to destroy the mind, thought will arise. With any effort, there is a rising of thought. So if you are trying you are creating your thoughts, and with those thoughts you are trying to remove thought. How is it possible? So, if we don't have the grace of Self we will never destroy the mind because our effort is always an illusion; our effort always creates thoughts, our effort always creates illusion. Only one who has grace has the eligibility to destroy his mind and thoughts, without effort, very naturally and very easily. If there is no 'I' thought it is not a mind, it is called the Self.

Bhagavan said, and all holy persons are saying, that surrender and trust, are necessary. If you don't trust, you are always creating illusion; the 'I' thought is creating all thoughts. I can follow the advice of a *guru* and so I say, 'I am observing my breath.' But I am creating the breath; I am creating the observer; I am creating the observer and the breath and I am seeing. Then I get peace: Oh, that peace also I am creating. I have no peace: no peace is created by me. I saw God: that God is created by me. No problem: I am creating no problem myself. What is necessary for destroying the mind? How is it possible? Where is it?

It is possible only for one who has no mind, who has no 'I' thought. This is only possible by grace, by a holy person's grace. By your effort, by your ego, too much is created. If you have any experience – 'I had an experience' – who had? Who had the experience? I had. Who is 'I'? Where is the experience in deep sleep? Where is 'I' in deep sleep? Where has 'I' gone? This is a great drama, it is called illusion. Your death, illusion; your practice, illusion; your birth, illusion. So Bhagavan said one time, 'I have no birth. You are doing *jayantis*, birth celebrations, to me – I had no birth at all.' How can you understand this? 'I see him moving and talking – why is Bhagavan saying he had no birth?' But it is true; there is no reality anywhere, within you or outside. So we must have trust, surrender.

To surrender to God one must first give up likes and dislikes. One who has like and dislikes, he never trusts, he never surrenders to God. It is true. If you have likes and dislikes, your surrender, your trust, is only drama. If you trust, you surrender immediately. To have no likes and dislikes, that is the symbol of surrender.

What about* vasanas, *the tendencies of the mind? Must these be removed before Self-realisation can become permanent? Could it be enough to achieve a* sattvic *(calm and peaceful) mind?

Before realisation you must remove *vasanas*. That is enough to achieve the peace. There is the idea that Westerners have more tendencies than Hindus or other people but this is not so. Everyone has a mind which creates. But a *sattvic* mind is needed. How do you understand calm mind? How can you tell if it is pure? Is speaking about Truth pure mind? Following service or prayer, is it pure? The Self knows, God knows the purity of us. Gradually, day-by-day, without your effort, you will become pure. That is grace. Grace is always here, so don't think about your purity. Don't think about anything. Don't give any work to your mind. That is purity.

Give up your thinking. Don't try to understand what purity is, what meditation is. Bhagavan said, 'There is grace always within you. Keep quiet.' When you think about yourself you say, 'Oh, I am a bad fellow. I have these habits. I have this confusion. I have these *vasanas*.' If you don't think about it, you are alright. Who told you you are bad? Did God ever tell you this? No, it's the mind's creation. Stop your mind's creation only – that is enough.

All people who come here to Arunachala have eligibility for enquiry, for Self-realisation. Bhagavan said we came here because we have already done so much and here we do nothing. Grace is always within us and surrounding us. Be peaceful, joyful; all will be done perfectly, correctly. No one who came here ever failed, so trust the power that is guiding you. When grace enters us, it removes all illusion, all mind. Self-realisation becomes permanent.

Many Western seekers come to India looking for enlightenment as if it is an experience. What is enlightenment?

Whoever is seeking enlightenment must disappear. That is enlightenment. (laughter) Visions, powers, light, forms, experience – this is not enlightenment. Enlightenment means permanent peace, no death problem for you.

Such a short answer? (laughs)

Only one sentence. (all laugh) Enlightenment means the one who wants enlightenment must disappear. (all laugh)

Are there any qualifications for enlightenment?

God selects those qualifications, never us. Naturally there is a power inside us and it is removing unnecessary thoughts, unnecessary habits. Leave it to that power, that grace. The grace itself is changing us. We never change with our knowledge or effort because when we have any habits or desires we are trying to fulfil them. But grace knows what is needed and what is unnecessary, what is preventing Self-realisation – it knows. So it is always removing what is unnecessary and this brings about change. Here at Arunachala this is a natural process.

We never completely love or trust any person. Service, devotion, meditation, love, trust, surrender, are never complete. Why? There is 'I' and it cannot allow these qualities. Trust, prayer and love are also difficult. So a good method is to think about your mind, about you, and don't think about anything outside – any philosophy, any god, any lectures, anything. Always observe your mind, not the world.

If your mind is negative all the people and the whole world will appear negative. Positive thoughts create a positive world. So, good thoughts, good perception, good mind – you are good. Bad thoughts, bad perception, bad mind – you are bad. But mind is not good or bad; remove those dualities, then the mind is pure. So, observe your mind with constant awareness. Then you will realise there is no mind at that state. God is correct, your thinking is at fault; so always observe your mind. If you care about your body and your interest is on the world, you don't recognise the grace. You are wasting your time. You are wasting your life thinking about others, thinking about the world; you are wasting your valuable life. Observe your mind always, don't observe others. Don't interfere in the lives of others. Always think about yourself, 'What am I doing? What is my mind doing now?'

Sri Ramana said that Self-enquiry is the most direct route to realising the Self. What do you say about Self-enquiry?

In other methods there is a seer, seeing and seen, and all experiences are going and coming – so many methods. But in Self-inquiry the mind will be completely burnt. In other methods the 'I' thought still remains. It subsides in the Self and again it springs up. The mind has so many experiences and *vasanas* and the 'I' thought gets stronger. But in Self-enquiry, gradually the mind is burnt; it has no chance to come back. When your mind is burnt, then you get peace. In Self-enquiry, Self-realisation, there is no chance for the mind to come back. Bhagavan said it is simple, suitable, and for ever; it is permanent. Self-enquiry means being without the 'I' thought.

Is there any difference between Self-realisation and enlightenment?

If anything appears inside, that is not Self-realisation. There is nothing to see, there is no appearance. Duality is helpful for greatness, to reach divine worlds, to see gods, divine places. But Self-realisation – it is everywhere. Wherever you go, there is the Self. Bhagavan said, 'All is within you.' So the Self is everywhere. This is possible for any person.

Methods may be different but you must kill the false 'I', then there is no longer a method; that is full Self-realisation. If you don't kill the 'I' there is duality. Self-realisation and enlightenment are both the same: two different words which mean the same.

At the end of his book,* Self-Enquiry, *Sri Ramana says, 'He who is thus endowed with a mind that has become subtle, and who has the experience of the Self is called a* jivanmukta.*' Is this the state that can be called Self-realised?

One who has realisation, who has reached beyond the mind, is a *jivanmukta*. Subtle mind means no tendencies, no attachment with the mind, no attachment with the breath, no 'I' thought.

It appears essential to meet a* guru *and stay with that* guru. *Who is the* guru*? What is the* guru's *role? How to recognise a true* guru*?

Peace is Self. Peace is *guru*. If you sit before your *guru*, you should have peace. Then he is a true *guru*. A Self-realised person helps others attain realisation. If one has peace always within him, automatically that peace enters into others. That peace is grace, that peace is the Self.

Anyone who speaks with the mind or from memory, if he tries to learn, to know, if he is doing practice, he is not the *guru*. If he thinks any person is separate from him, he is not the *guru*. If he thinks good or bad of a person, he is not the *guru*. If he tries to understand others, he is not the *guru*.

In all states – wakening, sleep, deep sleep – he is the same and never loses his state of Self-abiding because he has no differences. That is *guru*. The Self-realised person's grace will enter directly into the Self, not into the mind. When we sit in meditation, peace, emptiness and calmness are increasing inside. Though we hear the outside sounds and there are always thoughts, there is no disturbance from them inside; that is grace, the *guru's* power. There is consciousness within you; there is full awareness within you. The *guru's* grace is going directly to the Self, Self-awareness, Self-consciousness.

Self-awareness is gradually killing your mind; it changes without your effort. Naturally grace is removing everything which is unnecessary, without your knowledge and effort. That is the grace of the *guru.* If you make any effort, it will stop. So keep quiet, be still, and the *guru's* work will be finished very soon.

With the mind it is impossible to select the perfect *guru.* You have some opinions and you see the *guru* according to your opinions. If your opinions match your ideas about a *guru* then that is the one you choose. That is a mind trick. No, this is not the correct way to choose. Peace is God, peace is grace, peace is *guru.* Bhagavan also said this. Peace is not available by our effort, by the mind; it is only possibly through the grace of the *guru* or the Self.

Seekers often have curious ideas about the enlightened state. Can you describe your typical day and how you perceive the world?

Many devotees came to Bhagavan and he advised them according to their maturity. But Bhagavan never saw anyone; he was in a thoughtless state. His personal advice is not from the mind because he sees only the Self. Divine grace flows without effort, without reason, without purpose and action. He has no world to perceive.

Is there something you would like to add?

Every person is God but they are all thinking with their mind according to their opinions. We are created by God, we are God, but through our desires and our belief that this world is real we forget our God consciousness. Remove your thoughts: 'I am the body', 'This world is real', then it is very easy to know that I am God. You are filled completely with garbage but you think it is very valuable. You are talking unnecessarily, you are living unnecessarily, you are collecting unnecessary garbage. So, day-by-day, we lose our natural state.

These thoughts are disturbing us. In the present, do good, see and speak good, then there will not be disturbances inside. There will be peace; it is very easy.

Swami

Dayananda

If the mind is momentary why do you want to control it? Who will control it? The controller is also momentary. The whole thing is wrong thinking. You are Self-evident. You exist. If your existence is to be arrived at, then to whom is it to become evident? The existence of the Self is evident to the Self.

DAYANANDA

The guru is one who makes you see
that you are not any different from him.

Swami Dayananda

Swami Dayananda

Swami Dayananda Saraswati has been teaching *Vedanta* in India for more than four decades, and around the world since 1976. In his public talks abroad, Swamiji has spoken at many of the most prestigious American universities and has addressed international conventions, UNESCO and the United Nations where he participated in the Millennium Peace Summit. He has large teaching *ashrams* in North and South India and in the USA.

Swami Dayananda Saraswati is a distinguished, traditional teacher of* Vedanta, *a thorough and highly professional man devoted to traditional* Vedanta *values. During the last four years, the groups I have taken to visit him as part of the Arunachala Pilgrimage Retreat have always been rewarded with long lively question-and-answer meetings. His interview is one of the most thorough, clear and comprehensive. He speaks with the full authority of his seventy-eight years.

There is the fundamental question, 'Who am I?' Who are you?

If somebody wants to know more about oneself, psychologically, who am I? is a valid question, because one has certain experiences, childhood experiences, buried in the unconscious. One doesn't really know what they are but one has the experience of being lonely in the midst of people. One is prone to anger, prone to varieties of emotions for which there are no real external causes. The same situations can be met with objectivity. So why this anger and fear over which you have no control?

If I am asked to clap, I can clap (claps) or I need not clap. The freedom is with me. The action is based upon my will. I do it, I need not do it, I can do it differently. So that is will-based. Suppose I ask you to be angry – you can't be. It doesn't mean that you don't get angry. You get angry, but not consciously. So there is a cause for anger that lies in the unconscious. So, if one wants to know about oneself more, one can undergo psychoanalysis, then, having found some problem, one can undergo psychotherapy.

One can ask this question: 'Who am I?' but it presupposes that there is an 'I' that we don't know. Then, if I know, what do I gain? We begin to analyse what it is we really want. Everybody is a seeker. Who is not a seeker? Some want money, some power, some want money and power. Everyone wants pleasure: simple sensory pleasure, aesthetic pleasure, satisfaction. If the head of a corporation wants to buy another corporation it is not for money, it is for ego satisfaction and comes under *karma* (result of all actions). Money, power and status come under *artha*. *Artha* is that which gives you security. So these are the two very common, universal pursuits.

In our Indian culture we include one more value, one more end – that is *dharma*, the righteous way of living. One should be able to conform to *dharma* – not to hurt others, to treat others in the same way we would wish them to treat us. That is *dharma*. Why are we not able to follow this? Because of the pressure created by other pursuits like *artha* and *karma*. We cut corners, go against *dharma*, and seek what we really want. But, through experience and one's own personal initiative, one learns and grows to conform to *dharma*.

These are all *purunartha*, human ends that we need and want to accomplish. Can I change the status of being a seeker? That is where the enquiry begins. That question – 'Who am I?' – can it change my status of being a seeker? I have a certain self-identity. In this self-identity my body-mind-sense complex plays a very important role. I am as good as the body is, the mind is. How much I know, what I know, my past, all this constitutes my individuality. This is me. But this me, any way you look at it, is limited, wanting, in fact insignificant. You see, it all depends upon the perspective from which you look at yourself. If it is a small perspective you become very big, but if you look at what is, Mother Earth cannot even be represented by one pixel. The continent, the country, the state, the county, the street, the house, the room and the place where you are sitting become insignificant.

I am insignificant, small. Just compare yourself with others: money wise – wanting; skill wise – wanting; power wise – wanting; health wise – wanting. Human beings are self-conscious, self-judging, and therefore have many complexes – height complexes, colour complexes, eyebrow complexes. (all laugh) I am wanting. All through my lifetime my unfulfilled desires are more than my fulfilled desires and therefore there is no chance of taking myself to be a successful person.

If I am a person who is globally aware, I want the people to be different, I want the governments to be different, I want the political leadership to be more enlightened, the religious leadership to be more enlightened. All these are desires, unfulfilled desires, and some of them cannot be fulfilled. I want more equal distribution of wealth. I want everything to be different.

The more I am aware of what is going on the more desires there are. There are many spheres of desires, therefore I am a dissatisfied person and self cannot be accepted. This is me and I can't accept myself. When I can't accept myself, the whole of life is a seeking of accepting myself. The self I am conscious of is not acceptable, it is wanting – this is the truth. Therefore, in life I am seeking myself to be acceptable. Through money I won't accept myself, through others I won't accept myself, through the societal concept of success I won't accept myself. Even if I achieve this success I am still unacceptable because I am limited, I am wanting – nothing will free me from being limited – no additions. This is the truth.

It is very important we understand these things before we jump on the 'Who am I?' question. Self non-acceptance is the issue, self-acceptance is the goal. I am embellishing myself to become an acceptable self. A broomstick is always a broomstick, no matter how you embellish it. You can put a diamond necklace around it, but it is a broomstick wearing a diamond necklace. This is exactly what happens to this person: no matter what he adds to himself it is the same – either he gets rid of things or he adds things – it is the same. Therefore there is no such thing as freedom from seeking. So we must ask what we are seeking freedom from. To ask 'Who am I?' is the wrong approach. What I am seeking is freedom from being small. Freedom, not from myself, but from being small. That accounts for all our pursuits. I want to be free from being nobody. Everyone wants to be somebody. If nothing can be accomplished then one dies one's hair green. In New York I saw a woman with green hair. (all laugh)

What kind of freedom am I seeking? I want freedom from being a seeker. But if I attempt this as a limited being, as an individual, any subtraction or addition still equals a limited being. If you are not an individual you are not going anywhere; if you are an individual, wherever you go you are there, therefore you have to deal with yourself. The smallness will not go. Therefore, there is no *moksha*, no liberation. Alright, there is no *moksha* – so can I accept myself now? To look at it another way, perhaps my conclusion about myself, that I am a wanting person, is wrong. If I look at myself through my body, my mind, my senses, I am bound to be wanting. I am designed to be wanting, but the body doesn't have an 'I' sense, the mind doesn't have an 'I' sense, the senses don't have an 'I' sense. The judgement is centred on me, on 'I' – the source of the problem is 'I', and the solution to the problem is 'I'. If I am wanting I cannot accept myself. So, the only solution, the only way out, is that maybe I am not wanting.

My own experience is that, occasionally, I am not wanting. Occasionally I am at home with the world, with myself; I'm happy. I pick up a moment of happiness looking at the stars, the trees, the birds, the mountains, listening to music or enjoying something. I feel I am okay! So, in spite of my having all the unfulfilled desires embedded in that very personality that is me, with all angularities, in spite of all that, I just see myself in a desirable light. So this experience of being different – desirably different – is enough. That's a window through which I can make a supposition: perhaps I am that one who is there when I am happy. This happiness has not come from the fulfilling of a desire. You read a comic strip – you are happy. You listen to a joke – you become happy.

A woman received a bunch of flowers from her husband who was travelling. The message written on the card was 'No'. She phoned her husband:

'What is it that you have written?'

'What did I write?'

'The message.'

'What message? I didn't give any message.'

'But there is a message: "No".'

'The florist asked me, "Do you have any message?" and I said, "No".' (all laugh)

You laugh, at least some of you laugh. Some of you require a little more, perhaps, to make you laugh. It is easy to make anyone laugh. What happened when you laughed? Did you fulfil all your desires? Is the credit card paid off? Is the mortgage paid off? Are the problems solved? No, nothing is solved. And yet you can be happy. It is a great thing to really examine. An experience is as good as what you know about it. An experience is dumb, dumb like a stone. You have to know what it is all about.

Our whole *samsara*, life of becoming, is experience-oriented – we are all experience hunters. These good experiences, acceptable experiences, are few and far between and they keep us going. In these experiences I see myself as acceptable – therefore the world is acceptable. This occurs in the same world in which I am unhappy, in which I am searching for my acceptance. So in the same world where I am unhappy, I see myself in a light in which I would like to see myself. Then again I want to repeat the experience, I want a better experience. I see a flower – a flower is an object – and I am happy seeing the flower, but happiness is not in the flower or in me – it is me. That's what experience is – centred on me. Is this really me? Or is the other wanting me really me, because that seems to be more lasting than this one? The unhappy, unacceptable wanting self is seeking to be this self, this happy self. If you cannot suspend the wanting self you can't be happy.

Our self-consciousness is meant for complexes. In fact these complexes drive us to the solution. Maybe there is a solution. That is why you cannot stop seeking. Why? Because if I am a wanting person intrinsically, then there is that sense of want that can never be given up. What is intrinsic to an object cannot be negated, cannot be suspended as long as the object is there. Fire is hot and you cannot remove the heat and still have fire. Not possible, because heat is intrinsic to fire. If this limitation of wanting is centred on the self, it cannot be negated. I negate in a moment of joy, therefore maybe that is what I am. That is why nobody complains that they are happy. Nobody comes to me and complains: 'Swamiji, I don't know what to do. I am too happy these days.'

Many Western seekers come to India looking for enlightenment as if it is an experience. What is enlightenment?

An experience is only as good as your interpretation. It has to be understood. We don't lack experience. I am seeing you, you are seeing me. This is one experience. In this experience there is a subject, there is an object. Subject and object are opposed to each other. This is duality. And this is going to be there all the time. If you resolve it for the time being you don't become enlightened. You can resolve subject-object in sleep – the head is empty. An empty head is not an enlightened head. An enlightened head is one in which the subject is also the object – that is enlightenment; that is knowledge.

What the subject can objectify, the subject can know. If the subject and the object are both one and the same, the person doesn't have a means of knowing; he needs another means of knowing. That's what *Vedanta*, the *Vedic* philosophy, is. That's why I say that we need to know certain basics before we seek anything, then our seeking is very well directed and pronounced. Otherwise we still remain in darkness, groping.

In its own reality the Self is acceptable, it is *purna*, all-pervading. There is nothing more secure than the Self. So Self is acceptable, and if the Self is accepted then it is not a question of experiencing the Self, because all experiences are strung in the Self, and the Self is in and through all experiences. Therefore, you don't require a special experience of the Self, the Self is already experienced, it is the content of all experience.

Are there any qualifications for enlightenment? Is* sadhana *(spiritual practice) necessary? If yes, what form do you advise?

A human being should become human first, then all these things will come. You have to say, 'I am the whole,' you have to discover, you have to know. So what is the qualification? For any knowledge you require preparedness. Suppose there is a child of a mathematician and a physicist. His grandparents are all professors. This boy is only three years old and the mathematician wants to teach him maths – a simple five plus four – and he can't make him understand what it is all about. Why? There is an age for everything. What time can prepare nothing else can prepare. Age is very important at this level. Anything can be understood if the preparedness is there.

I have to understand that I am the whole. Both the subject and object, whether the object is a micro-object like an electron or whether it is the whole universe, are One. Both come from the same, both are the same. That takes a lot of learning, it takes a lot of understanding and a lot of clearance of mistakes and confusions. So what are the qualifications for this? We would say a person should be rational in thinking – irrational conclusions should be seen as irrational. That capacity, that intellectual discipline, you gain by your own experience, by your own thinking and some discipline, or by schooling. That is not negotiable; you are a rational being and of course you have to be rational – nothing irrational. I can be above reason but there is nothing unreasonable.

Therefore, the qualification of simple right thinking is taken for granted. In *Sanskrit* (language of ancient Indian scriptures) we have a list of attributes, of qualifications. You grow into humaneness, into being a human being, through consideration for others, not hurting others, compassion, giving, sharing, friendliness, being non-judgemental, objectivity, dispassion. Practice is involved because you have to sometimes 'fake it to make it'. (all laugh) If compassion is not there you can't be compassionate, but even though compassion is not there you can act compassionately; even though love is not there you can act lovingly. Act it out. You act it out as though you have love and love will come. Cultivate friendship by being friendly. Caring comes by acting caringly. These are all your natural traits. They are all connected to your own wholeness, completeness. That's why they are desirable qualities.

So a lot of practice is needed, but before that a lot of prayer, devotion, because you have to bring *Iswara*, the Lord, into your life. The more *Iswara*, the more objective you are. That is a big topic and is part of the preparation. The pursuit of knowledge goes along with this and a teacher is required. One has to go to a teacher who is well informed, who himself had a teacher who also had a teacher because there is a certain methodology involved in this. The secret is that the methodology is never handed over to you in words, it grows upon you under the teacher. Like Indian music, it can never be taught. You can't write it out. It has to grow upon you over a period of time. So the teaching methodology is very important.

When Sri Ramana was asked, 'When will the realisation of the Self be gained?' he replied, 'When the world which is what-is-seen has been removed, there will be realisation of the Self which is the seer.' What is the true understanding of the world? How to remove the world?

When Bhagavan Ramana is answering the question, obviously he means something more than the words convey. I, the subject, is opposed to the object. What is 'not I' is much more than what the 'I' is. If both are one reality, then the reality should transcend both the subject and the object. So when the subject withdraws from the object and falls back on its own lap, all that would be there is the content of the objects which is the Self-revealing content of the awareness which is the content of the subject too.

There is no literal destruction. The world, if it is real, cannot be destroyed. If it is not real, it need not be destroyed. Understand that.

Elsewhere, Bhagavan Ramana says one's mind, when withdrawn from all objects, is Self-revealing consciousness, which is the Truth, the Truth of everything. This is knowing the Truth.

It has been suggested that the mind must be destroyed for liberation to occur. Do you have a mind? Sri Ramana used the term **manonasha** ***to describe the state of liberation, meaning destroyed mind. How to destroy the mind?***

By the word mind, Ramana means the 'I' thought. All thoughts form the mind and they are centred on the 'I' thought. If the thoughts are mind, (and if the thoughts are based upon the 'I' thought), the 'I' thought is the mind. The *manonasha* is therefore the isolation and destruction of this I that alienates you from everything else. The mind is reduced to I, and that I alienates you from everything else. But in fact the Truth of the I is this alienating I, and also what it alienates itself from. The subject is I, and the object is I. The whole subject-object is called *Iswara*, the Lord. The whole thing is you. This is what we teach.

Manonasha is only a *prakriya*, a method, to turn one's attention to the Self. You withdraw from *drisha*, from the world of objects, and you turn towards yourself, the Self. We use this method to separate the I from *drisha*, from what we objectify. The Self is not what we objectify. The Self is the one that objectifies. Then what is the Self? Then follows the whole enquiry. So it is a methodology. It is not *manonasha* – mind is not an issue. If mind has to be destroyed, then after destruction how is the person going to talk? (all laugh)

Swami, this is a very important point because, as you know, in the Buddhist tradition they are looking for 'no-mind'.

When they say 'no-mind', what do they mean? They mean 'thought-free mind'. A 'thought-free mind' is an empty mind.

Not a destroyed mind?

Not a destroyed mind. If it is a destroyed mind then you cannot have a thought afterwards! Their whole lives are gone working for a no-thought mind. There will always be thought. Only in sleep is there no thought – no particular thought. In dream there is thought. In waking there is thought. When you close your eyes there is thought. When can you stop thinking? Why should you stop thinking? No-thinking doesn't solve the problem. The problem is wrong thinking. A person makes a mistake in simple arithmetic and then the teacher says, 'It is your mind.' Will 'no-mind' give him arithmetic knowledge? (all laugh) His wrong thinking was the problem, not his mind. The whole thing is that there is a problem with the problem. You are solving a problem that doesn't exist. If it exists, you can't solve it. If it doesn't exist then you should see that it doesn't exist. To solve the problem of wrong thinking requires an entirely different approach. It requires a means of knowledge which has to come from outside. It is an epistemological problem. That is why this neo-*Vedanta*, this modern spirituality, is all moving in circles. I would say they are all innocent. They don't know what they are about. What does it mean to say you are lost in the ocean of bliss? Who is lost? And who comes to report that? Their words do not come from knowledge.

To see me sitting here you have to use your eyes, you have to use your ears. You are behind the eyes and the ears – the mind and you. And the eyes and ears are a means of knowing. Therefore, Swami is. Anything which is, is arrived at like that. And then what do you see? Is it Swami Dayananda or is it Swami Iswarananda? (We look very much alike.) You have to employ your valid means of knowledge to know. Anything that is and anything that is not has to be known to you, that's why there is no emptiness. Emptiness is known to you. There is no emptiness.

You can spend a whole lifetime meditating and looking for emptiness, looking at the mind or at something else. If you look at all these, what will happen? Enlightened? When you look at the mind all day you loose your linear thinking and afterwards you become dull. Every day you do meditation like that you become duller and duller. Useless! It is good to just be aware. That is a good thing; that much alone. Alertness; not fidgeting. Being conscious about what you do and what you say, especially about what you say. In our culture you are required to have discipline over talking. Loose talking is not allowed, so first be sure you have a worthwhile topic. Second, be sure the person is interested to listen and last comes your urge to talk.

The knowledge that removes *dukha*, this sadness, pain, the seeking, centred on oneself, is possible. That *yoga* of knowledge will take place for the one whose food intake is moderate, the one who is very conscious about all activities, and the one who doesn't waste one's energy in fidgeting and is alert during the waking hours. (*Bhagavad Gita* chapter 6.17) Nothing more.

If the mind is momentary why do you want to control it? Who will control it? The controller is also momentary. The whole thing is wrong thinking. You are Self-evident. You exist. If your existence is to be arrived at, then to whom is it to become evident? The existence of the Self becomes evident to whom? Everything becomes evident to the Self. The existence of the Self is evident to the Self. That is what is called Self-awareness. Now we are removing from the Self-evident Self all wrong notions. That is called Self-knowledge. First negate what it is not and then recognise what it is.

The negation itself will be arrived at. Negation is total. Any part of the Self that is available for objectification is not the Self! It is not Self. That is the first stage. The second stage is 'not Self is Self'. Where the Self is, there is also 'not Self'. The 'not Self' is Self, but the Self is not 'not Self'. In other words, a thought (not Self) is myself – but I am not the thought. This includes the 'I' thought.

In *Upadesa Saram*, Bhagavan Ramana wrote: *Vrttayas-tvaham vrtti-masritah, Vrttayo mano viddhayaham manah.* All thoughts form the mind, and they are centred on the 'I' thought, *ahamvrttim*. If the thoughts are mind, and if the thoughts are based upon the 'I' thought, then the 'I' thought is the mind. Therefore the real mind is *ahamvrttim* – this is Ramana's thesis.

Then, when you enquire into the 'I' thought, the thought goes away and only *vastu*, the Truth, remains. *Aham-ayam kuto bhavati cinvatah, Ayi patat-yaham nija-vicaranam.* When you begin to enquire 'What is this I?' with the help of the teaching, *ahamkara*, the ego, the enquirer himself, dissolves into the Self-evident being leaving no one who can answer the question. He is the whole, he is everything. This is Self-enquiry.

Later, Bhagavan Ramana says: *Ahami nasa-bhaj-yaham-ahamtaya, Sphurati hrt-svayam parama-purna-sat.* If you enquire what exactly this *aham* is, you discover this *ahamkara* – the knower – is himself *mithya* (false, apparent), is dependent upon the known as well as the knower – both depend upon the one whole, one whole *sat* (Truth) which Self-exists. That is called whole – both subject and object are one and the same Truth.

Whatever you see in front of you plus yourself, both together are the whole. The hearer and the heard; the seer and the seen, are one whole. Subject-object are one whole. That is why any small thing can make you happy. Whether it is a microbe or whether it is the cosmos, it's one reality – subject-object.

Bhagavan Ramana says that in that very place where this 'I' resolves, the Self-evident being reveals itself as limitless. It is Self-evident. All the notions drop off. That is the nature of knowledge, Self-knowledge.

What about* vasanas*, the tendencies of the mind? Must these be removed before Self-realisation can become permanent? Is it enough to achieve a* sattvic *(calm and peaceful) state of mind and to know one's* vasanas *so that they no longer bind? How to remove the* vasanas*?

This is another thesis, the *vasana* thesis. *Vedanta* talks about three *vasanas*: *vishaya vasana* is subject-object orientation, which is removed by enquiry, *vichara*; *deha vasana* is the body *vasana* and we are born with that; *sastra vasana* is the need to study more, a sense of not enough scholarship. All these go away by consistent contemplation. You are the whole. You will never become the whole. You don't lack experience of the whole. Whatever you experience is the whole. There is no such thing as 'wholeness will appear'. The wholeness always is – what is, is the whole. It is one hundred percent cognitive. That is traditional *Vedanta*.

Having a good traditional teacher is important. With a teacher, when you are studying the *Upanishads*, you are studying yourself; the *Upanishads* are a mirror. A person who no longer has any more wrong notions is called a *jivanmukta* (liberated soul in this life). He has the body-mind-sense complex; he has thinking-hunger-thirst – normal life! In fact, the difference between the *jivan* (individual soul) and the *jivanmukta* is that the former is normally abnormal while the latter is normally normal. Normally abnormal means that also everyone else is confused, therefore he is okay. (all laugh)

It seems essential to meet a* guru *and surrender to that* guru*. Who is the* guru*? What is the* guru*'s role? How to recognise a true* guru*?

The *guru* is the one who teaches the *mahavakya*, the equation, that you are the whole, you are *Iswara*. That sentence raises a contradiction because you are an individual and *Iswara* is all. You are small knowing and *Iswara* is all knowing. How can I be *Iswara*? This contradiction is raised and then resolved.

If I tell a wave, 'You are the ocean,' the wave will ask, 'How can I be the ocean?' Then I will say, 'You are born of ocean, sustained by ocean, go back to ocean, you are never separated from the ocean.' The wave will say, 'That is true, I am part of the ocean, I cannot be the ocean.' Let us try to find out about the ocean. The ocean is water. Then what is the wave? The top of the wave is water, the middle of the wave is water, all of the wave is water, there is only water. Therefore water is the *atman*, the Self of the wave, the *atman* of the ocean – H_2O. The wave has to know that. The wave cannot know, as it doesn't have a Self-evident Self. It does not have any problem. If it has a human mind there will be Self-evident Self, and it can know. Then it has to know immediately: 'I am the Self,' which is Self-revealing and reveals everything: 'I am the whole.'

So the one who teaches this is the *guru*. Go to a teacher who is very well informed, who has teachers. If someone says, 'I have not studied anywhere,' leave him alone. Do salutation to him and leave him alone – don't learn from him.

The *guru* is not one who says, 'I am the *guru*, you are nobody.' He says, 'You are the whole.' Not only does he say that, but he also makes you see that. He makes an honest attempt to make you see. If one doesn't see that then there must be some problem; either the teaching lacks something or the one who is listening has some problem, perhaps some emotional or authority problem.

The people who are afraid of *gurus* have an authority problem, a problem centred on father, and they have to solve it; it is a psychological problem and it means that they are afraid of authority. The *guru* is not authority; the *guru* is one who makes you see that you are not any different from him. Where is the authority in this? Anyone who resents authority has a psychological problem and he or she has to look at his or her own mind. Looking at these problems is *sadhana*.

Swami, can I ask you how to recognise a teacher?

A lineage is important, so first you should verify if the person is a very well-informed traditional teacher who knows the methodology of teaching. If so, you should then expose yourself to the teacher. If he can make you understand and see what he is teaching, then he is a teacher. Trace all the sources of help. At every stage somebody is necessary, somebody helps us. Someone who is lucky has just one teacher, usually one has many. Learn from all of them. In my case it was like that.

Does the teacher come when I am ready or do I look for the teacher when I am ready?

They say that if you are ready the teacher will come. That's not correct. (all laugh) If you are ready you will spot the right teacher, you won't get carried away. If one is half-baked then he easily gets carried away. You go by the length of the beard!

Would you suggest that the sincere person should renounce and become a* sannyasin*, a renunciate, and live day-by-day in a way that prepares him or her for Truth?

Yes. True. One need not be a *sannyasin* but have the quality of a *sannyasin*. A *sannyasin* doesn't want anything – that freedom from a sense of ownership is a very good thing. That sense of ownership is a big factor. The *sannyasin* doesn't think of tomorrow, and that is very important. It can be accomplished by anybody but requires a certain maturity. Living one day at a time is very helpful.

Traditionally, devotees had tremendous devotion to the* guru*. Please say something about devotion in the pursuit of awakening.

Devotion is trust in the capacity of the teacher to make me see. The teaching is a means of knowing. I am not talking about knowing an object beyond me or within me, it is me, and so I can expect from the teaching immediate knowledge and therefore, as I use my eyes, I have to use the words of the scriptures. It is a means of knowing.

Suppose I say, 'Look at this banana. It's a green banana,' (holding up an orange) you will say, 'What has happened to Swami?' (all laugh). Even if you wish the swami to be right, you can't oblige your own thinking because Swami is not right – why? You don't will this to be a banana or an orange. It is an orange. Your will has no place, it is knowing. Will doesn't play a role in knowing. Your eyes are open, the object is there in front of you, lighted properly, sight explains. If it is an orange it is an orange, if it is a banana it is a banana. You don't have a choice.

You surrender totally to your eyes. Your ego, mind, everything is just at the altar of your eyes. That's how knowledge takes place. The teacher is like that. While teaching takes place, there is no teacher or taught – only teaching is there; only the topic. And you see the topic while teaching takes place. The topic is you. This is what we call surrender. It's only a means of knowing. This total surrender to both the teaching and one who handles the teaching is called *shradda*. It is not surrender to an authority. Because knowledge is involved, then questions are allowed. One can raise questions and they are answered. You don't dismiss the teaching if you don't understand. Benefit of doubt is given to the teaching and to the teacher. You remove the hurdles in understanding.

Seekers often have curious ideas about the enlightened state. Please describe your typical day and how you perceive the world. (Dayananda laughs)

Suppose I look at you. I should see you as you are. What is, is seen. No projected values. No judgements. That's what is true. Totally objective; you have a certain reality and the reality is evident, Self-evident. Therefore, there is no real contention. There is only subject-object. Have you been to a 3D film? You put on special glasses. It starts with a brawl in the bar. Somebody throws a soda bottle – it comes directly towards you. You have gone there for entertainment, you have a bag of popcorn on your lap and then the soda bottle comes flying towards you and you duck. And then afterwards you realise, 'Oh! Three dimensional.' You ducked into your popcorn and then remembered it was the theatre, then you wanted to know if somebody had seen you ducking. (all laugh) But luckily the others also ducked; you are relieved. You are in good company. This will take place for sometime, correct? Then afterwards you know it is three-dimensional and then you can relax and enjoy, but never lose sight of the three-dimensional movie. That's what it is.

Can I ask something Swami? We have been sitting together for some time now and from the very beginning it felt very energetic here. There is speaking, and the question is 'Who speaks?'

Who speaks?

Yes.

I speak. (all laugh) The speaker is I. But I am not the speaker. The difference must be seen. When you want to say 'touch wood', what do you do? Touch wood. The table is wood, but wood is not the table. So B is A but A is not B. Like on the stage; a person playing a role. The role is the person, the speaker is I. The role undergoes all kinds of changes according to the script. The role is a beggar. The actor plays the role of a beggar and all the way through he knows he is not a beggar. A is not B – the actor is not the beggar. The beggar is the actor. I am the speaker, otherwise there is dissociation.

An actor on the stage is playing a role. He is the actor and he transcends the role while simultaneously repeating all the lines. The person stands transcending the role because he is aware of the fact that 'I am not the role, the role is me'. That is called enlightenment, that is what we call *jivanmukti*. It is as simple as this! The actor recognises himself to be free from the role while at the same time playing the role.

The beggar is the role and it is not separate from the actor – the beggar's body is the actor's body. Beggar talks, actor talks, but there is space between beggar and actor. The space is not physical. The space is Self-awareness, awareness of Self-identity. Even while talking, begging, he knows he is doing well. When crying, he knows he is doing well. A is not B, B is A.

In *Sanksrit* I can say:

Naiva kincitkaromiti yukto manyeta tattravit
pasyansrnvan sprsanjighrannasnan gacchan svapausvasan.
Pralapan visrjan grhnannenmisan nimisannapi
ndriyanindriyasthesu vastanta iti dharayan.

The one who is together, who knows the Truth, thinks: I do not do anything at all, even while seeing, hearing, touching, smelling, eating, walking, sleeping, breathing, talking, realising, grasping, opening and closing the eyes, knowing full well that the organs are engaged in their objects.

Seeing, I don't see; hearing, I don't hear; I perform no action, but I act. Action happens, without me there is no action, but I do not act – it is an amazing thing. This is what we call liberation, freedom. You can call it enlightenment or freedom, but I will say it is normal living. (all laugh) I don't say enlightenment is anything special, it's normal living, That is the truth. This is the secret of *Vedanta*. This is the secret of the teaching.

It is sometimes said that the enlightened sage is like a radio, that the words are coming from…

That is true. There's only topic, deal with the topic. But still there is language involved, there are anecdotes which all come from his or her own individual knowledge, *buddhi*. If one doesn't know oneself then B is A and A is B. Therefore there will be an agenda. Here there is no agenda. B is A, A is not B. That awareness makes the whole thing free.

During these last hours, it's like talking to nobody.

Talking to nobody? That is not true. I am talking to you. I am talking to all these people. 'Nobody listening' means I will be crazy. (all laugh) I am talking to people in a way that they can understand. If I talk to some of my old students I will talk entirely differently, in a way which you will never understand. There are levels of talking. I am talking to you at a level which makes sense to you. There is nothing wrong. I am not talking to nobody. In fact you should respect your audience and you should talk to that person with love and care.

You have given a profound discourse on awakening. When you meet someone with a passion for awakening, what would your short advice be?

Be alive to what is. What is, is what you see, what you know – that is called what is. Awakening is not anything special. It does not take place sitting under a tree. Sitting under a tree, after some time, you will get a drop on your head. (all laugh) Therefore the best awakening, enlightenment, is don't sit under a tree, because there are birds sitting above! That is awakening. Awakening is seeing more than what I see. Seeing more about myself and at the same time more about what I see. That is awakening, being awake to what is. Have a good lunch. Thank you.

Om shanti, shanti, shanti. Hari om.

Ganesan

'Who are you?' Robert Adams shouted. John Wilkins knew that Robert's moods changed often because of his illness. He thought that Robert had really forgotten him, so he said, 'I am John Wilkins!' Robert gave one of the most beautiful smiles I have ever come across in my life. He said, 'John, in that I Am is Truth, John Wilkins is the untruth. I Am is Reality, John Wilkins is the unreality.'

This moment is the only Truth.

Ganesan

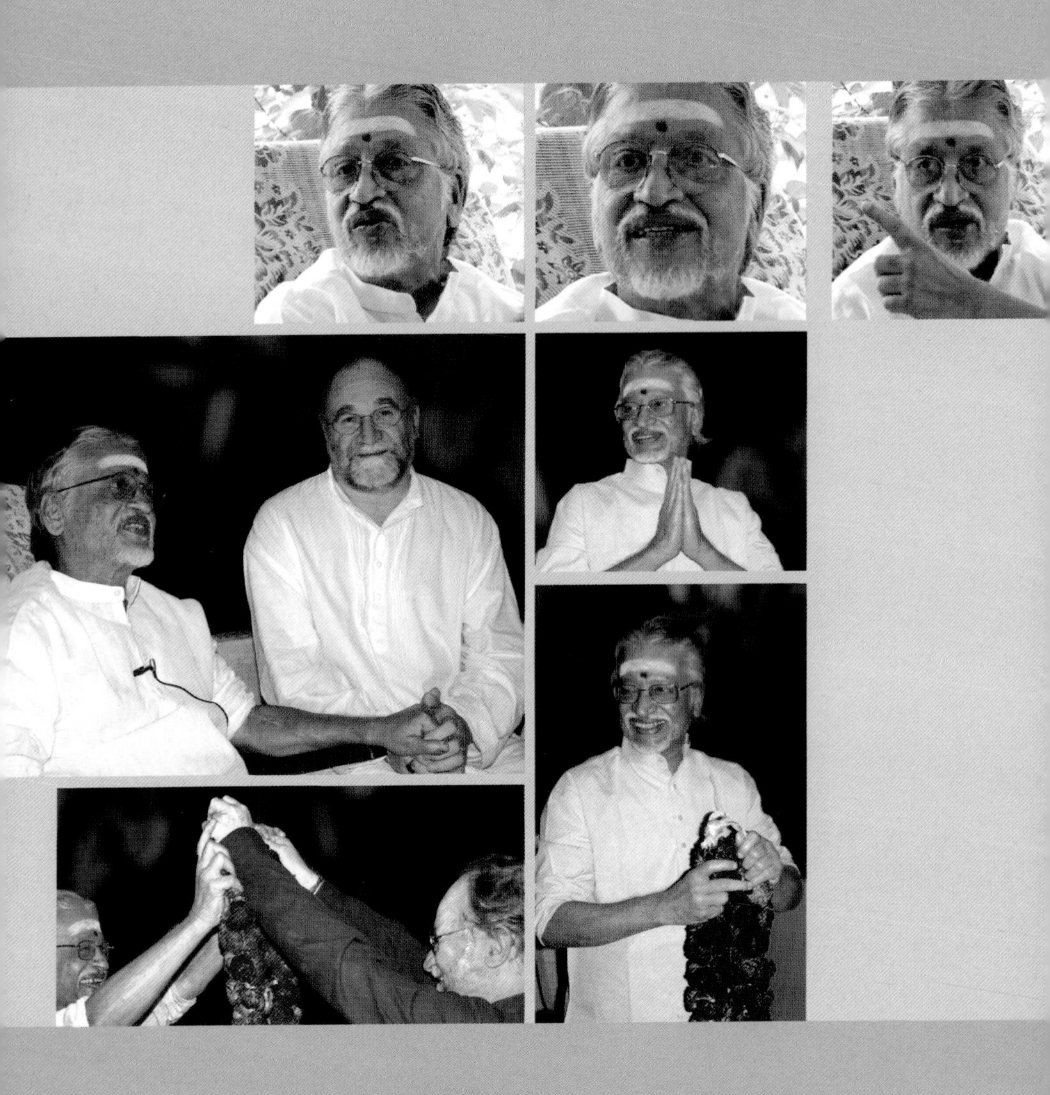

Ganesan

For thirty-five years Ganesan was the manager of Ramana Ashram, Tiruvannamalai, and for twenty-five years he was the managing editor of *The Mountain Path*, the *ashram's* newsletter. He looked after the old devotees of Sri Ramana as his *sadhana*, allowing him to absorb little-known reminiscences of Sri Ramana. His sessions of spiritual sharing are given at his home in Tiruvannamalai between nine-thirty and eleven every morning. He has authored several books on Bhagavan Sri Ramana Maharshi.

Ganesan's grandfather was Sri Ramana's brother, the first manager of Ramana Ashram. Ganesan grew up, until the age of fourteen, in the presence of Sri Ramana. I enjoyed my interview with Ganesan as he exudes an atmosphere of calmness and peace. It is touching to feel his love for Sri Ramana and to hear his beautiful, finely-worded reminiscences.

Sri Ramana proposed the fundamental question 'Who am I?' Who are you?

The same I Am which has aroused the question induces the I Am to give this answer: that which exists is only I Am and nothing but I Am.

Many Western seekers come to India looking for enlightenment as if it is an experience. What is enlightenment?

The question itself is wrongly worded: there are no Westerners, there are no Easterners, there is no bondage and there is no enlightenment. The English have a proverb: you raise the dust only to put it down.

We imagine – when I say we, it includes the speaker – that we are in bondage, proven by our ignorance: I don't know *Sanskrit* (language of ancient Indian scriptures), I don't know the *Bhagavad Gita* (classical Hindu scripture), I don't know the Bible, I must be ignorant, I must get enlightened. In this ignorance, which is not real, we raise the question: 'How do I get enlightened?' as if there is enlightenment separate from ignorance. You are told you go to India, a very sacred country, a holy place; strive hard there for a minimum of three years, then you will find enlightenment. All this is raising more dust. What will happen if you don't raise the dust at all? Why raise the dust and then say, 'I want to put down the dust'? For thousands of years we have been playing the same trick upon ourselves. Why do we play this game that we are ignorant, that we are in bondage? The brain will immediately give us reasons: I have misery, sorrow, inadequacy, illiteracy, poverty. As long as we presume we are in bondage we will always be seeking enlightenment.

Bhagavan Sri Ramana Maharshi said, 'From the standpoint of non-truth you will never reach the Truth.' We presume we are in non-truth and we try to seek the Truth. Is seeking the Truth a movement? We presume that we are in a state of ignorance, and we will find plenty of reasons in the scriptures: What are your impediments? What are your obstacles? Why you are in bondage? Then fifty pages later they suggest how you get released from this. This is merely sales talk!

We think we are in bondage and we want enlightenment. We think we are non-truth and we are marching towards the Truth. Again, the intention is beautiful, the efforts are all genuine, but we have wasted three thousand years. From Buddha onwards we have played the same game. Perhaps even before Buddha, but for the sake of convenience we will only go back three thousand years! (Premananda laughs) We are past masters at not following the master's instructions! So we left Buddha and we moved on to Jesus Christ, two thousand years ago. Now I will reach the Truth. And again we missed it! One thousand years back we were all there with *Adi Shankara*, remember? This is not just fanciful thinking! And we missed it again. We have come to the same Buddha, the same Jesus Christ, the same *Adi Shankara*, the same Ramana, the same Premananda, the same Ganesan ... fill in the blank with all your names!

We have taken the wrong path, we are going in the wrong direction. That's why we have not got it. And today, here and now, we are taking the correct direction. We are here, and right now we are the Truth. Give up the thought that there is movement from non-truth to Truth. Find out who has suggested that you are in bondage, that you have to get freedom, enlightenment. Who? A book? A so-called master? And even so, why did you accept it? Find out! And even if you have accepted it, why were you not given the right direction? As long as you seek the Truth outside, you'll be travelling in vain. Do you know the Mullah Nasruddin story? I'm very fond of it.

Mullah Nasruddin was seated just a few steps outside his village on the side of the road. A man came along looking very tired, but very sincere. He said, 'Sir, I have come two hundred miles searching for Mullah Nasruddin's village. I have not yet found it, but I am determined not only to find it but to find Mullah Nasruddin too, because he has given me a revelation. I am prepared to take any amount of strain! Tell me sir, how long must I walk? I am prepared to walk even two or three hundred miles more.' Mullah Nasruddin answered him, 'You want to know when you will reach his village?' The man said, 'Yes sir, look at my eagerness!' Mullah Nasruddin said, 'If you take this path I don't know when you will reach him because you will have to go all the way around the world. If you turn around, there are only a few steps; you have just come out of Mullah Nasruddin's village. I am Mullah Nasruddin. (Premananda laughs)

This is all that we need. Give up this hallucination-self created by you, that you are in non-truth, that you are in enslavement, in bondage. I seek enlightenment, from whom can I get it? When, where will I get it? Who will give it to me? We have done this clown's job for three thousand years. From *ashram* to *ashram*, from one *guru* to another *guru* we go. It is spiritual entertainment, spiritual tourism. Sir, I am not making light of this.

Ramana Maharshi said, 'You are taking a candle to help you see the sun. You are God, God is within you.' As long as you seek God outside, you will be seeking eternally. Here and now, wake up! There is no enlightenment because there has never been bondage. You were never ignorant! You are the I Am. The question was put by the I Am, the answer has come from the I Am and the listeners are all I Am. (laughs) There is nothing but I Am! So where is the question?

Many people start on this journey from a feeling of suffering. They have some pain, their life is not really working and they suffer. They are looking for something that will bring them peace.

If you want instantaneous release from suffering Maharshi says, 'Go to sleep!' (both laugh) In sleep nobody complains about any suffering. Maharshi says that is your real state, not this waking. Waking is business hours! Making money, engaging yourself with the exchange of 'I will give you a little entertainment, you give me money'. The moment I get money somebody robs it, so I suffer! Enjoyment, suffering, pleasure, pain, pleasure, pain. You can never stop this. There is no release from suffering because there is no suffering. (laughs) It's not a concept. Don't give attention to your brain which says it is a concept! Don't accept it as a concept, pay attention to the Truth.

Truth is that which should be available to all, under all conditions and at all times. If it's only available to Jesus Christ or Bhagavan Sri Ramana Maharshi, that's not Truth! Don't think it is a big puzzle, it's the simplest puzzle I have ever come across. It's simply the feeling of being alive that's always there, what the scriptures call I Am. I Am is not just words; we convert it into words because we are mad for conversation. 'Where are you going?', 'I am going to the *ashram*', 'I am going up the hill'. I Am is not words, it's a feeling of existence.

I was with Robert Adams for three years. Have you heard of Robert Adams? A great American master. A *jnani* (one who has realised the Self), fully realised, a beautiful *jnani*. I had the great opportunity of visiting him in America, first in Hollywood, then in Sedona, Arizona. I loved him so much! He had Parkinsons disease so he had to be seated, just as I have to now since I had open heart surgery. (indicates his comfortable chair) I like *mahatmas* (great souls), not only their words, their presence too. Their every movement; a finger movement, even the movement of the moustache hairs I love! Because everything is Truth. Truth is what?

Bliss. And there was that bliss in Robert Adams; for a fool like me to be seated next to him, I was swimming in bliss.

There was another friend of Robert's, John Wilkins. One day he held Robert's knee and said, 'Robert, we have been close friends for twenty years. I have been listening to your talks all this time. Today I want you to make me understand what is Truth and what is non-truth, what is Reality and what is non-reality. Please don't play the game of saying it's omnipresence, it's omnipotent; I have heard enough of that! Make me understand at my own level.' Robert, being a *jnani*, was a very happy man! So he was smiling as he listened to John.

Then suddenly he assumed a very serious look. 'Who are you?' he shouted. John Wilkins knew that Robert's moods changed often because of his illness. He thought that Robert had really forgotten him, so he said, 'I am John Wilkins!'

Robert gave one of the most beautiful smiles I have ever come across in my life. He said, 'John, in that I Am is Truth, John Wilkins is the untruth. I Am is Reality, John Wilkins is the unreality.' There were seventy or eighty people in the hall and everyone went into *samadhi* (absorbtion in the Self); absolute silence. John Wilkins, myself, everyone there was put into that state of ecstasy. For five minutes there was nothing but joy. I Am is Truth. John Wilkins is the untruth. John Wilkins can never know the Truth, he can never get it, he will become a donkey in the next birth! (laughs) Or a monkey!

As long as you are holding on to John Wilkins, or any name, you cannot know the I Am. You are the I Am! When you experience the I Am, here and now, the I Am that is now talking, the I Am that is now listening, that experience is Truth! Right now, not on video two months later in your room! You are not going to be the Truth; right now you are the Truth. From that state of Truth try to raise this question: Is there enlightenment? Then the enlightenment will dawn. As long as you're going to hold on to John Wilkins this interview has no end! (both laugh)

We have to move to the next question then! Are there any qualifications for enlightenment?

No qualification is necessary except giving up the standpoint of untruth. The entire non-truth has to be given up; why are you holding on to one section of the non-truth? Maharshi gives this example: Does the barber bend down and start measuring all the hair that has been discarded on the floor? Does he sit there and start counting and weighing the hair? In one sweep he sends it all away! (laughs) The whole non-truth has to be rejected, right now.

What qualification do you need to be the Truth? Or to know that you are a human being? Truth doesn't need any qualification. Non-truth needs lots of proof. If you were to say, 'Excuse me, it is now evening,' this is a fact; it is evening. Look at it simply, don't complicate it. We are masters at complicating ourselves. (laughs) Become simple like a child, that's what Jesus Christ said, then you can enter the Kingdom of Heaven. We all want to be adults, educated people.

Two things to notice: suppose I say this is early morning, sunrise. This is non-truth so I have to prove it. If I say it is evening there is no proof necessary as we all know it is true. It is very simple. It needs no qualifications. If I say, 'This Saturday evening is very, very auspicious for worshipping this particular Hindu god,' I have to prove it. I have to show you Hindu scripture: 'I am not saying this, Lord *Shiva* is saying this. Look at this book.' If I say your friend is a woman, that is a truth, a factual truth. Suppose that I go on to say she is a good woman, you might say, 'No, you don't know her!' (laughs)

Non-truth is conceptual, thought-oriented concept. This Truth about yourself, the I Am, needs no support, no confirmation from anyone else. And we have forgotten this Truth. The *guru* in human form, in the form of Ramana Maharshi or Papaji or Nisargadatta Maharaj, is only there to remind us. 'Hey! You are going in the wrong direction, take a right about-turn!'

What about twenty years of meditation? (laughs) Is* sadhana *(spiritual practice) necessary?

Not twenty years, I am talking about three thousand years! (both laugh) We were at the feet of the great master Gautama Buddha; he said, 'Wake up!' We did not. We took the wrong direction because there lies pleasure. The very first Indian *Upanishad* (ancient Indian scripture) describes very beautifully, very poetically, that we have two choices. A bird is seated in a tree with two fruits. It has the choice to eat one fruit but not both. One of the fruits is called *preyes*. *Preyes* is the outward path of pleasure, achievements, success, accumulation and enjoyment. The other fruit is *sreyes*. *Sreyes* is the inward path of no success, no achievements, no time, no space, no causation, nobody! This way we will always be happy, we are just *prem* and *ananda*: love and bliss. Maharshi said they are not two things, *premananda* is a rhetoric. This second fruit is *premananda*. We have the choice to eat that *preyes* fruit, which is what we have been doing. That fruit has not given us anything; three thousand years we have wasted. Choose the other fruit, the path of *sreyes*.

Your whole attention should only be on Truth, and Truth will express itself. You cannot define Truth! The moment you try to define Truth, it is untruth. What is untruth? That which comes and goes is untruth, that which permanently stays is the Truth. The aliveness, the being, the I Am, is undeniable. If you want to take the path of *preyes*, if you want to extend yourself once more into the world, you will be living for another five thousand years!

It is said that it is helpful to have a* sattvic *(calm and peaceful) mind in order to see the Truth.

These are all words! Again, anything that the mind suggests, that books suggest, that somebody else suggests to you, are all untruth.

Don't you think that for many people it's very difficult to see this inner Truth with busy, stressed minds caused by so much suffering and pain?

Sir, can you conceive of anyone more compassionate than the Buddha or Jesus Christ or Ramana Maharshi? Have they wiped out suffering? As long as you think there is suffering there will continue to be suffering. As long as you think there is pain there will be pain.

Sri Ramana said that Self-enquiry is the most direct route to realising the Self. What do you say about Self-enquiry?

I like this analogy. You see the huge tree at the entrance? It is a peepal tree. It has a small fruit, a very tiny fruit, and if you had a precision instrument you could cut it. Inside there are very, very tiny seeds, very, very tiny, and if you took your precision instrument to break that tiny seed there would be nothing inside. One seed is so small but it can produce many peepal trees. This is the creation, this is the world. This is the outward path of *preyes*.

Instead of looking at the trees look at the seed, the Truth. When you pay attention to any Truth you find there is nothing there. From nothing, not only this peepal tree but thousands of peepal trees can be produced. Maharshi says take the inward path of *sreyes*. Focus attention on this tiny seed that can produce a tree; break it open until there is nothing left. Maharshi says to 'scorch it with attention'. If you cut the branches and the leaves off, the tree will come up again. When you scorch the seed with attention it can no longer sprout. Like the tree, the body cannot be denied; spirituality doesn't mean you should commit suicide. But when you pay attention to this I Am, the seed, nothing more can come from it. Focus attention on the I Am, the Truth; don't seek anything else. Why not go straight to the Truth?

This is Self-enquiry, going right to the seed. This way you know the Truth for yourself, not as knowledge. Ganesan, son of so and so, born in such and such year, aged sixty-eight; these are all the branches of the peepal tree, the outer life. Self-enquiry is the way to know where all this sprouted from. Not the technical thing of 'Who am I? My body I am not!' This is a toy that Maharshi gives the children to play with so that other activities will be given up. Self-enquiry is to go within oneself and to know that there is nothing but Truth, the I Am. The I Am that speaks, the I Am that listens; focus the attention on the seed. Focus the attention on the Truth.

How to conduct Self-enquiry? You have written a very nice little booklet on the subject. Perhaps you could summarise it for me?

If you want words that is where to find them. (laughs) Right here and now why not just be the I Am? Why do we want a technique? Because we already assume that we're not the Truth for multifarious reasons. Begin with the Truth. Don't try to understand. As Jesus Christ said, attain the Truth first! And the Truth will set you free. Jesus Christ did not give a definition of Truth and he did not say to first have a correct understanding of Truth. He didn't say to know or understand Truth, he said attain the Truth! We can only attain that which is already there. You are alive, you are existence, *sat* (Truth); the feeling of I Am. How happy you look! That's the I Am expressed through the face with a smile. The I Am is happiness. When you pay attention to the Truth you completely bring back all your wandering thoughts, your doubts, your wrong ideas that you are in bondage, and, like the barber, you sweep them aside! Focus attention on the Truth, the I Am, right here and now! All the rest is untruth. This moment is the only Truth.

When you are working in an office in Düsseldorf there are many distractions. It is very easy to forget and believe you are John Wilkins again. Then Self-enquiry is helpful.

That is still the wrong way! If you are paying attention to the I Am, it doesn't matter whether you are in Düsseldorf or in Siberia or in prison! I am sure you have read the stories of the Desert Fathers. They were tortured, they were put in prison, but they kept chanting Jesus Christ's name. All this time they were in the I Am, the Truth. If you start paying attention to the Truth, even in Düsseldorf, I assure you, all this distraction will simply be happening.

Did you meet Papaji?

Yes, I spent five years with him.

I was with him once watching cricket on TV. Somebody asked him, 'Why are you watching that?' He said, 'I am just looking.' The I Am is just looking; it is not the other way around! When you are rooted in the I Am, whether you watch cricket or whether you are in an office in Düsseldorf, it will all just happen! Ramana woke up at three o'clock in the morning and was very active till eleven o'clock in the night. And everyone was in a happy state, not just him. When you are in that state of I Am the office workers will feel happy. 'My master Premananda is so happy, I want to be with Premananda.' Why are they sticking to you? Figuratively, I mean. Why does your *sangha* (spiritual community) follow you to Arunachala? Here you are in the presence of your Self. Here, like a mirror, Arunachala shows that you are the Truth. Once you are established in that Truth here and now, as Nisargadatta Maharaj said, the now is always, the here is everywhere.

What you say is of course absolutely true.

Yes.

***Particularly for* mahatmas.**

Yes.

But in Düsseldorf there are many who are not* mahatmas, *or they do not know they are* mahatmas. *Would you say that Self-enquiry could help those people?

It is very simple. The I Am within you wants to be recognised; it always has the urge to go back home, to be itself. You have corrupted the happiness within you by thinking that you are German, you are Indian, you are Christian, Jew, Zoroastrian or Hindu. These are all obstacles to your happiness. 'Come on, recognise me!'

Maharshi gives this beautiful example – you have a headache, why do you take aspirin? Why do you have this very serious urge to get rid of the headache? Because you already know you were happy when there was no headache. If you did not know you would accept this headache as your natural state. This applies to all pain. Why do we want to get rid of the pain? Because we already know there is a state of happiness.

When you read in the newspaper of the thousands bombed to death in Iraq you feel pain. Why do you want to get rid of that pain? Because you already know there is a state of peace, which has been disturbed by this news. You want to go back to that state of peace and you cannot bring about peace in the outside world. Are you stronger than Buddha? Or Jesus Christ? Buddha could not bring peace to the world, even Jesus Christ could not bring peace to the world. Outside there is no happiness, inside there is always happiness. That's why Self-enquiry is important. Turn within, you are always happy there. Buddha says the wheel of birth and death has to stop. It can be stopped only by Self-enquiry. Not as a technique, but knowing that you are the Truth right here and now. Düsseldorf can be the here; the now is always. There are no two I Am's, there is only one. There are six billion bodies in the whole wide world belonging to different countries, each with a different name. How do they all refer to themselves? What is the word in German for I?

Ich.

Ich. In Hindi it is *mein*, in Tamil it is *naan*. Everyone says I. Maharshi asks, are there six billion I's, just as there are six billion names? Are there six billion I's, or is there only one I to which all these bodies are referring? Find out. This is Self-enquiry. Who can say I Am, except in the present tense, here, right now?

I have another question.

Yes, I am ready!

When Sri Ramana was asked, 'When will the realisation of the Self be gained?' he replied, 'When the world which is what-is-seen has been removed, there will be realisation of the Self which is the seer.' What is the true understanding of the world?

You have to answer this question in deep sleep! Is there a world? For the waking state, all the scriptures give different answers to this. Ask! The word for world in *Sanskrit* is *lokaha*. It's not just a word, all *Sanskrit* words have a deeper meaning. *Lokaha* means that which is seen. Anything that is seen must have a seer. When you pay attention to the seer, the I Am, the seen drops off by itself. And what is the proof? In deep sleep there is no seen object at all, but the seer is alive. That's why the next morning you say, 'I slept well.' The seer is the Truth, the seen is non-truth. Your sleep is not my experience, so find out in your own experience if this world is real; see if the world is there in your sleep. Has the world ever come and told you it is there? Has this fan told you 'I am a fan, I am a fan'? (laughs) It is you who says this is a fan! Everything that is seen depends on the seer and if you find out the truth about the seer, the seen becomes accepted, not rejected. Jesus Christ says the Kingdom of God is at hand. What is the Kingdom of God? Everything! It is not somewhere else, in Heaven. Everything has been created by God, including this body. When you attain the Truth, that Truth will lead you to the Kingdom of God. You will be the happiest person!

How to remove the world?

Who wants to remove the world? Why do you want to remove that?

Sri Ramana is suggesting that only when the world is removed will the Self be realised.

That is because the question was put by a professor rooted in book knowledge, untruth, so he has to be given this removal thing to talk about. Elsewhere, Maharshi says, 'Who has created the world, he will take charge of it. Why are you bothered about it?' Man's only creation is thought. He can't create anything.

Permit me to share something with you. In 1952 there was a conference of scientists in Geneva to evaluate scientific progress. All branches of science were represented. On the first day each speaker gave a synopsis of what they were going to talk about for the seven days of the conference. Each one was claiming how much we have achieved. Then Einstein came to speak. I remember very well reading this in the newspaper, it stuck in my heart. He said, 'It is true we have discovered many things, but please be humble. All of us scientists put together still cannot create one blade of grass, yet it rains and the next day there is grass everywhere. God is the creator. We only adjust.'

When you are established in the I Am, all your works are attended. Pay attention to the Truth and the Truth will take charge of all the non-truth aspects.

It has been suggested that the mind must be destroyed for liberation to occur. Do you have a mind?

The mind which manufactures the doubts takes you back to the source by itself. The mind is the only link between the body and the Self. You don't achieve anything by denying the mind. Make it a servant and it will take you back to the Truth. Make it a master and it will take you away from the Truth. By denying the mind or asserting the mind we are not going to achieve anything.

Sri Ramana used the term* manonasha, *meaning destroyed mind, to describe the state of liberation. How to destroy the mind?

By staying in the now! Premananda, what state are you in?

(Silence) Good, you can't answer with words, only with silence. That is *manonasha*. The brain immediately says that this no mind should be permanent. 'Can I have this *manonasha* always?' The now alone is the Truth. You may call it decorative words like *manonasha*, *samadhi*, ecstasy; these are all mere words. It is just Truth. Every moment there is *manonasha*. Ramana Maharshi was living every moment, he was alive! He was answering questions, reading the newspaper, cutting vegetables and cooking. His mind was a servant. In *Sri Arunachala Ashtakam*, Maharshi starts with the statement, 'If you are in silence, don't disturb it. Stay in that state. If a thought arises ask, "To whom has this thought come?"' Wherever you are, even in meditation, if you have thought then you are not in *manonasha*. When there is no thought, then it is *manonasha*.

When you are in this silence, as you were when I asked you Premananda, that is *manonasha*. But *manonasha* is not a permanent state. When you start your interview again, the mind comes back. Then if you stop and ask, 'Who asks these question? To whom?' You go back to the *manonasha* state.

Maharshi has defined *sadhana* as descending from the brain to the heart. The brain distracts the attention; descending to the heart means to pull it back to its source. No one else can do this for you, you have to do it for yourself. No book can do it, no technique can do it.

Non-recognition of the passage of time is *manonasha*. It is the mind which records time. Time only has movement because mind has created time.

I have a special wristwatch which just says 'Now!'

Yes, that solves the problem! (laughs)

What about* vasanas, *the tendencies of the mind? Must these be removed before Self-realisation can become permanent?

Yes, as long as you identify yourself with the body. I am a Hindu non-married man, sixty-eight years old, senior citizen; as long as I identify with this, these *vasanas* will be there. When I pay attention to the I Am, and when I pay no attention to the 'I am Ganesan', there are no *vasanas*.

Maharshi says to find out if you are just the body. What happens to the body in deep sleep? Where is the body then? Find out. Experience it. Not intellectually, because no intellect works in deep sleep. Paul Brunton said, 'Maharshi, why do you ask me to look at the state of deep sleep? It is a state of dullness, there is nothing in deep sleep. It can't teach me anything!' Maharshi smiled and said, 'See, it has already taught you one lesson: that in deep sleep you cannot learn anything!' (laughs) So experience always teaches us. There are no *vasanas*.

I have a very strong* vasana *that comes up when I'm empty.

Because you pay attention to that!

It is that I must save all those people in Düsseldorf.

Yes, that is because you like to have enjoyment in *vasanas*! (both laugh)

I don't enjoy them, they just come!

Otherwise you couldn't enjoy them! There was a lady cook in Ramana Ashram – a child widow. A child widow, from the age of six or seven, is fed and cared for and given spiritual teaching, and she does not indulge in the world in any form, even when she is grown up. This lady lived a very upright, moral, ethical life. At the age of forty she asked Ramana, 'Bhagavan, I've been following your path all my life. Why have I found no fulfilment?' Maharshi's answer startled me: 'Is it because you have not had enough of the world?' That single thought was her creation. And the moment that Bhagavan said this to her it dropped, and she became established in the I Am.

I have met sixty old devotees of Bhagavan who became established in the I Am while the *prarabdha*, the body, was going on. There is one famous incident I witnessed. There was a great astrologer. He could predict absolutely one hundred percent correctly. He was so convinced of his ability that he asked Maharshi, 'Is not astrology a perfect science?' Maharshi gave the reply, 'The science of the Self is superior to all sciences.' On that day he left astrology and started seeking. He became a beggar in the streets in Tiruvannamalai for nearly fifty years. In his last days we had the great good fortune of looking after him. He was a saintly man, very beautiful. He was ninety-six then, and he had fallen from his bed and broken his thigh bone. All the doctors said that nothing could be done for him. They said gangrene would set in and he would die in excruciating pain. I am an emotional man, I used to cry to see him suffer. I used to ask, 'How is your leg?' He would say, 'Ah, when you ask me that question there is pain in the body.' He just gave this simple answer, that when you draw my attention to the body, yes, there is pain. Then I asked, 'What state are you in?' And he told me, 'I am happy. All the time I am in this blissful state of I Am.' This was at nine o'clock. At eleven o'clock he died.

Could you say something of your own establishement in I Am?

This speaker woke up in 1960. I'm not claiming that I'm realised, all that is nonsense! The realisation is a continuous now, and it is always available to all. It is not just one person seated here. In no way am I better than you.

Can you tell me what you mean when you say that you woke up in 1960?

Just the same I Am, the now. There is no passage of time. When you shift your attention from time to the now, time loses all its importance. As long as you pay attention to time you are going to be born for another five thousand years, I assure you!

It appears essential to meet a* guru *and stay with that* guru. *Who is the* guru*? What is the* guru's *role? How to recognise a true* guru*?

I Am is the only *guru*! (laughs) Because He is the only permanent Truth. All other *gurus* are imaginary. Moses was told by God, 'I Am that I Am.' Jesus Christ said, 'I Am the way, the Truth, the light.' The I Am has no religion, no caste, no body, no country. Anywhere, everywhere; all the time you are I Am. And that's the only *guru*. *Guru* means removal of darkness. Holding onto time is darkness. Removal of time is I Am. So, I Am is the safest *guru*. Nowhere to go around seeking, no travel, no payment, no photograph, no video, no book! You are That! That's the *guru*.

How to recognise a true* guru*?

You are already a true *guru*! What is there to recognise? How to recognise the I Am? Who asks this question? Maharshi has already answered all your questions. Do you have to say, 'I am a man'? Do any of us need to say, 'I am a man or a woman'? We already know! The I Am is always there.

How to recognise the I Am? It's a funny question! (laughs) Maharshi says a person who is asking how to recognise the I Am is like a man without a tongue saying, 'I have no tongue.' If you are not I Am, how can you ask the question: How to recognise the I Am? How can a corpse put this question to a corpse? This person is alive! This aliveness is the I Am. Simple being is the Self.

Others give definitions of Truth, Self, everything. In Hinduism there are volumes written describing the Self. My master said, 'Simply being, you are alive now, whether asleep or awake, you are alive.' This simple being is the Self, this simple being is the I Am, the one who raises the doubt and the one who pretends to answer the doubt.

Sri Ramana's devotees had tremendous devotion to him, and he to Arunachala. Please say something about* bhakti*, devotion, in the pursuit of awakening.

Yes. Unless you love something you cannot pay attention to it, even your child, your wife. This attention is *bhakti*. What can be dearer to you than your own life? That's why we are all spending so much energy and money on awakening; that is love, that is *bhakti*. Each one is interested in himself, that's why we are all here to find out the Truth. Ramana Maharshi paid attention to Arunachala, and we all pay attention to him. Always turn to yourself. Your paying attention to Ramana or falling at his feet is only an expression of that *bhakti*. This longing to love Ramana, that is *bhakti*. Everyone has *bhakti*, everyone wants to know the Truth, and this wanting to know the Truth is *bhakti*.

Seekers often have curious ideas about the awakened state. Please describe your typical day and how you perceive the world.

Why are you accusing only the seekers of having curious ideas? Even so-called enlightened people who announce, 'I got my enlightenment on

February 7th 1977,' have a curious idea! The idea that we have to attain enlightenment is an illusion. It is postponing the understanding that we are the Truth. Postponing means what? Paying attention to time! Somebody tells you, 'Follow this path; I will give you step one, two, three, all sixteen steps. After three years you will get enlightenment!' Time oriented! All this is fooling yourself because the Truth is not bound by time and space. The moment, this moment, is the Truth! We may say, for the sake of convenience, that this speaker awakened in 1960. I request that everyone let this moment now, 8th January 2005, be recorded in their life as the moment of awakening. Now! This moment! Maharshi once said – this is quite often quoted – 'A time will come when you will laugh at yourself, that you struggled all these years for this!' Let that time be now. For this speaker it was the past, for others it may be the future, but whether it is in the past or the future, only the awakening is important.

You will laugh at yourself! Thinking that you have followed, or not followed, stumbled, achieved, not achieved; it's funny stuff! (laughs) I once heard Papaji say, 'When you laugh there is no mind.' This is because when you laugh you are the I Am. You cannot laugh if there is a mind. At the moment of laughter there is no mind. That is the state of I Am; happiness, bliss – *ananda. Premananda.* We are love, always enjoying love, immersed in bliss. We have failed to recognise it. What is the time to choose to recognise it? Now! Don't believe this fool or anyone who says he had enlightenment in 1960, or 1977! (laughs) There is no time! Tell me, what happened to five-twenty? It has already become five minutes to six! (both laugh) Look at that fellow (indicates the clock), he's fooling us!

You have a very fast clock!

Yes!

My watch still says now!

That's why you're happy! I'm unhappy because I'm looking at the clock!

We could swap if you like.

Now I am so happy, Premananda! Extremely happy!

You have given us a profound discourse on awakening. When you meet someone with a passion for awakening, what would your short advice be?

There is no short or long! (laughs) People used to tease me, saying, 'Don't you give initiation and *mantras* (sacred sounds)? In other places they initiate you, the special chosen disciples, and give you a *mantra*.' They expect me to do that! So I say, 'Who says so? I also initiate into *mantra*!' 'Oh! We never heard that! We were told that Ganesan just talks of this dry Self-enquiry.' I say, 'I initiate into this *mantra*: be happy!' (laughs) This is my *mantra* path, *bhakti* path, *jnana* (knowledge) path, yoga path, *dharma* (righteous way of living) path: be happy!

It includes everything and it is so alive, it is the Truth. It is not separate from Truth, happiness, bliss, whatever you call it. And you are that, so I am not going to add anything more. You are already *ananda*. I am only saying direct your attention to the Truth, that you are always the Truth; be happy! That's the greatest *mantra*. Be happy. Have you ever heard a better *mantra*? (both laugh)

I quite like 'Don't worry, be happy.'

That is mind, to add the negative! I asked Mother Krishnabai, 'What is mind and what is Self?' She told me, 'Any positive feeling is Self, any negative feeling is mind.' She advised me to never use any negative terms. I asked, 'How is this possible?' She said. 'If you pay attention to the positivity of yes, you need not say no at all. The no comes from the mind and the yes comes from the heart.' Suppose you invite me to your *ashram* at eight o'clock in the evening. The mind may immediately say no, and support it with: 'I've got some other engagement.' This may be true or it may be false, it doesn't matter. This negativity is the burden of the mind. What is negativity? It is escaping from being in Truth. It's very heavy! But when I say yes, this positivity is the language of the heart.

It just so happens that I was going to ask you to tell us a few stories about your meetings with Sri Ramana. Would you like to come over for dinner at eight o'clock tonight?

Will you be disappointed if I say no? (both laugh)

It could be any evening of your choice.

I am going to say yes! Any time. Stories you want? I have just told you so many stories. The biggest story, the longest story, the strongest story, the best story, is the story of the I Am.

Am I right in saying that when you were a little child you grew up in the proximity of Sri Ramana Maharshi?

Yes. He was my great uncle, and I saw him as my grandfather.

I would love to hear a few of those personal stories, if you would like to share them.

I knew Ramana Maharshi only as my grandfather until after my graduation, after I had a massive spiritual experience. Then he was no longer my grandfather; he was and still is my *guru*, one with myself. But when I was a child I looked upon him only as my grandfather. I was very short until adolescence. People used to call me Shortie, in Tamil. (laughs) Very short. Grumpy and Shortie.

There would be one or two hundred people eating in the dining hall in the presence of Bhagavan. Everyone would be served first and Bhagavan would be served last. He used to pay so much attention to the food servers. I loved to see my grandfather watching them; I wanted him to look at me with the same attention. So I thought that if I served food Bhagavan would give me the same look of affection and attention.

I went to the kitchen and said, 'I want to serve dinner!' All the cooks were elderly child widows, and they were all very fond of children, especially me because I was so close to Maharshi. The vessels were so big, and I was so small, so the cooks were saying, 'No, no, no. That's only for grown up people, not for children. You go and sit with Bhagavan and eat.' When they refused I was crying and throwing a tantrum, 'Boo-hoo-hoo!'

Bhagavan heard this. 'What is happening in the kitchen?'

One of the cooks went and told him, 'Our child Ganesan is having a tantrum.'

'What? What is he doing?'

'He insists that he will serve.'

'What is wrong there?'

'Bhagavan, he's so short! All our vessels are bigger than him!' (laughs)

'That's your problem, not his problem. Put salt and a small spoon in a cup, give it to Ganesan and send him to me!'

So they gave me a small cup of salt with a spoon and said, 'Go to Bhagavan, he will teach you how to serve!' I felt very proud. I came to Bhagavan. He looked at me and said, 'You want to serve?' I said 'Yes, Bhagavan, I want to serve'. Of course, what I wanted was his attention.

'Do you know how to serve?'

I said, 'No.'

'Do you know why to serve?'

I said, 'No.'

'Do you know what to serve?'

I said 'No.' Then I understood. My ego was crushed. Bhagavan took pity on me and said, 'I will teach you.' He said, 'Do you know what is in the cup?'

'That I know! It is salt!' I said proudly.

'Do you know how much to serve?'

'No, that I don't know,' I said, rather ashamed.

He said, 'Take some in the spoon. No, no, not that much! Aah, that's it! That's it. Do you know where to serve it?'

'No, Bhagavan.'

'You put it on the banana leaf on the top left hand corner.' I was very happy because Bhagavan was paying so much attention to me. I immediately put the salt on his leaf, just as he instructed. 'It doesn't matter today', he said, 'but you should serve this leaf last.'

I looked at all the others in the great dining hall. Then I went and served them. And Bhagavan watched me! (both laugh)

We did not have any toys at the *ashram*, so one American visitor sent a hundred different beautiful toys, with a request to distribute them among the children in Bhagavan's presence. The manager called me and said, 'Go to the hall and choose a toy now. In a few minutes all the other children are going to come. Whichever toy you like, you tell Bhagavan.' So in I went, and only Bhagavan and I were there. I was so short and my eyes were so wide; I had never seen so many toys in my life! My eyes went straight to an airplane, something I had never seen before. I used to occasionally see some small tiny thing in the sky making a lot of noise, but I didn't know what it was. This airplane was big, not really a toy, it was made to scale.

Bhagavan called me, 'Ganesan, come! Some American has sent all these toys. Whichever toy you like, come and show it to me, but you can choose only one!' I ran and then picked up that airplane.

'You like that?'

'Yes, Bhagavan! I like that.' I was so excited.

'Come, bring it to me.' I went to where he was seated. He said 'Do you know what an airplane is?'

I said, 'I don't know, Bhagavan.'

'See, this is the propeller,' and he touched the propeller to make it spin. 'We start this first. These are the wheels, the plane will be running along on them, and then zoom!' My excitement and joy were increasing. He said 'Look at this! These are all the passengers!' He pointed through the window. 'And this man here is the pilot!'

I tell you Premananda, at that moment he became me! I was in such tremendous excitement, and I could see the same thing in him. A *jnani*, a realised sage, is like a mirror. I was in heaven. Then he said 'Don't break it!' (both laugh)

To live with a realised person is the most natural way of living, something we have forgotten. We fill our life with worries, plans, desires, and they all disturb us. A realised person like Ramana Maharshi or Poonjaji, established in that inner Truth, they are always happy. And they make everyone else happy. Like a mirror, they reflect what you are, both the Truth and the untruth. If you are mislead by *vasanas* they point out, 'This is your *vasana*, come back to the Truth!'

Ramana gave me joy by simply explaining a toy airplane to a child. I can never forget this, even now I can see how he became me and expressed my joy. It's so beautiful.

More stories later! (both laugh)

D. B. Gangolli

In deep sleep even the ego goes out of existence. Nobody will be able to say in deep sleep there is duality of any kind. It is absolute absence of duality. In other words, it is non-duality, it is pure consciousness – which can never be understood by the mind.

Naturally mind must not be destroyed. There is no question of destroying a thing which doesn't exist.

D.B. Gangolli

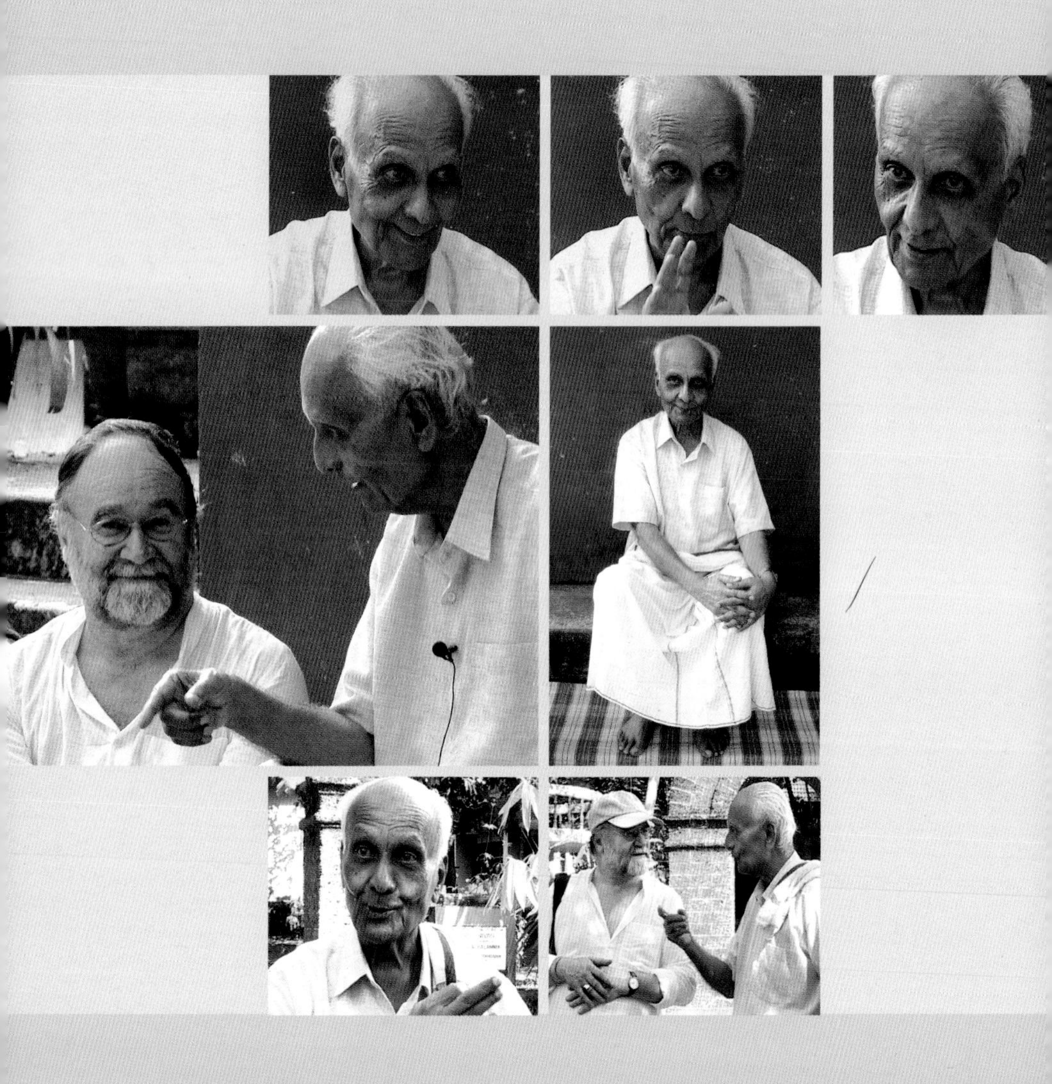

D.B. Gangolli

I met Gangolli in 2003 at his simple apartment in Bangalore. He was in his mid-eighties, a little frail, a gentleman in the British mold. We dialogued about his beloved *Vedanta* for three days. In 2006 I invited him to speak at our Arunachala Pilgrimage Retreat where I experienced his joy to share *Vedanta* with a large group. He lived his life as a householder, raising a family and working as a senior sports writer for the *Times of India*. He authored many books on *Vedanta*. He left his body in 2006.

Sri Ramana proposed the fundamental question 'Who am I?' Who are you?

This is one of the most powerful and popular questions known all over the world in spiritual circles. Ramana Maharshi was a very great sage of India who hit upon a method of taking any person directly towards the ego, the 'I' notion. The *Advaita Vedanta* (non-dual teaching) of *Shankara* (religious teacher) explains, in a slightly different way, but with full force, this sort of powerful question. Many people couldn't answer that by themselves. Ramana, being a sage and a spiritual teacher also, could give certain tips on how to go about analysing this 'I' and in the process go behind the ego. Behind the ego is the pure consciousness, the *sakshi chaitanya*.

It is also called *sat-chit-ananda*. *Sat* means pure, absolute existence and *chit* means pure, absolute consciousness or knowledge and *ananda* means pure, absolute bliss. We have these three words: existence, knowledge or consciousness, and happiness. In the dual world people understand these three things in three different ways – they are not equal, not synonyms. But in *Vedanta* these three mean the same thing.

Existence means pure consciousness only, pure consciousness means pure bliss only and pure bliss means pure existence only. All the three words are borrowed from the world of duality, given some special significance and rolled into one. They mean and point to the same Absolute Reality, *Brahman*.

Ramana Maharshi, when he was asking this question, 'Who am I?' didn't give all the already known details. It is already known to everybody that 'I' is in the world, is born with a body and has some dealings in this body, in this world. There is no need to write a big book about it.

He was referring to this 'I' which is a projection of pure conciousness. He knew that this 'I' is a doorway to know, to cognise its very source that is the pure consciousness. So he adopted a method and would put this question to anybody coming to him: 'Have you concentrated your mind and tried to know who this "I" is?' And then followed a method of Self-enquiry which is given in his book, *Who Am I?*

Shankara, who came much before Ramana, was a teacher belonging to a very ancient tradition coming down from Narayana himself. In the *Bhagavad Gita* (classical Hindu scripture), *Krishna* passes the tradition to *Arjuna*, saying, 'Now I am again giving it to you.' The complete line of teachers is given in the *Bhagavad Gita*.

The ego is beautifully described by *Shankara* as *ajyasa* which means misconception or wrong knowledge. This ego is delusory, but unfortunately it happens to be the very focal point of all empirical tasks. So naturally, what happens is many people in the world do not know how to analyse this 'I'. *Shankara* has written three pages about this misconception as an introduction to the *Brahma Sutras* and there he says it is a very peculiar combination of the reality and the false appearance. So actually it's a reality-unreality (*atman-anatman*). These have been combined together, and the child born out of the unholy marriage is this ego. Beautifully put by *Shankara*.

This ego is the effect of a combination of two things which are totally opposed. In the *jiva* (an individual embodied being) itself, the ego itself, there is a combination of the Truth and the false appearance. This ego itself is a false appearance. When this is taught by the *Vedic* scriptures, and also by *Shankara*, it is rather difficult to understand. Once you understand this it opens up everything like a master key, opens up the doors of the treasure trove of *Vedanta*. Naturally, what happens is this ego, if it is a combination of two completely opposed things, reality and unreality, will be very highly delusory. Delusion in the sense that delusion is subjective, and illusion, *maya*, the world outside in front of me, is objective.

Shankara's beautiful explanation of *maya* (illusion of the conditional world) is that a person who has this subjective delusion can always see the world because this ego has the means of cognition of the duality outside, the world. So naturally this triad is there in us – the cogniser, the means of cognition and the cognised world. The ego is to be analysed, and if you know ego very well there is no need for you to analyse the outside world for the simple reason that the outside world, in a manner of speaking, is a projection of the ego. The ego becomes a focal point on which the whole of duality hinges. So we try to analyse this ego and separate it from this triad.

Unless there is an ego there is no world because the ego is the subject which is aware of the world of duality. So naturally, if the ego turns its attention away from the world and, with the introverted mind, turns towards its very source, then it merges in its very source because it is the subtlest part of the mind. This is the very basis of *Vedanta*. Though *ajyasa*, this misconception, is the experience of everybody, the moment you cognise it as delusion it never continues to be a delusion. This is just like a spell: as long as the person is under a spell he doesn't know he is under a spell. Whatever is dictated to him by whatever is controlling his mind, he does it. But the moment he comes to know, 'I am under a delusion,' it is no longer a delusion; he is no longer under a spell.

Just as in the example of the rope appearing as a snake, the moment you come to know the reality of the rope, the falsity of the snake is spontaneous, instantaneous. There is nothing extra to be done to know the falsity of the snake. It goes out of existence. The moment you come to know the falsity of the ego, the world goes out of existence and the ego also becomes falsified, sublimated.

When Sri Ramana was asked, 'When will the realisation of the Self be gained?' he replied, 'When the world which is what-is-seen has been removed, there will be realisation of the Self which is the seer.' You have explained the true understanding of the world. You have also explained that when the ego drops, the removal of the world is instantaneous.

If the ego itself is delusory and if the world is illusory there is no question of 'getting'. Now what remains for us to do is to be rid of the delusion. As I said just now, spontaneously delusion goes out of this thing. The world is more delusory than the ego because it is far away from us and it is something outside us. Here, at least, we have got something very close to us, intensive. As long as the 'I' is there the world is there. This is a universal experience. When the 'I' is not there the world can never come into existence. We have the belief that I was born in this world. This is a belief born out of wrong knowledge (*avidya*).

It's a belief. When the scriptures tell us to analyse if the 'I' is there or not, do you think there is any duality? In other words, 'I' is the very focal point on which the whole of duality is hinging, sort of superimposed.

Perhaps we can get rid of this delusive ego, or analyse how it came into being and compare it to the Absolute Reality. In deep sleep this ego goes out of existence. Nobody will be able to say in deep sleep there is duality of any kind. It is an absolute absence of duality. In other words, it is non-duality, it is pure consciousness – which can never be understood by the mind. If Ramana had wanted to use the *Vedantic* method he could have said, 'You are asking a question about a thing which doesn't exist. Where is the question of getting rid of it?'

The moment I come to know the reality of this 'I' – from where it was projected, its very source, pure consciousness – the idea of duality was never there. It was an illusion and now it has gone. It had never had any existence at all and hence, there will be realisation of the Self which is the seer. What Ramana means by 'seer' is pure consciousness, the witnessing consciousness. He has called it seer. I use the term witness, witnessing consciousness. You can also say, 'He is the seer.' All this duality is something seen by Him, but never outside Him. He pervades and illumines whatever is there in front of Him. That is the quality of pure consciousness.

Iswara, the Lord himself, became the *jiva*. He entered into our bodies. He created from the outside. He combined all the five elements then prepared the body. Then he saw it was inert. 'If I don't enter into it, it will never become sentient.' To make it animate and sentient he entered into it. This is a beautiful explanation of creation. Having created it, he said, 'Now I have satisfaction. I have done everything beautifully. This human being is alive and I have become this and I know everything is, and I am everything.' In that way he got satisfaction through his creation. Creation is a pretext in *Vedanta* for the scriptures and the teachers to turn our attention towards the creator, and once that purpose is served, the rescinding process starts – I am not this, I am not that (*neti-neti*).

Many Western seekers come to India looking for enlightenment as if it is an experience. What is enlightenment?

Enlightenment is a synonym for your beatitude, liberation and then Self-knowledge, your intuitive experience of the Self. All these expressions are there. Actually, enlightenment means knowledge of the Absolute Reality. Enlightenment happens to be the very core of our being and is called liberation, *moksha*.

A person who is Self-realised or who has attained Self-knowledge has intuitive knowledge of the Self, not mental or intellectual – it is intuitive knowledge. To differentiate we have used that word 'intuitive', that is pure consciousness as the Self, *sat-chit-ananda*. If this is called enlightenment it has to be experienced. It is not something to be believed in. The scriptures talk about universal experiences and comprehensive consummate experiences, *purna*, which means all-pervading. There is nothing outside this. So naturally this is an experience, which happens to be the very core of our being. All human beings can experience this. In fact, every moment of our life this experience of the witnessing consciousness is there behind the ego, supporting it, and that is why the ego is so conscious and powerful in the empirical world.

There is some conflict in this word 'experience'. I understand what you're saying, that it has to be an experience, but implicit in the word 'experience' is something that comes and goes. What you are pointing to is our very nature, so it is eternal, it doesn't come and go.

This is the empirical sort of experience. But here when we use the word 'experience' it is not in that sense. Here, at best, we can say it's a universal experience without the experiencer. Or you can also say it is the triad of the experiencer, the means of experience and the experienced object, all three rolled into one, and that is called pure consciousness.

Are there any qualifications for enlightenment?

Yes and no. If enlightenment happens to be our essential nature, where is the question of any qualification? For what? There is also no need of *sadhana* (spiritual practice). There is no spiritual practice to be done, no qualification to be had. If you look at the very core of your being, you are That. Whether you know it or not is a different matter, but you are That. 'That' means the ultimate Absolute Reality. If that is so, do we mean to say that any Tom, Dick or Harry can get this experience automatically, without doing anything? No. He is very much in this dual world as the ego, and the ego is naturally extroverted. It is always going outwards through the intellect, through the mind, the memory and the five senses, in contact with the world. The ego, the mind and the senses are called the *triputi* or the triad. This triad cannot be broken.

Any one component cannot be selected leaving the other two. See for yourself. The ego is always to be found along with these other two. If the ego becomes introverted, the other two go out of existence. The ego is directed towards the source now. So naturally the qualifications are only for the mind, which is extroverted, to be given exercises like *karma yoga* (activity as practice) and some other purifying practices that are mentioned in the *Bhagavad Gita*. There are twenty qualities to be practised positively to keep the mind introverted, and the introverted mind is directed towards its very source. This is called *mumukshatwa*, and unless a person qualifies himself as a *mumukshu*, he will not be qualified to have enlightenment.

Is that the same as a* sattvic *(calm and peaceful) mind?

Yes. A *sattvic* mind naturally minimises the *rajas* (active) and *tamas* (sluggish) aspects of mind but the three will always be there. Like the triad, these three *gunas* (qualities of nature) will always be there, but the person who is a *mumukshu* will try to keep a maximum of *sattva*. His mind is so very subtle, introverted and concentrated that it can think in terms of analysing all the teachings of the *Vedanta* scriptures, and naturally it can concentrate even on the Self. An introverted mind is a very concentrated and powerful faculty. So naturally those are the qualifications.

So you're saying that there is a preparation needed. What would be your advice? What kind of preparation would you suggest to achieve a quiet, introverted mind?

The *Upanishads* (ancient Indian scriptures) have given some wonderful advice. They suggest *yagna*, meaning sacrifice, and including some rituals which are conducted when you try to give up all that you possess; *dana*, meaning charity; and *tapas*, meaning austerity, where one sits in meditation for long periods, chastening or cleansing the mind. Many people are doing these *sadhanas*.

In the *Bhagavad Gita*, *karma yoga* is given as a wonderful exercise and anyone with a little discriminative power can do it without difficulty. There are four aspects of it. The first is to give up the hankering after the fruits of action. The second is to accept any work that comes and offer it as worship of God. The third is to minimise and give up attachment to and identification with the ego. Fourthly, attachment towards outside things must be minimised. If these four qualities are introduced into whatever you do it becomes a *karma yoga*, and in the course you become an introverted person and a qualified person for Self-knowledge.

After that there is what is called *sakshat sadhana*. Its three aspects must be carried out in the presence of an adept teacher. First, he explains to you the interpretations of the *Upanishads – shravanam*. The next step is reasoning based on those teachings – *mananam*. This is followed by reflection and intensive introspection – *nididhyasanam*. Ramana has said the same about all these direct *sadhanas*.

But these last* sadhanas *that you've mentioned, aren't they going to increase rather than quieten the activity of the mind?

No. For that very reason, perhaps, some people don't go through the *Upanishads*. In fact, all the *Upanishads* teach you about a method of superimposition, and in the process they take the mind away from the dual world and direct it towards the Self, the non-dual reality, the very source of all duality. It brings about the conviction that this is reality, not the other. That's very powerful, so naturally discrimination is very important, but in the process the mind becomes concentrated. It directs all its energies towards pure consciousness.

Sri Ramana said Self-enquiry is the most direct route to realising the Self. What do you say about Self-enquiry? How to conduct Self-enquiry?

Self-enquiry means *shravanam*, *mananam* and *nididhyasanam*, listening, reasoning and deep contemplation. When you do these under the guidance of a seasoned, adept teacher, he teaches you how to go stage-by-stage from giving up the ego, identification with the ego, to being one with the Self, which is the very essence of being.

Let me take the example of the three states of waking, dreaming and deep sleep. The teaching is to analyse the waking state in a different way than previously understood; then attention is turned towards the dream and then towards the deep sleep. First, by the way of superimposition, a relationship is built up between the three states. The waking and the dream states are seen as projections of something which is in the seed form in the deep sleep. So all three are connected. There is a cause and these are the effects. Then slowly the teacher and the *Upanishads* teach you these three are independent, not connected at all. This is also supported by universal experience. When we are in the waking state we are not in the deep sleep or dream state. When we are in the dream, waking is not there, deep sleep is not there. When we are in deep sleep, waking and dream are not there. So naturally they are independent experiences that are projected by pure conciousness, for your benefit, to know Him. All the three are projections, superimpositions on pure consciousness. If that is realised the teaching is completed.

Could you explain, in a step-by-step way, this* Vedantic *method of Self-enquiry?

Yes. This is capital 'S' Self-enquiry, and according to the scriptures it is actually a giving up of your identification with the small self, ego, and switching over to identification with the Self, which is your very essence of being that you can never lose. When you come to know this is real and the ego is just a false projection, a misconception, this is called Self-knowledge, Self-realisation. *Vedanta* teaches us capital 'S' Self-enquiry, and in the process it analyses everything that we have understood about the small self, the *jiva*. The *jiva* itself is the *paramatman* (supreme soul). *Paramatman* has projected itself as the *jiva*. There are not two things at all. The snake is not there independently from the rope, and in the same way the *jiva* can never exist independently from the Self, the pure consciousness.

It has been suggested that the mind must be destroyed for liberation to occur. Do you have a mind? Sri Ramana used the term* manonasha *to describe the state of liberation, meaning destroyed mind. How to destroy the mind?

'It has been suggested that the mind must be destroyed...' You see, mind, at present, appears to be there. Mind means ego; the subtlest aspect of the mind is ego and the intellect is there. The memory aspect of it is also there. So mind means all these four aspects – the ego, the intellect, the memory aspect, and the volitionary – all these comprise the mind.

Now we in the empirical sphere, we accept that the mind exists, don't we? But when we come to know the reality of the Self, mind is not there at all. It was never there. So naturally the mind need not be destroyed – there is no question of destroying a thing which doesn't exist. World can exist only when the ego is there. Without the ego the world can never be experienced, can never exist. It's the same here, the mind cannot exist apart from the Self. It is a projection. But, at the same time, it is a misconception, a false appearance. So there is no question of destruction of the mind. Many people, including Ramana Maharshi, talk about this *manonasha*, destruction of the mind, but it is not the correct word. *Manonigra* can be used. *Manonigra* means you give up the identification with the mind, give up grasping anything, and when there is no grasping, the grasper also is not there.

What about* vasanas*, the tendencies of the mind? Must these be removed before Self-realisation can become permanent?

Vasanas are latent impressions. These latent impressions are taught in a beautiful manner. You know, it's a vicious circle. As long as you have got *avidya*, ignorance of the Self, the ego will be there. *Avidya* itself is *ajyasa*, misconception, so the ego will be there. Can you find an ego without any desires? Never. An ego without desires can never be found.

If you analyse the ego properly, according to the *Vedantic* scriptures, it is a bundle of desires, and when these desires become very powerful they prompt you into action because the desire is towards acquiring something from the outside world. So we are prompted to take action – go there, procure it, secure it and then take it in our possession. So desire leads to *karma*, action. *Karma* leads to *karmaphala*, the result of an action. Any action has to reap its fruit, and whether it is good or bad, you, the agent of the action, has to enjoy it. When you enjoy the fruit, there is a latent impression created in the mind and that's called the *vasana*. The *vasana* is lurking even in the unconscious mind, where it becomes very powerful. When favourable conditions are created here in the world, those latent impressions come to the surface in the form of powerful desires that prompt us again into action.

So this is how, like the dog trying to catch its tail, we are going through the vicious circle of repeated births and deaths. This is called *samsara*. But this can be removed very easily with Self-knowledge. The moment the ignorance of the Self goes out of existence, there is no *samsara*. You have gotten rid of the *samsara* and all the problems of life.

Self-realisation means getting rid of all these false appearances. You must never give that same stamp of reality as you give to the Self to anything from the ego or the mind.

During the time I spent with my master, Poonjaji, there were people, who, in his presence, had a very strong awakening to the Self, and he would say, 'Your work is finished.' They would be glowing in bliss and they would feel their work was finished. Then they would go away for some months and when they came back a lot of these people would say, 'It's gone!' Often Poonjaji would say, 'If it's gone, then you never found it in the beginning.' And at the same time, I can remember Sri Ramana saying that strong* vasanas *can pull you out of that awakening, that understanding. Can you comment on that?

There are many people who speak in terms of *shaktipatta*. Have you heard of it?

Yes, it's a kind of transmission of energy.

Vedanta never approves of that. These things cannot be transferred from one person to another. If you speak in terms of transfer at all, it is the *guru* telling you to find it in yourself. There is no transfer, so this *shaktipatta* is a misnomer and is totally wrong. It is never taught in the *Upanishads* and I don't know how Poonjaji and all these people got this understanding. *Vedanta* doesn't approve of any mysticism. There are many mystics.

I didn't experience Poonjaji as a mystic. He would simply sit there and people would come and ask him questions.

Self-knowledge doesn't need any certificate from any mystic. The *Upanishads* are supposed to be of divine origin. The *rishis* (seers) became the medium through which the *Upanishads* were heard and articulated and given to the world. It is divinity itself that is called the *Upanishad purusha*, the Self. It is to be known only through the *Upanishads*, nothing else. So, if this is what *Shankara* teaches us, and what *Vedanta* teaches, then the mystics cannot be trusted. There is no such thing as an experience which can be taught in terms of universal experiences.

I understand what you are saying in one way, but surely if the seeker is ripe and he comes to a master who turns the thing back around to the student with a certain force in that moment, then surely it is possible that that is the moment when the student finally sees the Truth and there is no magic in it.

I don't agree with that because it is there in him. Nothing is given to him afresh by the *guru*.

No, nothing is given, but just by the* guru's *presence there is an end, there is a finality.

Alright, in that case, the moment I know the Self I have gained Self-knowledge. I don't see anything, no world at all. I don't hear *om* (sound of universal consciousness) and see brilliant light everywhere; nothing of the kind. If that were so, *Shankara* would have mentioned it somewhere. The *Upanishads* would have mentioned it.

In the Japanese Zen tradition there is a whole history of stories where, at a certain moment, the master touches the student in some way and the student wakes up. This is similar to what I am describing.

Anything that is created afresh is created in time and it will go out of existence. But Self-knowledge is not of that kind. It is beyond time, space and causation. It is neither a cause nor an effect.

I don't think these people experienced any transfer of energy from Poonjaji to themselves, but more they experienced the end of the search. Perhaps they were mature people who had been looking for understanding in many places, for many years, and in this particular man's presence they were taken back or forced into the deep recess inside themselves and then experienced the Self.

I can accept that, in a qualified manner. Let us put it this way: the adept teacher invokes, kindles, that Self-knowledge in the student. But when the Self-knowledge is attained, he realises. That is called Self-realisation, isn't it? When he realises that Self, should there be any sort of superhuman symptom or symbol that is occurring in him?

If realisation has happened, the student will attain *sirvatmabhava* – everything is nothing but *atman*, the Self. Ramana had that understanding; we can't doubt it. This was the reason for his blank expression. He was completely identified with the Self. That is where he was looking from, and he had separated the Self from the not-Self. Unless you do that you can't have that blank look. He was identified with the Self in every moment. He was not registering any experience.

I would like to tell you my own experience with Poonjaji. After more than twenty years of searching, doing sadhana *and so on, I was suddenly sitting in front of this man who had a tremendous energy and was the focus of two hundred people. He talked to me personally in a way that seemed to turn all the energy back inside me. I didn't feel any transmission from him, but something occurred inside me. There was whiteness, nothingness. Suddenly I discovered I couldn't open my eyes. They physically wouldn't open. I was transfixed in that place. At the end of all this, when I had been given some water and was just resting, there was tremendous bliss. There was no Premananda, there was no mind. There was a tremendous expansion of consciousness.*

In *Vedanta*, we dismiss these individualistic things; they are not universal experiences. *Upasanas* are meditations which are mentioned in the scriptures. You perform them as they are given to you, to the letter, very carefully. You get such mystic powers and each one gives rise to a different kind of experience. It's an experience, it is individualistic, but we are not talking about that. It is a sign that you are on the right way. It is a certificate that you are getting your mind clarified, but these meditations can never give you the ultimate. You have to come to *jnana* (knowledge, wisdom) only, which is an intuitive experience of the Self and is based on universal experiences like waking, dream and deep sleep. Deep sleep is an experience which is experienced by everybody, and, in deep sleep, pure consciousness is in its purest form, not having any superimposition nor any projection. There is no white light, nothing of the kind. That is taught by the *Upanishads*. Why not accept it? It is based on universal experiences. You can never deny that.

But why would I deny my own personal experience?

You see, the point is many people have followed Poonjaji and others. They have had all sorts of brilliant experiences. First and foremost, Self-realisation is a thing which is not to be got afresh. Secondly, it happens to be the very core of our being, whether we know it or not. There's no choice for it and hence, in that light, it is destined. You are destined to be one with it. From that point of view you can call it destiny. You are destined to be That only.

From one day to the next all the questions went and I saw that the ground of being was always there, the Self. From that moment it seemed as if I was thrust deeply into the ocean of Self, which I have never left.

A Self-realised person expressing the same thing would say: 'The moment I get *jnana*, my identification with the ego is minimised. I don't seek anything. There's nothing, no purpose in having anything.' He speaks the language of a renunciate. He has renounced everything, all of duality; he doesn't possess even the body now. The greatest fear one can have is the fear of death. He has already gone beyond death, so he is not afraid of it. He can say, 'Death, you can come and take away this body. I have already discarded it.'

That's also my situation.

Actually, many people have got it, but they didn't have this special thing that you had. The understanding is more important than the light and other experiences.

I should be clear. I never considered that actual experience of light and expansion, in itself, to be important. The thing that seemed to be important was the entrance into the ground of being, which has never left.

Yes, that is more important.

It has never left.

Yes, it will never leave. It never came and it never left. It was always there.

This was always there. The duality, and other things which I believed to be true, they were never there – well, they seemed to be there.

They seemed to be there, but they were never there.

Right, but the thing that changed in that moment was a clear knowing of the ground of being. In that moment, it changed everything in such a way that there were no more questions. The knowing hadn't been there before, but has been there ever since.

Yes, correct. Knowing the Self is not the usual knowing by the intellect. That's not knowing – you can never know the Self that way, as an object. It can never become the object. The Self, pure consciousness, at best can become the subject in the form of the ego, which goes to show the concessions that the *Upanishads* give to us. It is the pure consciousness, the Self, coming in the form of the ego. Beyond that, it can never become an object, but, at best, it can become a subject which is conscious of the object. That's all; it can never be made the object. So naturally 'I' itself, in its own realm, can never be objectified by anything else. The only thing that can objectify the ego is the pure consciousness. But in the sphere of duality, ego can never be objectified. It is the subject; it will remain like that. For that very reason 'I' can never give up the ego, the subjective consciousness in me; 'I' can never jump out of it and become the object. 'I' can always remain the source of awareness in the duality sphere. I know everything else, but that ego, such a powerful ego, even though it is in the presence of the Self, it is sort of a misconception. It never really existed apart from the Self.

The Self itself appears as the ego, and when the ego seeks its source, that is called Self-realisation. That's all. And Self-realisation doesn't mean Self is objectified, experienced. Nothing like that. You remain as the Self. Are you aware of the Self, the ego? Supposing we put that question to ourselves: Are we aware of the ego? What will the answer be? In the sphere of duality, ego is the basic focal point on which all duality is mounted, or superimposed. Now ego itself, is it self-aware? Yes! It is self-established and it can never give up its self-awareness. Very true. In the world of duality, Self can never be objectified by anything else. Hence, it has the stamp of certainty, even though it is a misconception. Wonderful! This is something fantastic. The ego itself, in the sphere of duality, has the stamp of reality. It doesn't need any certificate of being real, yet from the viewpoint of the pure consciousness, it was a misconception of Truth which was superimposed.

So, it is the Self trying to show its excellences – it can project the world through the ego and again take it back. This is His *leela*, His divine play. The play of the Self, of *paramatman*, God. He is doing this in every moment. Should He create the world? Is it true? It is given in the form of a story, but it is not true that way. These are all pretexts for the teacher and the scriptures to turn our attention towards the Absolute Reality. That's all. Nothing else.

At the end of his book,* Self-Enquiry, *Sri Ramana says, 'He who is thus endowed with a mind that has become subtle and who has the experience of the Self is called a* jivanmukta.*'

This kind of subtle mind has become One with the ultimate Reality. The *Vedanta* scriptures say that spiritual instruction given by a teacher who knows the tradition can result in some sort of a refinement in the mind, which happened in your case in front of Poonjaji. Ultimately, when the mind becomes refined by these teachings it becomes no-mind. It merges in its very source. So a *jivanmukta* can be interpreted as a person who has established himself in this pure consciousness. Although he is still in the body, he feels he is no more embodied – as if he is one with the Self, not with this self. This self has been sublimated, falsified, and even if he carries out any transactions through this ego he fully knows that he is acting. The *jivanmukta* is acting as an actor, wearing the role of this small self. Ego and he know, 'I have nothing to gain here. I have to keep this body going as long as it can because it has taken a shape, and let it go on as long as it lives. Let it live.' In the *Bhagavad Gita*, *Krishna* says to *Arjuna*, 'Don't harm this body because this vehicle helped you to come to this stage. It has helped you. It has become a medium for you to achieve this wisdom and so many other arts.' He didn't say, 'Now your job is done so throw it out.' Don't do that. Let it fall off of its own accord.

***Sri Ramana goes on, 'And when one is immersed in the ocean of bliss and has become one with it without any differentiated existence, one is called a* videhamukta.'**

Videhamukta means without the body. You see, *mukta* means with the body, *jivanmukta*. *Videhamukta* means that after giving up the body he becomes One with the Ultimate. This is a thing which is not accepted by *Vedanta* and if it was said by Ramana, he is going against the *Upanishads*. *Videha* (without the body) is not taught at all by the *Upanishads*. This was introduced by the people who came much later than *Shankara*. *Jivanmukta* occurs at any time while in the body. The body may continue but you are not identified with the body. You have identified with the Self and you have separated the not-self, the body, and the reality of the consciousness. So you are established in the reality. A *jivanmukta*, while in the body, has known the essential nature of liberation, freedom, and that is called the Self.

***It appears essential to meet a* guru *and stay with that* guru. *Who is the* guru?**

The *Mundika Upanishad* – *mundika* means shaven head, so it signifies it is meant for the *sannyasins*, the renunciates – says you must find the *guru* who is a *shrutriya* and a *brahmanishta*. *Shrutriya* means he must be very well versed in the traditional method of teaching, and *brahmanishta* means he must be established in the ultimate Reality. So these are the qualifications of a *guru*.

And what is the* guru's *role?

The *guru's* role is only to teach the methods for giving up identification with the ego, the embodied self, and realising one's essential nature. That is his role. He has studied the scriptures, the methods; he has been taught by his *guru*, so he was also at one time a student. Then he remembers all the impediments, the difficulties he experienced as a student and how he got rid of all his doubts. Now he is in the position of the *guru*, and he teaches the student according to that method. The student also will become a light kindling another light; so this goes on in a series. That is the *guru's* role.

***And how to recognise a true* guru?**

When you come in close contact with the *guru*, you see how he behaves, what he says, what he teaches, how he himself practises. You see how he follows all those precepts which he has taught you. Supposing he gets up early in the morning and does some meditation, you are at liberty to ask, 'Sir, what is that meditation you perform? Can I do it?' If he says you are fit for that, do it along with him. So he is a guide in every respect – he makes his student go through all the necessary steps to achieve the same result that he has achieved. He has followed the path and he has become a teacher now, just like a professor who has undergone some training. Now he is in a position to teach other students. But was he not a student? He was a student, and from his *guru* he learned this *vidya*, this knowledge, wisdom. Now his expertise is such that he can share that knowledge and give it to another person. He should be open, without any reservations or inhibitions, and answer any question that the disciple asks. He must very willingly, lovingly, compassionately teach him everything, not keeping any secret from him. That sort of *guru* is a true *guru*.

Sri Ramana's devotees had tremendous devotion to him and he to Arunachala. Please say something about* bhakti, *devotion, in the pursuit of awakening.

Bhakti is the equivalent of devotion. Devotion always implies devotion to something, towards something; so you are a devotee and there is a deity, a god. You will devote all your time to the deity and you invoke his blessings; you invoke him and you want his grace to flow towards you. You are asking for something. *Bhakti* is always towards a deity who is in a position to grant something that you desire. So in *Vedanta*, even though they are quite different, *bhakti* is definitely equated with *jnana*, which means aquiring knowledge, aquiring intuitive knowledge.

Would you say it's important that the* bhakti *and the* jnana *are woven together? Could you say that it's a necessary attitude towards your* guru, *this devotion?

Instead of saying necessary attitude, we can say that we are devotees from birth. *Bhakti*, a belief in something, is natural in man. It is something which is within your control – you can do *bhakti*, you need not do *bhakti*; you may do it in a different way than it is mentioned in the scriptures. But *jnana* is not like that. *Jnana*, aquiring knowledge, depends on another who has the knowledge. So that is the difference between *bhakti* and *jnana*. *Bhakti* is worshipping God, seeking His grace.

***Can it be the* guru's *grace? Can the devotion be towards the* guru?**

We have a *Sanskrit* verse:

Guru Brahma, Guru Vishnu, Guru Devo Maheswara.
Guru sakshat parambrahman tasmayi Sri Gurumay namaha.

That's the prayer we recite before we start any class. *Guru Brahma* – *guru* himself is the ultimate Reality. Look at how it is: *guru's* position is eulogised. It is praised to such an extent that *guru* himself is a living god before me. You must have that much faith in him. Supposing the disciple doesn't have any trust in the *guru* – the *vidya*, the knowledge that he gets, will be of no consequence.

So then* bhakti *is an essential part of the* guru*-disciple relationship?

Yes, a very essential part, and this is natural. Man, in his nature, is devoted. He has devotion towards his parents, devotion towards his teachers, devotion towards his *guru* or a deity. The scriptures, the priests, tell you to invoke the blessings of this deity and you will get what you desire. So like that, all these things are happening. But the *guru* must be trustworthy, and he should not cheat the student.

Seekers often have curious ideas about the enlightened state. Please describe your typical day and how you perceive the world.

When the seeker gets the final knowledge of the Self there is no change, except his identification is shifted from the ego to the Self. Now he knows the Reality. Formerly he was thinking something was real which was not real. Hence, it was a misconception. Now he has conviction that this is the Reality, and this Reality can never cease to exist. It is eternal, non-dual, beyond time, space, causation, beyond *dharma* and *adharma*, the merits and demerits, all the things that are mentioned in the scriptures. It is something which he can never think of as ceasing to exist. It can never go out of existence. It is the Reality, the One Reality, yet we don't call it One – we say non-dual, absolute, eternal.

So in your typical day are there no special fireworks at all?

No. I can put it this way – when one becomes a *jnani*, one who knows, there is a vast change in his perspective. He is not to be found behaving as others; he is not seeking the society, the company of people. If he seeks company at all it is with like-minded people or the disciples. Otherwise, he keeps to himself, he seeks solitude. That's a symptom even in a *mumukshu* (one whose mind is introverted), before becoming a *jivanmukta*, even at that time he seeks solitude, and what does he do during this solitude? He is always training the mind towards the ultimate Reality.

You have given us a profound discourse on awakening. When you meet someone with a passion for awakening, what would your short advice be?

A true seeker has passion. A true seeker is very devoted; he is prepared to give up everything except this one knowledge. In other words, he is not like the others. He seeks this and this alone. So naturally, we have to tell such a person, 'Seek it from a *guru* who is a *shrutriya brahmanishta* (one who is well versed in the traditional method of teaching and is established in the ultimate Reality) and your success will be very fast.' It will be a short trip to success. He must find a *shrutriya brahmanishta* and find out for himself. He must trust the teacher and get all the experiences here and now so he can experience those things himself.

Thank you. Is there anything else you wish to add to this dialogue?

Approach a *shrutriya brahmanishta* and, from close contact, you can find out if your caliber is good. There need not be any doubt that he will definitely deliver the goods, bring you that sense of conviction after which you will never waver, and you will never have any doubts.

That was so in my case. (starts to cry) When I saw this teacher I got it. I was convinced, and I need not seek anybody else's advice. In fact, a stage has come when I can give advice to others. Such a powerful personality I came across – I was lucky.

You have been brought to tears a few times today.

I don't know. It happens so quickly I have no control over it. It overtakes me because I have done a lot of *bhakti*. I used to cry like a child.

These tears are not the tears of sadness. They are the tears of joy, which is the language of the Self. Thank you.

Kiran

Enlightenment is not something that you can search for. When all searching ends, when you just stop, when you're still, then something opens up from inside. The search is from the mind, and awakening, the clarity that you see, the inner state of awakening, is when the mind ceases.

Sit with yourself. You'll find it inside,
not somewhere outside.

Kiran

Kiran

Kiran was born in 1941, he studied Hindu philosophy at the Sanskrit College in Thane. In 1967 he became a disciple of Osho while pursuing the life of an industrialist and a householder. Following Osho's 1981 departure from India for the United States, Kiran sought out a number of other *gurus*. The one who influenced him most was U.G. Krishnamurti. In 1993 he began to teach. He left his body in March 2006, aged sixty-five.

This interview with Kiran was conducted in 2004. It was our first and only meeting. He sat relaxed on a sofa swinging from the ceiling in a large airy living room. Some of his Indian disciples were present. When asked about his biography, Kiran immediately replied: 'I have no biography.' He felt very much with himself. Kiran was a modern spiritual teacher, a businessman, householder and family man.

Sri Ramana proposed the fundamental question 'Who am I?' Who are you?

The right answer is silence. There is no answer to this question. Any answer that you get from asking the question 'Who am I?' is not the right answer. The answer that you get to this question most of the time is from the knowledge that you have about yourself. Then you reach that point when this knowledge about yourself ceases and knowing dawns upon you; there is no word which can express who you are. There is just silence. You are that silence. You are that nothingness. There are a lot of labels that you have coined from your language, your profession, your acquaintances, your relations, all the conditioning that you have, but these are not the right answer. Your question is 'Who am I?' I would say that the I dissolved and there is nobody there. There is nobody. There is no I, there is nobody there. That is my answer.

So for example, in this moment now, who is speaking?

The speaking is happening. It is not somebody speaking. So far as you are speaking, the mind is speaking through your knowledge. This moment now, it is happening. It's just speaking; there is nobody who speaks, just speaking.

Many Western seekers come to India looking for enlightenment as if it is an experience. What is enlightenment?

Enlightenment is not an experience. It is an expression of the inner state. It is our natural state; that means it is not separate from us. Enlightenment means the total knowing, total understanding of who you are in the real sense, not through knowledge, not even through knowing. When you reach that total unfoldment of knowing it cannot be an experience. It is something like waking up in the morning. When you wake up in the morning you experience a lot of things. You see the sunrise, the beautiful colourful morning sky, you listen to the birds, you feel the cool wind. These are the experiences, but they come through the awakening. The awakening is an inner state, your natural state. Through this natural state you experience the way it is, the way the life is, the way it is expressing, the way it is demanding, the way it is giving you answers to respond. This state of clarity inside, this awakened state inside, is an enlightened state. It is not an experience. Through the state of awakening there are a lot of experiences that we can claim. Those who claim awakening or enlightenment do not know it. It is not that the experience confirms your awakening. Awakening is coming back home, coming back to our natural state of pure consciousness, the state of clarity. That is what I understand as enlightenment.

You say that many Westerners are coming in search of enlightenment. It is the misunderstanding of the Western mind that this is a search, that you can reach, you can achieve, you can become enlightened. Enlightenment is not something that you can search for. When all searching ends, when you just stop, when you're still, then something opens up from inside. The search is from the mind, and awakening, the clarity that you see, the inner state of awakening, is when the mind ceases. The rejection of mind. That means that when the whole area of knowledge dissolves, the clarity of knowing is available to you. This cannot be reached through any search. But still people are wandering around knocking on each door, asking who will give me enlightenment as if it is something somebody can give you. It is like a blind person searching for the light. How can he search for the light? He has to do something to his eyes, not fight in the darkness. If you understand and do something to open the eyes, then the light is already there. Only that is required.

Enlightenment is not something that we have lost. It is our natural state; clarity is our natural state. If you really do something in the right direction then it is available there. When Buddha was asked, 'What did you get when you became enlightened?' his answer was, 'I came to know that I never lost it, I never lost it.' What does that mean? You do not know now. What is required is to understand what the hindrance is to that clarity. If you come in search of enlightenment without understanding what is hindering your clarity, your understanding, your knowing, how can you reach the summit?

That's why the meaning of enlightenment has been totally misunderstood by the Western mind. Enlightenment is not an experience. I have seen many of the Western masters who claim themselves enlightened, but are actually claiming some kind of experience certified by their masters, getting the certificate and starting to give *Satsang* (meeting in Truth), the holy business. The one who is really enlightened is not like that; there is nobody there who can claim enlightenment, and there's nothing to claim. There is nowhere to go, nothing to reach, nothing to become. How can you claim something if you are not That? You can claim climbing Everest, you cannot claim coming back to your home. This is coming back home. Such a relaxed state. Everybody misunderstands, and a few in India also want new business out of this whole hotbed of enlightenment. They want to sell this, make money out of it, and the rest of us are exploited.

Could you say something about what it is that prevents us just being in our natural state?

It is *ajnan*, not knowing, in the ancient scriptures. What is *ajnan*? What is not knowing? When I was there in Ramana Maharshi's *ashram* I felt so pained that in the same room where Ramana used to sit on the sofa, people now just sit in the corner and chant 'Who am I? Who am I? Who am I?' Is Self-enquiry a matter of chanting? It's not a *mantra* (sacred sound), it's an enquiry, a very serious enquiry. The belief system that you can accept something as Truth without going into your own knowing is the first weakness.

There are so many things that we have accepted as Truth that are not our own knowing, including most religious beliefs and spiritual beliefs. The answers people give from asking 'Who am I?' I am *Brahman* (absolute reality), I am *paramatman* (supreme soul), I am consciousness; these are the answers which come from your beliefs. Somewhere you have read it, somewhere you have heard it, somebody has told you this and you accepted it. How can you say 'I am consciousness'? There is no other consciousness which can say 'I am consciousness'. This belief that we carry, and we just repeat without understanding, has to be questioned. The scientific approach should be taken. The first hindrance is your belief system, that frozen part of your mind where you do not question. There are a lot of things there which are used as a reference point to understand things. If you have a frame to understand something, that frame is coming from the frozen part, the reference point. We are not even aware that we are not actually seeing the way it is, but seeing through frames. These frames are a hindrance to our knowing.

Would you say that the basic frame is the idea that I am somebody?

All that knowledge that you have about yourself, all that has been kept inside without questioning, that you don't even dare to question, this is the point which is the hindrance to your actual awakening, actual clarity. It includes all your knowledge about yourself, the way you recognise yourself through the opinions of other people and then start to believe that is who you are, the answers that you have accepted without question from religion, culture, tradition, the spiritual influence; this is the hindrance, it's a disease. That is where you have to start questioning.

Are there any qualifications for enlightenment? Is* sadhana *(spiritual practice) necessary? If yes, what form do you advise?

Qualifications, what qualifications? You need to be alive, that's all. Most of the time we are not, we are so dead. We are so connected to the past. The first requirement to be awakened, to be enlightened, is to be alive like a flower, alive like a bird, alive like a child. Look at the child. Can you do it? How can you be alive unless you are just totally free from that whole dead past, unless you are available to Now, this very moment? If you connect here then you are alive. But we do not connect here, we connect to the past. We see the present through the past and dream about the future. To be alive means to be available now. To be alive means to be bubbling with life inside, with all your problems, with a dance inside, with a song inside, with all your being. Be spontaneous. This is the qualification.

Is there any *sadhana*? Is there any path? There is no path. The path is created by the mind. It's like flying into the sky. It's an open sky, free sky, you just have to open your wings and take a jump. When you fly into the sky there is no path. There is no *sadhana* that you do. Do it, it's your inborn gift. To be enlightened is not something based on some *sadhana*. *Sadhana* is meant to direct the mind, you take the journey through the mind. The mind has to get so tired that at a certain point it drops dead. Real *sadhana* is to make you so tired, physically and mentally, that you realise that you have done so many things to reach nowhere. That is the point where you start questioning the search itself. There is nothing that takes you there because there is nothing there. Then begins the journey which starts from stopping. The outer journey begins when you start walking, but the inner journey, the *sadhana*, begins when you stop. There is no movement. Sit silently and do nothing. You are just doing *sadhana*.

Another path which is attractive to the mind is *yoga*, the path of the seeker. There you are doing something so that slowly, slowly, this mind acquires a lot of power, and at a certain point it explodes. But when it explodes it is an explosion of power, so it becomes more powerful. Some *yogis* (practitioners of *yoga*) have a lot of powers, *siddhis*, a very, very strong ego and very strong mental powers. They can control people, they can mesmerise, they can show so many miracles, *chamatkar*, and this is an attraction for the mind. Most of the people attracted into the path of *sadhana* are thinking that enlightenment will happen there. They reach a certain level of *siddhis* and they misunderstand that this is a part of enlightenment. Enlightenment is to reach the state of a *buddha* (awakened one), of order and total understanding, a total awakening, not the state of the *yogi* with *siddhis*. My question is: are you searching for power or are you searching for peace? Really we all search for peace.

If you really understand the path of peace, it's possible to relax. Accept yourself as you are. For the last ten years I have been sharing this with people. Accept where you are and accept what you have. Acceptance of yourself the way you are finishes all spiritual journeys and all *sadhana*. You are doing this *sadhana* because you are not happy with yourself, you are not accepting yourself as you are. You want to become somebody, you want to reach somewhere, you want to achieve something. You want to become like a *buddha*, like something you have created as a goal, so you take a path of *sadhana*. When you accept yourself as you are, what is the need of any *sadhana*? You are as you are. Stay within yourself, with yourself, and love starts flowing. All *sadhana* begins with hatred, with rejection, with non-acceptance – otherwise you cannot do any *sadhana*. Accept yourself.

You may call this the beginning or the first step where you are just relaxing within. When you relax inside with the total acceptance of the way you are, then something starts coming up because this mind, who is a doer, has no job. Otherwise mind has a spiritual job, a worldly job, so many jobs that mind creates according to the goals it creates. The *sadhana* also is the mind's job. The moment you accept yourself, there is no job left for the mind, so there is no doer. When we start living with the understanding that the way I am is absolutely fine, then automatically the mind is helpless and the ego is helpless. As Ramana used to say, to whom is this happening? There is no answer to this question. You start seeing it, you start seeing that your mind, where this is happening, is a mirage. You come to that witnessing centre which is your natural state, which is what you are. Then you start living with this understanding. This acceptance is automatically the unfolding of understanding; the clarity starts happening without your *sadhana*.

I don't encourage *sadhana* and I don't discourage *sadhana*. You have to make up your mind. I have gone through this whole journey of *sadhana* and at a certain point I got fed up with it. But one has to be very, very honest. Mind is very cunning and tricky, it starts telling you that you are getting somewhere, some imaginary experience starts happening and you start believing that you are close to enlightenment. 'Come on! In one year you are going to get enlightened, maybe tomorrow!' This is all the mind's game. I have gone through this, I know it. It's all the mind's game.

The spiritual life demands honesty with yourself. Only life demands honesty to the other. The spiritual life demands honesty to yourself. Be honest with yourself that even after doing years of meditation, years of *sadhana*, nothing has changed. Who has the courage to say that nothing has changed, that you are the same? We have some vision that something has changed. Some momentary change that you see is not a change. You take a painkiller and wow! all the pain disappeared. So what? The cause of the pain is still there. All *sadhanas* are functioning like a painkiller, they give you some temporary relief and the mind is fooled, and the mind is also fooling you that it is happening. Understand that you have to be absolutely clear about what you are searching for. What are you searching for? Be honest and look there. Am I relaxed when I connect with the life? What is the point of disturbance in my connection with the life outside which creates a reaction in my mind? Am I relaxed? Look inside and see for yourself. You will find that you are not. You get so tired, so fed up. How long? How many years? How many masters have you gone to? How many years of begging for enlightenment?

A Sufi master woke me up suddenly: 'What are you searching for? What do you want in life?' I said, 'I want happiness. I want peace.' He said, 'Then question why you are unhappy. Don't search for the peace. You have to stay with yourself. You have to observe, you have to watch, you have to enquire: Why am I unhappy? Why am I sick? Find out. Don't search for health.' This is the whole *sadhana*. I don't say that it does not help. It has its own limitations. If you are full of pain and frustration and unbearable suffering, then you need some painkiller. You need some kind of technique or method or medication which can relieve you from the immediate pain, but it is not the cure. If you don't understand then you get addicted to the painkiller. Why should you do meditations every morning for twenty years? What for? If it is a cure, at a certain point it has to drop out. It has to make you healthy. But if it does not, then it is becoming an addiction, like a drug addiction.

The whole day you stuff so many things inside. Why are our minds so full of frustration, so full of tension? Understand this: *sadhana* can work up to a certain point and give you a temporary relief, but it is not a cure. I am saying this because I have gone through it, I know it and I have seen many of my friends go through it. Understanding is the only awakening. Understand why you are sick, why you have frustration, why you are unhappy; understand it. Find out the cause of your unhappiness. The moment you understand it, you understand also the remedy. Then you are free. That freedom is your natural state. It is not that you have to find the freedom.

Sri Ramana said that Self-enquiry is the most direct route to realising the Self. What do you say about Self-enquiry? How to conduct Self-enquiry?

People have misunderstood Ramana's message of Self-enquiry – it does not mean chanting 'Who am I?' Self-enquiry means to look back at yourself without any frames of reference. The word 'enquiry' comes from science; when a scientist enquires into any question he keeps aside all the past answers and looks into it as if it is a new, fresh problem that he has to understand. Understand the problem layer by layer.

Self-enquiry as a technique brings a momentous way of repeating the answers and coming to a conclusion, an answer which is already there. Slowly, slowly, look into yourself, observing yourself, and observing the life around yourself. This I, which is connected within and outside, look there. Once you start looking, observing, then you start getting the clarity of something which is there in its own natural way.

My understanding of Self-enquiry is that we have to observe. Anything that you are trying to understand, first observe, then through that observation you start getting some knowing of it. Slowly, slowly, you come to the root of it. I tell my friends to observe the life outside, look around. When you look around what do you see? You see the expression of life around. You'll observe and understand that the life is changing and moving; it's all changing and moving. You'll also see that life is insecure, life is uncertain, life is unknown. That also comes through our enquiry and observation, that this is natural play. Each encounter that we have, each moment that we are connecting with life, reflects this nature, the nature of changing and moving, of insecurity, of uncertainty, of the unknown. Through your observation and enquiry you understand something: that this is the life which I'm connected to. Enquire why there is any action and why there is reaction. The mind is reactive; observe and enquire. Go deep inside. Go deep inside this problem of why there is a reaction. You'll understand that this is the nature of mind.

Not accepting the natural life is the nature of mind. Mind does not accept the life which is changing and moving. Mind always demands a permanency, a stagnancy. The way it is now has to be permanent, has to stay the same. The mind is trying to hold, to possess, to control, to reject. Insecurity is the nature of life; mind wants security, mind demands security, mind demands certainty, mind demands a known future. You'll observe, you'll enquire why it is like this, then you'll understand that this is the nature of mind. As you understand the changing nature of life, you will also understand the permanent nature of mind, and you cannot change either. And through this enquiry you'll understand that this is the way that this Self has to remain in balance. If I fight with the mind, which is the spiritual life, can I change it? If I fight with the outside life, which is the worldly life, can I control it? I cannot control my mind. I cannot control life. Then what is the way? To accept the way life is. To accept the way mind is. Accept yourself as you are. The outside life, the way it is acting, accept it. The inside mind, the way it is reacting, accept it. When you accept, the balance happens. And then in that Self, the result of the enquiry, there is a state which is there inside which Ramana calls the state of silence. This is what I understand.

When Sri Ramana was asked, 'When will the realisation of the Self be gained?' he replied, 'When the world which is what-is-seen has been removed, there will be realisation of the Self which is the seer.' What is the true understanding of the world? How to remove the world?

I already answered this question. The world which we see is the reflection of our own conditioned mind and we see the world from that frame. So when Ramana says the world dissolves, he means that the frame disappears. Then you see the exact total reality; the Self is reflected. We misunderstand Self-realisation as meaning that something is realised. There is no realisation. The moment this world dissolves there is nothing remaining. There is no realisation of Self.

The mirror realises its emptiness because all the time there is a reflection happening on the mirror. The reflection on the mirror is the world, and this is not going to go away. Understand this: the mind, which is the world inside reflecting the outside, is not going to go away. This is where I don't agree with Ramana. The reflections are not going to go away, because something is going to reflect each moment on this mirror. So the emptiness is not going to be revealed as a realisation; the realisation is awakening to this understanding. The mirror comes to the understanding that it is on this emptiness that the reflection happens, and this is not the understanding that 'I am that emptiness'. There is no I separate from the emptiness. This is awakening. The mirror is born out of the reflections but has been given the misunderstanding that emptiness can be experienced when all the reflections go away. So the mirror is all the time trying to wipe out the reflections. There is no point, the mirror cannot wipe out the reflections because the mirror itself is reflection. The moment it comes to I, it is reflection itself. The moment it realises the whole futility of the game and then accepts the reflection as it is happening, awakening inside happens. This emptiness is me. I never lost it. It is not that I have to remove the reflection and then emptiness will come. The moment when this understanding dawns on the mirror is the moment of realisation.

This realisation of Self is the realisation of your natural state, the way you are, but we misunderstand that unless we remove this world there cannot be a realisation. Let it be there, let it be there. There is no way that we can remove the reflection, there is no way that we can remove the world. It is not possible. Understand this and drop the effort. Sit silently and do nothing. This state just comes, and it goes by itself.

There is a whole body of spiritual people who are trying to remove the world, which means trying to remove the mind, and they struggle for many years with this, without any result.

It's not possible. That's what I'm saying, it is not possible to remove the mind because the mind is not separate from consciousness. Mind is not separate from the Self. The Self, which is home to this knowledge part, and the past, is the mind. So if you are making an effort to drop the mind, the mind survives. Drop the effort. And how do you drop the effort? By accepting the mind itself.

This is very important. My next question is on the same subject. It has been suggested that the mind must be destroyed for liberation to occur. Do you have a mind? Sri Ramana used the term manonasha to describe the state of liberation, meaning destroyed mind. How to destroy the mind?

This is the question people are asking, how to destroy the mind, and the question is asked by the mind itself. The mind wants to destroy the mind. So even if the mind is successful in destroying the mind, the mind survives. This is the game of mind, understand this. This is the statement most misunderstood by people. Mind is nothing but an illusion; it's a myth. It is something which is created by life itself because the life demands a worldly attachment to the knowledge part, the past, where we have accumulated knowledge.

When you want to function, when you want to respond to life, you need a mind, you need some support of knowledge. Consciousness temporarily attaches to the part of knowledge and creates a temporary functionary mind. Functionary mind is temporarily created by existence itself to function. There is also a functionary ego which is also a demand of existence. We cannot live without the mind and without the ego because we have to function, we have to respond. For functioning, for responding, for acting, we need a mind and we need an ego, but that has to dissolve the moment the functioning is finished. We create a permanent mind because we create a desire which is not connected to the demand of life, but which is something in the future. The life demand is now, in the present, but we create the permanent mind because we have a lot of dreams, a lot of goals created out of our own knowledge, or the non-acceptance of the way I am. We create a lot of goals and these keep this mind surviving permanently. If we are living moment to moment the functionary mind is created, the functionary ego is created; when the functioning is finished, they dissolve.

I'm now speaking to you. This is a demand from existence, to sit here and talk to you as a spiritual master. So there is a functionary mind which is the mind of a master and there is a functionary ego, the ego of a master, but the moment this *Satsang* is over it just dissolves. But if I sit in front of my wife or my children and remain as a master, then it is a permanent ego, permanent attachment that I create. I go to my factory; I have to be a boss there, a businessman there. So I have to have a business mind, a business ego. This is how life changes your functionary mind, functionary ego. The characters that life demands us to play change accordingly, but they have to go when the demand is finished.

The one who understands this is free from all the identification of these characters. He knows that he is just playing a character. It is not that you are trying to dissolve the mind, just that you are not creating a permanent mind. You need a mind, you need an ego. That is a must, a requirement, a necessity of life. It is a misunderstanding that unless we dissolve the mind there is no realisation of Self. Your whole life you fight with the mind, and the mind survives because there is no other instrument you have to fight the mind with other than mind itself. So you create an imaginary mind which is fighting with this mind. Your whole life you just play a game. You're trying to catch your own shadow, that's all. Mind is a shadow of consciousness.

Would you say that it is the attachment to the thinking mind that has to go?

Thinking is required when the mind is there because to function you need thinking. It is not a thinking mind as you call it, it is the mind which is created because of something connected to life needed now. But you create a desire which is not connected to your actual requirement of life. Understand this, enlightenment is not what life demands from you. Life demands simple understanding. When you are hungry, life demands you find food and eat, that's all. But we create a goal; oh, I want to get enlightened so that I will be totally, permanently, free, permanently happy, permanently blissful. We want something permanent. The understanding makes you realise that nothing is permanent. Then the whole question of permanence and searching for the permanence dissolves. You don't create goals which are not connected to the life. When the life demands future planning, you plan it, but future should not be created by the mind itself because then the mind survives. This is where the mind is a hindrance. The permanent mind is a hindrance, but this permanent mind cannot be dropped through any effort. It can be dropped through understanding. Then it becomes a temporary functionary mind, that's all. I hope I'm clear.

Yes, it's very clear. I think this is a very important point because so many people spend so many years battling with the mind, using different techniques, and it seems that many masters have suggested this is a necessity, whatever their motive.

I'm just giving a very joking example: you ask a dog to catch his tail and keep it straight. Now look at the dog, what will happen to the dog? He will be all the time moving around trying to catch his tail and even if he catches his tail, how long can he keep it? Again it's gone and his tail becomes crooked again. This is the game that people want to play, and those who do not understand and want to make business out of it can make people dance with this whole game. Understand that this exploitation is happening. Not just now, for thousands of years you have been cheated. The whole of humanity has been misguided that you have to capture the mind, you have to control the mind, you have to dissolve the mind. It is not possible. Understand the futility of it and accept it, and in that acceptance mind becomes a very beautiful servant, a very obedient servant which you need to live. You need the support of that mind to survive; how to find the food, how to arrange for the basic necessities, the basic needs of the body, and to understand what life demands in reference to the greater cause. We are not just like animals fulfilling our basic needs. There is a greater cause that you and I have to respond to, the life's command. This mind is very important, a gift from existence. Mind as a beautiful servant is very nice but if we make the mind a master then it is very difficult for us, very difficult.

What about* vasanas*, the tendencies of the mind? Must these be removed before Self-realisation can become permanent?

That is the nature of mind! How can you remove it? When you are desiring to remove the tendency of mind, the desiring itself is a tendency of mind. Do you have any other mind to destroy this mind? One mind. It's all a game. It's beautiful to play a game, like chasing your tail. It's a nice game, but then at a certain point you get so tired, so tired. That's why the mind is capable of creating different games, not just one game. You see it changes techniques and changes methods and changes masters and changes the path. My understanding is, don't touch the mind, don't try to connect this mind with the Self-realisation. There is nothing that is connected with the mind. Understand this. Permanent mind is definitely a hindrance, but mind as it is created by life itself is not a hindrance. Understand that it is created, accept it and flow with it, that's all.

When you say permanent mind, do you mean the conditioned mind, the structures of the mind?

The mind which is following a desire which is not related with the needs of the life – this is the permanent mind. The unfortunate part is that from childhood we have been given a ready-made goal that we are all running after. Our whole life we all just run after that goal and so the permanent mind survives. Look at the goals which keep this permanent mind alive, the goals the mind is following to reach, to achieve, to become. What are you searching for? We are all unhappy because we are not in harmony with life, not because we are all unenlightened or because the mind is there. The cause is that somewhere we are not in harmony with life, with the way life is functioning, and this disharmony is making us unhappy. Understand how to be harmonious, that's all. The moment you understand and remain in harmony, you are happy. Why are we all running after happiness and fighting with the mind? No need.

At the end of his book* Self-Enquiry*, Sri Ramana says, 'He who is thus endowed with a mind that has become subtle and who has the experience of the Self is called a* jivanmukta.*' Is this the state that can be called Self-realised?

Sri Ramana goes on, 'And when one is immersed in the ocean of bliss and has become one with it without any differentiated existence one is called a* videhamukta. *It is the state of* videhamukta *that is referred to as the transcendent* turiya *(state). This is the final goal.' Is this the state that can be called enlightenment? I'm asking whether there's any difference between Self-realisation and enlightenment.

We misunderstand the explanations that Ramana gives as if they have to be reached as the result of some effort. Most of the people who read this paragraph have not reached the understanding and misunderstand it as if it is a description of a state which can be reached, then they start asking, 'How can I reach that state? How can I become a *jivanmukta*?' Any description of the state is misunderstood as if it is the result of some effort, or can be reached or achieved. This is the unfortunate part of all explanations of this state. Ramana has expressed very clearly what this state is. Your question suggests that when we reach enlightenment this is the state where we will get the total *jivanmukti*, or freedom from the attachments. This is a desiring mind which misunderstands and creates a desire to reach that state. I'm saying that it is a plain description of the healthy state of your being.

The description becomes a goal. When Osho described his enlightenment as feeling like thousands of explosions, each disciple was waiting for thousands of explosions to happen. I was one of them and all the time during my meditation I was waiting, and when I saw some little sparks of light I was so happy that now I'm getting closer. But a description cannot be a goal. That is a misunderstanding.

This state which Ramana is describing, *jivanmukti* or *videhamukti*, is when you are in the mind and free from the mind. Freedom from the mind is a witnessing state. You have seen the mind. The freedom is not that the mind disappears, but the identification that you are the mind disappears. Now you are seeing the mind. You are aware of the mind, that there is a mind having reactions.

It is like a circle, it has a periphery and a centre. The periphery is connected to the outer life which is changing and moving, all the time creating some movement on the periphery because it is so sensitive. The periphery of the consciousness is the mind reflected, the reactions that are happening. This is the mind. The centre is the witness itself where you are aware of the movement that is happening on the periphery but misunderstanding that once this periphery is totally silent and there is no movement, then there is a permanent silence. Then we are trying to silence the periphery, to silence the wind and the sun who are making the disturbance on the periphery – events beyond our control. You cannot control what is naturally happening on the periphery. It is natural, stay in the centre and watch the whole game. Just look at the periphery which is moving and changing, and the reactions that are coming. If somebody is abusing me there is going to be a reaction of anger disturbing my periphery. There is a ripple which comes, making a soft movement on my periphery. I am aware of it, I am aware of it. That awareness centre is the witness, and that is freedom itself. It is not freedom from something.

We started this question with *ajnan*, ignorance, the ignorance that is natural. This ignorance has brought us into the fight, into the spiritual life, the spiritual fight, the worldly life, the worldly fight. The fight, fight, fight. The fight creates a tension. The fight comes from non-acceptance, non-acceptance creates a fight, fight creates a tension and tension creates a frustration, frustration creates pain and when pain becomes too much it becomes suffering. Then for us life is suffering. Why it is suffering? Life is not suffering. Life is adventure, full of ups and downs. It is just going in its own nature. Awakening to this understanding is freedom. That is called *jivanmukta*, the one who is living, very much living, dancing with life, singing with life, but still not attached to the life. That is coming through understanding, not through any spiritual practice or chanting the *mantra* 'Who am I? Who am I?' or reading all the scriptures or sitting at the feet of the master and rubbing your head there. You are not going to get it. Wake up and understand. Understand where you have gone wrong.

Osho talked about 'beyond enlightenment'. Shivananda, a famous traditional master, talked about the seven stages of enlightenment. So for the Western mind this is very confusing.

They are describing the path which I told you about, the path of *yoga* where you go step-by-step towards the point where the mind explodes. The mind goes to a point where the pain and tension become unbearable. When you have a nightmare, when you're sleeping, that point when the nightmare reaches the highest point of fear, suddenly you wake up. The mind goes into the nightmare of all this effort, *sadhana*, to reach that point. When the *sadhana* becomes a nightmare there is the possibility of some awakening, but again there is the possibility of going back to sleep too. Or there is a possibility of changing the dream. Mind is very cunning, it immediately changes the dream. It doesn't allow you to reach the point of awakening. That's why I tell my friends that if you still believe that meditation can take you to that point of enlightenment, why are you only doing a one hour meditation? Sit for twenty-four hours. Don't get up until you are enlightened. Come on! Do you have that much trust? Do it, then this nightmare point comes very close. But nobody wants to. And even when you are practising some kind of meditation for a few years, your mind wants to change the technique. Let's go to some other master or other path. We change our dreams, we don't allow the dream to become a nightmare. Shivananda was a *yogi*, this is why he describes these seven stages. This is the *yogi* way. He was a *siddha*, one with powers.

A *buddha* is a different person. A *buddha* is a very ordinary person. What you see in this world, in the spiritual market, are all *siddhas*. If you really want to find a *buddha* you will have to seek him out. The real *buddhas* are hidden somewhere. The ones who understand, the ones who are absolutely alive, they are not claiming anything. They don't put a board out claiming, 'I am here. Come to me, I will get you enlightened, five hundred dollars. No ropes. No holdings in a German bank.' They don't have any publicity. You'll find this *buddha* sitting in the shops, or working in the factories, just ordinary people, but so much alive. They have no complaints. Very difficult to find these people. Their way is the way of hiding.

Gurdjieff was struggling hard to find a Sufi master. Somebody told him of a town where a real Sufi master lived. He arrived at the station and took a taxi to the town. He asked the taxi driver, 'I have come here to find the Sufi master. Do you know who he is?' This fellow said, 'I don't know anyone.' He stayed in a hotel in the town. He asked the owner of the hotel sitting at the counter, 'I am searching for a Sufi master. Can you help me?' The owner of the hotel says, 'I have no idea who the Sufi master is.'

He was wandering in the town asking everyone, 'Can somebody help me? I'm searching for the Sufi master.' Nobody answered. One day he was sitting on the corner, so tired. An old man came to him and said, 'What are you looking for?' Gurdjieff says, 'I am searching for the

Sufi master.' The old man said, 'I can see that you are tired of searching. Let me tell you who he is. The Sufi master is the owner of the hotel.' The man he saw every morning at the counter, the owner of the hotel, a real Sufi master! Gurdjieff went to the hotel owner and said, 'The old man says you are a Sufi master.' The hotel owner just laughed. He said, 'No Sufi master will declare himself. You have to find him, search him out. If you really want to see him, come with me. I'll take you to my master.' The owner of the hotel took him to the person whom Gurdjieff first met at the station, the taxi driver. He asked him the same question he asked when he arrived, 'I have come here to find the Sufi master. Do you know who he is?' The taxi driver said, 'I don't know anybody.'

These are the real *buddhas*. They are very ordinary people, very ordinary people. They are not much bothered about how to control the mind and how to realise the Self; no questions at all. Who cares? When you reach that understanding, who cares? You don't care about any enlightenmant. *Krishna* never claimed to anyone, 'I am a realised One.' In the *Bhagavad Gita* (classical Hindu scripture), when he spoke to *Arjuna* on the battlefield, *Arjuna* finally came to know that the one who was so close to him throughout his life, as a friend, was awakened. *Krishna* never conducted any meditation camps, 'I will take you to the meditation camp and change your mind.' He never asked *Arjuna* to fight with the mind or win over his mind. He never talked of Self-realisation. Let the Western people understand that they have been misguided, misled and exploited. This spirituality has become a holy business and it's very painful.

***This question follows nicely. It appears essential to meet a* guru *and stay with that* guru. *Who is the* guru? *What is the* guru's *role? How to recognise a true* guru?**

The *guru* to me is a guide, he is a guide. The whole concept of the *guru* is wrongly understood. The real master would not want his disciple to follow him. The real master wants his disciple to follow his own journey. He can guide, he can help, but you cannot just sit at his feet thinking that he is going to take you to your destination point. This is an escape. The reality is that there is nothing that you can do and there is no 'way'. The *guru* is the one who makes you understand that.

Where do you want to go? You want to realise your Self? Why do you wander around? Why go after so many masters? Just sit with yourself and you will understand yourself; that is the realisation of Self. Why do you have to go to somebody to realise? The one who guides you how to sit with yourself, to accept yourself, is the real master. We know how to go away from our selves, but we do not know how to sit with ourselves. We never sit with ourselves because we never accept ourselves, we hate ourselves. The moment you are alone you start feeling lonely. You don't like to be with yourself, you don't want to see yourself. All the time you want to escape from the way you are. Understand that there is no perfection anywhere; you cannot change yourself, you cannot change your mind, you are the way you are, I am the way I am and that's fine. You are a beautiful, unique creation of life. This is when the real enquiry, introspection, observation, starts. Here you don't need a master, you are your own master. Here you have to take the journey alone, you have to see your mind alone. The *guru* can only guide you in the right direction. Many have written all this praise about *gurus* because they want people to follow them. The real master does not want anyone to follow him. This is what I understand.

And how to find one of these true masters who doesn't want anybody to follow him?

That also is a good question, because again the problem is how to find the right master, the right guide. There is no way that you can find the right master because you don't know whether he is right or wrong. How can you know that the one who you are meeting is the right person? How can you know? I would advise that if you really want the right person to guide you, don't search, stay with your problem.

Would you say that it is when you stay with your problem that the master appears? So that in fact the master is finding the student?

That's the promise and that's what has happened in everybody's life. Those who really found the right master, it is not that they have searched for him and found him. The masters themselves found the disciples; that is the way. The life creates a situation where you meet that person and get the right guidance. Just stay with your thirst, stay with your longing, stay with your pain. If you accept it then you see that there is somebody who is always available. The mind doesn't have that trust, that's why the mind always wants to search for the right master. That's the promise, that someone is always there. Trust, have patience. *Shradda* is trust, *saburi* is patience. Trust life and have patience with your thirst, your longing. Just stay with it.

Would you say that this inner longing, this fire, is very important?

That is the root of it all. Most of the time we try to find a solution or an escape from that pain, that longing. If you have a longing, a thirst, a pain inside and a strong feeling that something is missing in your life, don't try to find out what it is that is missing – that is misleading and you take the route of the mind. Stay with the strong feeling inside that something is missing. Stay with the pain, just stay with it. It doesn't matter how long it takes, stay with your longing. Then you'll see that the *guru* gets to you. The mind doesn't like that trust, that patience.

Sri Ramana's devotees had tremendous devotion to him and he to Arunachala. Please say something about* bhakti, *devotion, in the pursuit of awakening.

I don't know whether you are using the word devotee and the word disciple to mean the same thing. A devotee is a different state of being. I don't see any devotees of Ramana, I see a lot of disciples. To me disciple means one who deceives himself, but a devotee is a different state. To be a devotee demands your devotion, not to the master, but devotion to an understanding that has been shared by the master. We misunderstand devotion as being to the physical form of the master, serving the physical existence of the master. That is not the right meaning.

The master is a medium who is expressing the message of life, the message of existence or message of God. Through him this message comes. The person who is sitting there in front of the master has to take the message and follow the journey. The master is the guide who gives you the message and the guidelines. You follow the message and the guidelines, you don't follow the physical form of the master. These are the guidelines for the guide. When we use this word 'disciple' we mean the one who is totally following the master, his physical expression or physical presence. This will not solve any problems, it will not take you anywhere. It will give you some mental consolation that you are doing something in the service of the master, and the master who wants to exploit this can get service from the disciple. There is a mutual exploitation that happens. Devotion to the message is very important, more than devotion to the master. If you are devoted to the message there is a transformation possible that can happen in the presence of the master because you and the master share the understanding, not the technique, not the method, but something beyond technique, beyond method, something beyond his physical expression, and his presence is very helpful.

I don't agree with the people who call themselves devotees of Ramana, all the time worshipping him. I have watched people worshipping Ramana's *samadhi* (tomb of a saint). Such blind worshipping. They offered him milk in the morning at the *samadhi*, they offered him food in the afternoon for lunch, they offered him a glass of water at night time. I was sitting quietly. What an unconsciousness! The man who was troubling hard his whole life to wake you up, and in front of his *samadhi* you are just showing your unconsciousness! Can't you understand that this dead person does not need any water or any food? And you call it devotion! This is all blindness, thinking that you are doing something spiritual. This is not true.

Ramana was there to deliver the message which can wake you up. Osho was there to deliver the message which can wake you up, not to put you to sleep. We just take this message and go back to sleep. I have seen many people snoring, chanting 'Who am I?' It becomes a very beautiful lover. You go on snoring. It has to wake you up, somewhere it has to touch you. Krishnamurti was eighty-five when he delivered his last lecture in Chennai. He was sick. He saw the same faces again and again and he asked, 'Don't you understand, sir? Can't you understand what I'm saying? I've been saying this for fifty years. I see you sitting in front of me every time. Don't you understand anything that I say, or am I doing a spiritual entertainment, sir?' And he started crying like a child. Fifty years of moving around the world, talking to people, delivering the message to make them understand the Truth of life. They sit in front of him, just listening. Is it entertainment? Was what Ramana was doing entertainment? Was what Osho was doing entertainment? Was what Krishnamurti was doing entertainment? Thirty years, Osho's effort. I don't know how many years Ramana lived. Were they doing entertainment? One word can wake you up. One word. We are not even available for it. Just understand. Don't go after all this nonsense of following people who don't really understand what spirituality means, what enlightenment means.

I sometimes feel very much pain that we are so confused with this very simple thing that life wants from us. We just wander around searching for answers, searching for Truth, searching for realisation. Sit with yourself. You'll find it inside, not somewhere outside. This is what I wanted to share.

Seekers often have curious ideas about the enlightened state. Please describe your typical day and how you perceive the world.

This is the question I am asked so many times. I don't agree with the whole experience of enlightenment, so I'm not interested in describing my day or the experience. I don't want to create a misunderstanding. I am an ordinary person, a living person, dancing with life, singing with life, with all the problems and all the pains – more ordinary than most people. I'm not a spiritual person, I don't do any meditations and I don't do any *sadhana*. I am just living the way life takes me up, the way it takes me down; I enjoy both. That's all. I don't claim myself enlightened. I don't bother much about what enlightenment is, I don't care. It's enough to be awake, it's enough to be alive. That's all, that's all. Why describe something which creates misunderstanding? Each day is the day of awakening. Each moment is the moment of awakening; it is not that some moment you wake up, so forget about the description. Every moment holds the possibility of awakening, of enlightenment. This moment is possible today, but forget that you are going to be awakened or enlightened in the next moment, or the next day, or next year or next life; forget about it. Any moment can be a moment of awakening. For the one who has understood this, no moment is very important. What time did I wake up? Seven o'clock. Why should I remember that it was seven o'clock when I woke up? It's not important for me to remember that I woke up. It seems very important to the sleeper, to the dreamer, but who cares? Who cares? What is important is the way that I'm living, not when I woke up. This is what I understand.

Thank you. You have given us a profound discourse on awakening. When you meet someone with a passion for awakening, what would your short advice be?

I've already said it. Understand the nature of life through your observations, through enquiry. Understand the nature of mind without any pre-conditioned ideas or answers. Look straight into the life. Look straight into the mind. Sit with yourself. And to sit with yourself you need to accept yourself. Accept yourself as you are. In any situation, in any condition, whether you are frustrated because of your pain or whether you are happy, however you are in this moment, say yes to it, accept it. This acceptance is not cowardice or because you're tired of doing something. This acceptance is from your understanding. Now you understand the nature of life, you understand the nature of mind, and you sit with yourself. There is no demand to change your mind, no demand to change anything outside yourself. Accept yourself as you are and in that acceptance the love starts flowing. In that love there is bliss, everything is beautiful. Then each moment is awakening.

Thank you.

Sri

Nannagaru

There is Truth, but the main thing is whether you know it or not. If you know it you will become happy and you will attain a sorrow-less state; if you don't know it then sorrow will haunt you and drive you, birth after birth. Only Truth is free from sorrow and free from bondage.

NANNAGARU

Truth is always there, whether you know it or not.

Sri Nannagaru

Sri Nannagaru

Born in 1934, Sri Nannagaru comes from a tiny village, Kommara, in Andhra Pradesh. Hailed by his devotees and disciples as *Nanna Garu*, meaning 'Respectable Father', he tours extensively, sitting silently. Sri Nannagaru's piercing looks turn the minds and thoughts from things external towards the heart center. His master is Bhagavan Sri Ramana Maharshi.

I first met and sat with Sri Nannagaru in silence at his gatherings at Arunachala in 2002. He has very kindly loaned me his ashram *for the last seven years to hold my Arunachala Pilgrimage Retreat. His was the first interview that I conducted. He sat on his bed with a translator and at the end said the book would be very successful. Sri Nannagaru is a simple man, devoted to Sri Ramana Maharshi and his many devotees.*

Sri Ramana proposed the fundamental question 'Who am I?' Nannagaru, can I ask you, who are you?

I am undying spirit.

Many Western seekers come to India looking for enlightenment as if it is an experience. What is enlightenment?

Enlightenment is Truth-realisation. If you realise the Truth, freedom will come. Freedom from rebirth, freedom from bondage. Enlightenment means Truth-realisation.

When Westerners come to India seeking enlightenment they have the idea that it is something for them to get, that it something to find. Is that true?

In India there are people who have attained realisation. India is a spiritual land with many Truth seekers, prophets and seers. Western countries should learn about spiritual things from India, and also India should learn about material things and welfare from Western countries.

India is a spiritual centre. There are many, not just one or two, realised souls in India. Some of these realised souls are known and others unknown. Certainly if you are in the presence of Truth-realisation you will be inspired to live in the Truth, to absorb the Truth and to know the Truth. That is why so many Western people come to India. There are many holy places in this country; India is a very ancient land. Thinkers, spiritual kings, noble souls, advanced souls and evolved beings are all here in India and so Western people come for guidance from these India seers.

You must know the Truth; unless you know the Truth you cannot get freedom. Freedom from the known and unknown is essential.

Can you tell us what this Truth is?

Truth means eternity. The nature of Truth is bliss, freedom, knowledge and undying spirit. The nature of Truth is that it knows neither birth nor death. Truth is above all troubles, customs and traditions. We accept Truth, accept *Brahman* (the absolute) and accept reality. Customs, traditions and cultures are created by the mind. The only thing you can't create is Truth – Truth is always there, whether you know it or not. Except for Truth, everything is created by the human mind.

So when people come to India seeking Truth, in fact they already are Truth?

Yes, you are already in Truth. Not just you, but everybody is in Truth. If one knows the fact, he is a seer. If he does not know the Truth that is in him, he is not a seer. In everybody's heart there is Truth. If you know it you become free and become a sage. If you don't know it then you become a slave to circumstances, likes and dislikes and so on. There is Truth, but the main thing is whether you know it or not. If you know it you will become happy and you will attain a sorrow-less state, if you don't know it then sorrow will haunt you and drive you, birth after birth. Only Truth is free from sorrow and free from bondage; only Truth is free from everything that is nonsense.

So there is a little joke, yes? That people come to India searching for Truth when they already are Truth?

That's right, they are already Truth itself, no doubt about it. But how to know the Truth that is already hidden in the heart? People come to India for guidance on how to know the Truth already in them. If you do not meet a seer, enlightened soul, or evolved soul, then you continue thinking that you are mere mind and body, not only inwardly but outwardly also. But if you meet a seer, an enlightened soul, then it is so nice! If you live for some time in their presence then you will get the thought 'Oh! There is a Truth in me, I have to realise this.' Such inspiration comes from meeting seers.

I understand. I think that is why we enjoy sitting with you. You have such beautiful eyes! Such twinkling eyes!

Ah very good! Thank you very much. (both laugh)

Are there any qualifications for enlightenment? Is* sadhana *(spiritual practice) necessary?

Are there any qualifications for enlightenment? Qualifications are essential in relative truth. The essential thing is that heart, mind, speech and deed must be one. Mind-word, mind-heart, mind-word-deed, these things must be one. That is the main qualification for Truth-realisation.

Also for enlightenment there must be purity. For purity the essential qualification must be mind control. Unless we can learn to control the mind we cannot concentrate it towards the Truth that is already hidden in the heart. Where the mind springs there is Truth, which is not relative truth. By Truth I mean actual Truth. It is absolute Truth!

Exactly what do you mean by mind control?

Mind control means that we have to arrest the wandering of the mind. Wandering of the mind brings unnecessary thoughts and sorrow and also brings physical and mental ill health. Too much wandering of the mind is very bad both for spiritual and material life, so power of concentration is essential.

Do you suggest some particular practice?

For mind control there is *upasana.* Put your mind on any god or *guru* you like and please remember his name and meditate on his form. If you like *pranayama* (breath control) you should also do it as it will be beneficial, but the best thing is *upasana. Upasana* means to constantly think about Arunachala, think about the hill and its name. If you think one thing, think God. If you think always about absolute Truth then automatically the wanderings of the mind will be stopped. *Upasana* is a *Sanskrit* (ancient Indian language of scriptures) word: *upa* means mind control. In the Indian tradition most Truth seekers and devotees say that unless you are accustomed to *upasana* you cannot get realisation.

Do you recommend meditation?

Upasana is a form of meditation. I recommend three things which I consider important: dispassion, discrimination and meditation. Meditation also will help to arrest the mind.

Is* sadhana *necessary for enlightenment?

If there is a *sadhaka*, a spiritual seeker, then *sadhana* is necessary; if there is no spiritual seeker then *sadhana* is not necessary! (both laugh)

So, if I think I am somebody then I need to meditate, and if there is nobody then I don't need to meditate!

Meditation is meant only for Truth seekers. Meditation is not necessary for realised souls. Meditation is not the destination, it is the means to go to the destination. Meditation is only necessary for the Truth seeker.

Who meditates? The mind meditates. If there is no mind then meditation is also not necessary. If there is disease then medicine is necessary, but if there is no disease then no medicine is necessary. Who is the meditator? Only the mind is the meditator, so if you have no mind then who will do the meditation?

Sri Ramana said that Self-enquiry is the most direct route to realising the Self. What do you say about Self-enquiry?

Ramana did not achieve realisation through Self-enquiry. Ramana taught not only Self-enquiry but also the path of surrender. He gave importance both to partial surrender and to absolute surrender. In the early state there is partial surrender and in the end state, automatically, absolute surrender will come. He laid much stress on two paths: Self-enquiry and surrender to the will of God. If you have complete trust that there is a God, that there is an Almighty, and you have complete trust about the controller of the universe, then the path of surrender is the best for you. If you constantly doubt the existence of the world and doubt the existence of God, then Self-enquiry is essential.

So could we say that by conducting Self-enquiry we are being constantly reminded of God?

If mind arises then there is also world and God, but if the mind subsides there is no world and there is no God; there is Truth. You put your mind in the Truth that is already hidden in your heart; that is real enquiry.

There is one Truth, there is undying spirit and there is the immortal state that is already present in your heart.

Simply put your mind in its own source, then you need not think about God or the world, because after the mind arises God will come and the world will come, everything will come. Fear will come, our separateness will come, other people will come.

Who is thinking about God? Mind is thinking about God. In Self-enquiry the world is not important, God is not important. 'Who is doing Self-enquiry?' The mind is doing Self-enquiry. You must let your mind subside. If you control your mind, if you are in a position to return the mind to the source, then there is no world and there is no God.

So these two paths, enquiry and surrender, are not really two paths, they actually become one path?

These are two paths, but in the end they lead to the same goal. There is no doubt they lead to the same goal, to the same destination, but people have many temperaments and many make-ups. Put the question, 'Who is this?' not the question, 'Who am I?' Put the question, 'Who is this mind?' If you constantly question the mind, slowly it will reach its source. Where the mind springs, there is eternity and there is Truth that knows neither birth nor death.

When Sri Ramana was asked, 'When will the realisation of the Self be gained?' he replied, 'When the world which is what-is-seen has been removed, there will be realisation of the Self which is the seer.' What is the true understanding of the world?

Like we have learned before, if you see the rope in its true form with correct perception, the rope is not a snake, it is only a rope that appears like a snake. Even if you think, 'That is a snake, that is a snake,' it is still only a rope. If you see the rope correctly then there is no snake. The snake is only appearance, it is not real, and after you see the rope the snake will have already disappeared.

World also just 'seems', there actually is no world at all, it just seems! When you see a rope for what it is, there is no snake. If you see the Truth, there is no world. Just like the snake seems to appear in the rope, in the same way the world appears as the Truth. If you see the Truth face-to-face then there is no world to see, and there is no mind to control.

How to remove the world?

Unless you realise the absolute Truth as it is, you cannot remove the world from your mind. If you see the world, fear will come, duality will come, lights and visions will come, and everything will come that is nonsense to us. Also the fear itself will bring death and sorrow. If you see the Truth face-to-face, then there is no world to see. If you can't realise the absolute Truth as it is, then do *dhyana*, meditation, and the world will disappear from the mind – whatever kind of *sadhana* you do.

It has been suggested that the mind must be destroyed for liberation to occur. Do you have a mind?

Yes, I have a *sattvic* (calm and peaceful) mind. My mind will work; it will act but it will not react, there is no reaction whatsoever under any circumstances. Yes I have mind, but it is a *sattvic* mind, it is a cool mind.

Sri Ramana used the term **manonasha** ***to describe the state of liberation, meaning destroyed mind. How to destroy the mind?***

If you constantly put your mind in the heart cave it will be destroyed. *Manonasha* is essential, there is no doubt, but *manonasha* means burnt rope. Burnt rope looks like rope but there is nothing; it is not useful for anything but it looks like rope.

So it doesn't mean that the mind is actually destroyed, it means that the mind is still functioning but has no power, no bite?

There is mind function but it is a burnt rope so it will not arrest you. Mind in purity is the Truth. The essential thing in spiritual practice is to acquire purity of mind.

Is what you are calling pure mind the same as what the Buddhists call no-mind?

No-mind is equal to pure mind. They are one and the same. We need not doubt it.

What about* vasanas*, the tendencies of the mind?

Tendencies of the mind come from previous births. Suppose you do work, you expect results, and you enjoy them. In enjoying the result a tendency will spring, from the tendency a thought will come, from the thought comes action, selfish action, and from that selfish body-bound action tendencies will come. If you enjoy the results of your actions, whether they are good or bad, certainly tendencies will come.

The main obstacle, the root obstacle to God-realisation, is tendencies. Good and bad tendencies will arrest our progress. In spiritual *sadhana*, tendencies create habits; our habits are our chains. All habits spring from tendencies; the tendencies must be eradicated and must be removed. There is no compromise here; they must be removed to get God-realisation. The purpose of spiritual practice is to eradicate tendencies. If you are in a position to move away from tendencies, naturally and normally, realisation will come. We may follow any path of Self-enquiry or devotion but the main thing is that our tendencies must be destroyed.

Could it be enough to achieve a* sattvic *state of mind and to know one's* vasanas *so they no longer bind?

No, that is not enough. A *sattvic* state of mind will show you the path to know the Truth. It is not the destination, but you should welcome this *sattvic* state of mind.

So when you know one of your* vasanas, *then this* vasana *doesn't bind you any more?

If the *vasana* creates a tendency then it is a bondage to you, but if the *vasana* does not disturb your mind, it is not a dangerous one and will not bring rebirth.

Are you saying that you don't have to destroy the* vasana*; you have to see and understand the* vasana *and then the* vasana *doesn't bind you any more?

We have to remove the *vasana* completely. If there is a *vasana* it will bring fear also. To reach the fearless state you have to get rid of *vasanas.*

My question is how to remove* vasanas*?

How to remove *vasanas*? This is the best question! If you are always thinking about *vasanas* you will not overcome them. By thinking about *vasanas* you are welcoming them. You should always think of God, think of Truth, of your *guru*, and then automatically the food supply will be cut to your tendency. If you stop the food supply to the tendency then automatically it will fade away.

At the end of his book,* Self-Enquiry, *Sri Ramana says, 'He who is thus endowed with a mind that has become subtle, and who has the experience of the Self is called a* jivanmukta.*' Is this the state that can be called Self-realised?

Jivanmukti (state of liberation) and Self-realisation are one and the same, you need not doubt this. In the *Bhagavad Gita* (classical Hindu scripture), *Krishna* described *jivanmukti*; he called it *stitha prajna* (deep understanding). You need not have uncertainty about it.

He goes on, 'And when one is immersed in the ocean of bliss and has become one with it without any differentiated existence, one is called

a* videhamukta. *It is the state of* videhamukti *that is referred to as the transcendent* turiya *(state). This is the final goal.' Is this the state that can be called enlightenment?

There is no difference between a *videhamukta* and a *jivanmukta*. Ramana Maharshi, Buddha and *Shankara* are all *jivanmuktas*. Jesus Christ was a *videhamukta*. The last words of Jesus Christ before he dropped the body were, 'Oh! My Father and I are One.' The *Jnani* (one who has realised the Self) and *mukti* (liberation) are One. Whether he has a body or not, that is the important thing. When your body is dropped, and at the same time you get realisation of the Self, then that is known as *videhamukti*.

If you are realised there is no mind to observe. With God-realisation there is no mind to observe and no mind to control.

It appears essential to meet a* guru *and stay with that* guru. *Who is the* guru*? What is the* guru's *role? How to recognise a true* guru*?

It is better to see enlightened, advanced and good souls and you will get inspiration from them. Goodness also helps us to realise the Truth. Goodness also is part of enlightenment; it is essential. If you seek goodness that is also part of *sadhana*; it is the keeping of holy company. If you are in the position to be in the presence of the *guru*, well and good, but if that is not possible then mental contact is essential; that will also help you to get enlightenment. In English there is a proverb – as you think, so you are. Mental contact with the *guru* is essential as it gives us much mental strength.

Who is the *guru*? Bhagavan says God, *guru* and the Self are one and the same. We need not see any difference; there is only one thing, and that is the absolute Truth. We may call the absolute Truth God, the Self or *guru*. Who is the *guru*? Suppose someone is a more advanced soul than you, you may then get guidance from him even though he may not be a realised soul. Suppose I am in kindergarten, then I may learn mathematics from someone in the tenth class and he need not necessarily have a PhD in mathematics.

Who is the *guru*? For the *guru* two qualifications are essential: he has to have a direct perception of the Truth and he has to be in the position to explain the Truth.

What is the *guru's* role? He is God's representative. *Guru* means he is in the hands of God. *Guru's* body is in the hands of God. The *guru's* role is to get humanity to a sorrow-less state.

Many people are coming to me; in my path everyday there are two or three hundred people. What do they expect from me? Do these people that come expect employment, power, money or good health from me? They come because they just want a sorrow-less state. We cannot buy this sorrow-less state in the market; the sorrow-less state will only come by the grace of the *guru*.

There is no market? (both laugh) I thought India was the market!

How do you recognise the true *guru*? Trust is essential. If you enjoy peace or bliss in the presence of Ramana, then he is your *guru*. If you experience feelings of peace or bliss, if you are getting some enlightenment or if you are ridding yourself from bondage to the body in his presence, then he is your *guru*. If you sit in the presence of a purified or enlightened soul then peace, happiness and bliss will come. Not only that, but everything that is good, both material and spiritual, will also come to you.

Seekers often have curious ideas about the enlightened state. Please describe your typical day and how you perceive the world.

Enlightened souls will see the world as a shadow of the Truth. It is only a shadow, it is not the Truth. If there is mind there is world, if there is no mind there is also no world. A *jnani*, one who knows, sees the world not separate from himself; there is no separateness from the world in his realisation. The *jnani* sees the world outside as himself. He sees the Truth in you also, and then you need not be afraid.

When you are looking into the eyes of your people, your devotees, what do you see?

I am seeing myself in those people, and then grace will work.

Is there something you wish to add?

Leave the body to destiny, to *prarabdha*. Our body and mind should be used to the maximum opportunity. We should use the gifts that God has given us. To some, God gave a good intellect, to others, God gave money, or speech facility, others are good writers; all these things must be used to realise the Self. And another thing is that to know God, to see him face-to-face, negative thinking must be avoided. Positive thinking is essential. That is my important message. We should not associate with negative thinking people; we should associate only with good and positive-thinking people. You have to associate with good, noble-thinking, advanced people and gradually self-confidence will come to you. From self-confidence springs Self-realisation.

Thank you very much Premananda.

Thank you very much Nannagaru, it was a very beautiful interview.

Swamini

Pramananda

There is no seen without the seer, but there is a seer without the seen. When there is nothing to see the seer is not called the seer; the seer is pure consciousness. Pure consciousness gains the status of seer when there is something to see. So the removal of the world means not giving the world an independent reality.

The role of a guru is to remove Self-ignorance, to guide the person to Self-knowledge.

Swamini Pramananda

Swamini Pramananda

Swamini Pramananda Saraswati received *sannyasa diksha* from Swami Dayananda Saraswati, and has studied *Vedanta* and *Sanskrit* with him from a young age. She has been a resident teacher at Arsha Vidya Gurukulam, Coimbatore, India, where she taught courses in *Vedanta* and *Sanskrit*. She has great integrity regarding the traditional teachings, combining deep respect for the ancient heritage of India with a modern, inquiring mind.

Swamini and I felt an immediate connection as our names are so similar! Her loving and attractive personality touches everyone she meets. Swamini has worked closely with her teacher, Swami Dayananda Saraswati, for many years on projects in the West and also in India. She has recently taken a rest from a large teaching commitment and has taken time to be in a personal retreat. It has been wonderful to know her and I would like to thank her for the invaluable help with the* Sanskrit *(language of ancient Indian scriptures) in this book.

Sri Ramana proposed the fundamental question 'Who am I?' Who are you?

I think this question is to be looked at from whichever level of reality we wish to consider. There is a basic transactional reality in living a human life, and there are metaphysical realities. At the ordinary transactional reality, yes, I am Swamini Pramananda, with this name given to me by my *guru*, Swami Dayananda Saraswati. For exploring the fundamental question, 'Who am I?' then you have the answers in Ramana Maharshi's book. Is that clear enough?

Yes. Thank you. Many Western seekers come to India looking for enlightenment as if it is an experience. What is enlightenment?

Enlightenment is knowing oneself. I suppose that one who has been able to know the Truth about oneself is considered to be an enlightened soul. I wouldn't say that it is just Western seekers who are looking for enlightenment, I think all of humanity is looking for some basic answers in life. Many of them don't even know what they are looking for. If you ask anybody what it is they are looking for, the answer is, 'I am looking for happiness. Whatever I do, I basically just want to be happy.' I don't think that one seeking enlightenment is looking for anything different. I think every human being's heart is in search of that: the free person inside.

Are there any qualifications for enlightenment? Is* sadhana *(spiritual practice) necessary and if so, what form do you advise?

I would say that any knowledge requires qualification. When you want to enter college you always have these prerequisites. Unless you cover the prerequisites in your credit courses you are not even given admission to the university. Self-knowledge is no different, it is knowledge after all, and like any knowledge there are prerequisites. When your *guru* speaks to you, you should be able to understand the language. I should have the capacity for attention, the capacity for assimilation and the capacity to be able to re-articulate what I have heard.

Self-knowledge is the wisdom we seek to discover happiness. The Self that is talked about in the scriptures is not the physical body. The Self abides in this form, it is consciousness reflecting in the physical body, and the body is looked upon as inert matter. The body and its attributes cannot be the attributes of the Self.

When I say I live in a house and the house is leaking, I don't mean that I am leaking. If I live in a structure, whatever happens to that structure doesn't happen to me. I am different from the structure: the form of the structure is not my form, the attributes of the structure are not my attributes. In the same way the Self is not the physical body and the attributes of the physical body do not belong to the Self. If I am identified with my body, if my self image is dependent on the look of the body, the colour of my hair, the colour of my eyes, the colour of my skin, then my life will be more 'materially' conscious. My whole orientation becomes external, and if my orientation is external, then I am not really ready or available to go inward.

Going inward requires my being able to suspend pursuits for the physical body, and therefore the first prerequisite in spiritual life is the suspension of external pursuits. Living in a consumer society, being drawn into and captivated by the media, advertising and so on, is not a prerequisite for Self-knowledge. It has to be a life of relative withdrawal. When I am looking to know and to understand myself, this means I am looking for the permanent. I am looking for something that is not temporary, something that won't go away from me. The Self is the One that doesn't leave you, because you are the Self; the Self is said to be the source of happiness. Dispassion toward the impermanent is *vairagya.*

The second important prerequisite for self-knowledge is the capacity to discriminate between the permanent and the impermanent. Once I have discriminated I move away from the impermanent and towards the permanent. These two prerequisites are called *viveka* and *vairagya* in *Sanskritam. Viveka* is the capacity to discriminate between the permanent and impermanent.

The third prerequisite is being human. The emotional growth of a human being means being a good person. My thoughts, words and actions are aligned. I don't victimise people in my anger against myself, against the world, against God. I can contain my emotional life, I have a relative mastery over my emotions. I have the capacity to reflect, I have an intellectual honesty, a commitment to be a better person, to grow, to forgive, to accommodate. All this comes under one qualification, one prerequisite.

So now we are looking at three prerequisites: *vairagya*, *viveka* and the third is the inner qualities. A person who is relatively kind can discover the nature of the Self as being all-kindness. One who is relatively compassionate is equipped to discover the nature of the Self as being all-compassionate. One who is relatively angry cannot do this. Understand this well; the third prerequisite is being a mature adult.

Do you suggest any practice that can help with the achievement of those prerequisites?

I would say that being with like-minded people, a support group, is conducive to knowing what is permanent and impermanent. If my friends are very worldly, that's not creating a support group. I would suggest a life of learning, a life of self-reflection, of quietening the mind, settling accounts, minimising my transactions with the world. It's endless, all the things we think we must do. By the time I have done all this it is time to sleep. I still cannot sit because I am too tired from doing things all day. Therefore, I suggest not packing the best time of your life with too many activities. Being more prayerful can help too. My search is to know the Self. The Self that I seek to know is no different from the cosmic Self, and therefore a certain prayerful attitude brings me closer to that quiet mind that is so essential for this knowledge.

I have noticed that in many Indian* ashrams *they do* karma yoga *(activity as spiritual practice), which usually means hard work.

Well, actually it has nothing to do with hard work. In fact, *karma yoga* has everything to do with attitude towards work. It's not about packing your day with work. It's about the attitude you carry when you do work, and for this you don't have to sit in an *ashram*. Wherever there is *karma* (result of all actions) there is *yoga*. (both laugh) Utilise that. *Karma yoga* is an attitude towards the results of action, how I handle life situations, how I handle the very doing of an action.

Either things can happen through me or I can make things happen. It's like the potter's wheel. When you put the right material on the wheel and you have the right spin, you only need to give it the right shape. You just allow it to happen. You don't do much, you are just there to make it come together. The thing keeps moving on its own; you are the facilitator. You tune your actions to a motion that is already set; you don't cut through that motion. You fall in line with a momentum which is already set in motion.

We have all come into this world with our own *karmic* package, and that *karmic* package is unfolding in our lives as our destiny through our relationships, through those we love, through those we hate, through all these intense emotions. We have *karmic* connections to land, to people and to animals. I am sure I have some *karmic* connection to you or else you and I wouldn't be here today. We are all connected. A person who is in touch with the *karmic* unfoldment of his own life also does work, but he uses his will and effort like that potter. The thing is already in motion, so he makes the choice to fall in line with the motion. If he pushes and pulls against the motion he will have high blood pressure, get stressed out and whatnot. This fighting with our *karma*, the results of all our actions, is like fighting with shadows.

Karma yoga is an attitude in action where I am so graceful in what I do that I am not really doing at all. I find myself to be just a facilitator within what is already happening. There is a knack, a beauty, in handling life situations with this attitude. Similarly, the results of my *karma* come back to me. Every action has a result. The law of *karma* is twofold. Firstly, everything that you do has a result; secondly, that result is in keeping with the action done. If you lift your leg to place it in front of you the result is that you have walked ahead, it will not be that you go backwards. The results, when they come, are twofold; one result is seen and the other is unseen. If I give charity, help a poor person, there is a seen result: my pocket is empty and his pocket is full. He is happy and I am happy I could help. Every *karma* also simultaneously has an unseen result which does not immediately come to fruition. It goes into your *karmic* account. If it is a good action there is a good visible result, and a good unseen result is credited to your account. The good unseen result is called *punya*. If it's a bad action, a wrong action, you get a seen result, such as you go to jail, and a bad unseen result is credited to your account. The bad unseen result is called *papa*. *Punya* and *papa*. At a future date your account will mature. That future date may be in this life, but not necessarily so.

If the bad credit matures while you are doing a good action, you don't see the result of your good action. You get a slap. Sometimes you do good to people and then they pull the carpet from under you. You don't see, but you are getting in life what you have put in. Therefore, *karma yoga* is the capacity to accept the results of my actions when they come to me. Not that I don't expect always the best; I expect it and I work for it, but what will come to me in life I do not know. Whatever comes, I trust the cosmic justice. I know that the law of *karma* will not fail because it is a law like the law of gravity; it never fails. I trust that so totally that I can receive any results with grace. The one who has brought into his awareness a certain attitude of graceful acceptance of action and its result, he is the one who is called *karma yogi*.

This is interesting for Western people because we have been brought up with the idea of a judgemental God, and many of us are carrying some kind of judge around inside us with which we judge ourselves every day. Would you like to say anything about this?

Yes, I would say that is very unfortunate, (laughter) because by the time we discover what we are doing to ourselves half of our life is already gone, and with the remaining half we need to undo our habitual patterns of thinking. That's not easy. We say that the creation is an intelligent creation; intelligent because it is predictable, because we can understand its patterns through the life forms, through the season changes, through the geography, through the geology. When I go into schools in India, when I talk to children, they think that knowledge is in the books in their backpacks. It is important to understand that knowledge is not in books. Knowledge is right here. Knowledge is in the creation; all that is here is knowledge.

This tree grows in intelligence. There is knowledge manifest here. There is knowledge manifest in this light. There is knowledge manifest in the seasons. It is very intelligently placed: when it comes, when it goes, when the seasons change, and so on. It is all knowledge. *Iswara*, the Lord, is in this breeze, in the air we breathe. It has just the right amount of oxygen, just the right amount of carbon dioxide. Everything is balanced. The body is the right temperature. Too cold you will be dead. Too hot and you will be ashes. Everything in and around you is nothing but knowledge manifest.

If we understand that knowledge manifests as the Lord, we remove all judgements. There is nobody there to judge. If there is no entity to judge us then why should we judge ourselves? Life is meant to be lived and owned up to. I own up to the Self as intelligence. I own up to the Self as omniscience. I own up to the true nature of the Self. I am not the physical body because the body is inert. The mind is also made of the same five elements; it is inert. All that we are looking at is omniscience manifest here in this physical body. Where is the entity sitting there to judge, and why would he judge? If I do a good action I will earn its result. If I do something wrong I will definitely earn the result. It's all set up in the laws. If I don't want to earn the result of my wrong actions, then I will do what it takes to rectify them. I will grow, I will own up to my mistakes, I will learn. If I am committed to growth and learning, there is nobody to fear. Why should I fear anybody, least of all God Himself? If He doesn't understand me I do not need Him. I don't need a God who judges me. I have had enough. There is no God who judges. The laws are at work, working within the cosmic order, the cosmic justice.

Do you have any technique that could help to drop this inner judge?

I would say meditation would help, meditation in which I tell myself, 'I trust the cosmic order.' The all-knowing creator, let's call Him omniscience, takes care of billions and billions of His creatures on earth, and in the rest of His vast cosmos, His galaxies. Such a huge universe is in His hands, in which 'I', a little soul, am not even a dot. It's like the president of a country. He may be sitting in one place, but his powers extend through the whole of the country through his ministers. God's ministers are the sun, the moon, the stars, the wind, the fire, the Earth and all the elements of nature that influence your day-to-day life, that give you your life's breath, that make this human life possible. He has order in His creation, everything works with laws, and in this, 'I', the one little individual soul, *jiva*, is naturally included.

Along with billions of *jivas* I am in His hands, and so let me learn to receive Him as my guide, my healer. Let Him manifest in me as divinity manifest in this body. Let my life expression never be seperate from the Divine. This form of meditation in which I receive the cosmic energy into myself, living in the moment, can be a very beautiful healing process. This is the final reality, you see? Working with the mind in this manner can really help us to heal and drop the inner judgements. As part of my healing I can understand that whatever has happened has happened and now it is past. I can learn to understand life situations not in terms of 'why is this happening to me?' This 'why me?' is the victimised mind. Let me live today as an adult; I am not helpless. Closing accounts means accommodating, forgiving.

The second thing that I consider very important to understand is the concept that every human being is born with a certain debt. We have certain debts that we have come to clear. You don't keep it going, it is not a credit system. You have to close your accounts. Sometimes a fellow keeps taking and taking and then pops off. He has a lot he owes to the world. He has to come back to give it back. The clearing of debt is a very beautiful concept in the Indian culture that helps in accommodating people, in outgrowing a relationship, in being kind, being human, being sensitive to others and their weaknesses and limitations. With this I can settle internally, there is no judgement. I just keep working towards clearing my accounts with the world.

Sri Ramana said that Self-enquiry is the most direct route to realising the Self. What do you say about Self-enquiry and how to conduct Self-enquiry?

We look upon Ramana as a rare person, a rare soul, a *mahatma* (great soul). He was able to know at a young age that he is not the physical body, that when the body is gone he will continue to be. This was something that came to him without a master, without any proper teaching. We would say that maybe this is because he had gone through the teachings before in his past lives. He had already done a lot of work before. All he needed was to live a few more years of a life of contemplation.

Self-enquiry in the *Vedanta* (*Vedic* philosophy) tradition is a composite of three elements. The first is *shravanam*, in which the nature of the Self is taught in a systematic, structured method of teaching. This the *guru* gives you when you go and live with him. It means listening to the master, learning about oneself, learning about the Self. As part of that learning, questions come up. 'You say I am not the body, but I feel pain in the body; what does this mean?' So there is a second component. Does my mind understand what the scriptures say and flow with it? If it doesn't, then those questions are addressed by the same teacher. This is called *mananam*, reflection. As you learn, you reflect. These two components are a process connected with the teacher. You do it with the help of a proper *guru*.

Having done this, having understood the nature of the Self according to the scriptures, I may still behave differently in my life because I have old patterns of behaviour. I know it's bad, but I still smoke. Similarly, body identification is carried by the *jiva*, the soul, through many lifetimes. If I want to drop my body identification I need to actualise these teachings with the help of a contemplative life. Sitting in meditation, enquiring into the Self or recalling the words of the scriptures I have learned is the third component: *nididhyasanam*, contemplation.

Traditionally we talk about Self-enquiry as having these three components – *shravanam*, *mananam*, *nididhyasanam*. The first two are with the help of a teacher, the third you do by yourself. Maharshi only talked about the third component because that's all it took for him; he didn't need an external teacher. So people think they don't need a teacher either. Ramana was an exception.

***Sri Ramana used to say Arunachala was his* guru. *He also advised people that it's useful to have a living* guru.**

Yes.

When Sri Ramana was asked, 'When will the realisation of the Self be gained?' he replied, 'When the world which is what-is-seen has been removed, there will be realisation of the Self which is the seer.' What is the true understanding of the world? How to remove the world?

We need to be very careful in understanding this, because removal can mean the absence of the world or it can mean seeing that the world is only apparent. If I understand that my shadow is a shadow, that it is not real, then I need not 'remove' the shadow because a shadow cannot hurt me. If it is there let it be so, if it is not there let it be so. Even though I don't remove it physically, cognitively I have removed its reality.

The traditional teachings say *Brahma satyam jagat mithya, jivo-brahmaiva na aparaha. Brahma satyam* means consciousness is the Truth. *Jagat mithya* means names and forms are apparent. Are you name and form or are you the Truth? The second half says *jivo-brahmaiva na aparaha*: you are the Truth. The name and form are not the Truth. So I don't give them a reality independent of the Self.

Removal of the world means you do not give the seen world a reality independent of the seer. There is no seen without the seer, but there is a seer without the seen. When there is nothing to see the seer is not called the seer; the seer is pure consciousness. Pure consciousness gains the status of seer when there is something to see. So the removal of the world means not giving the world an independent reality. The world doesn't exist independent of the seer, the consciousness. If consciousness is the Truth, the world is incidental; whether it is physically seen or unseen is incidental. Its reality is dependent upon the witnessing consciousness. That is what *Vedanta* teaches.

It has been suggested that the mind must be destroyed for liberation to occur. Do you have a mind? Sri Ramana used the term* manonasha *to describe the state of liberation, meaning destroyed mind. How to destroy the mind?

I won't call it destruction of mind even though it is called *manonasha*. The problem with the word 'destruction' is that it suggests that the mind will never come back. How do I transact with the world without a mind? *Manonasha* is really the removal of the problematic mind, the chattering, monologuing mind. By removal we mean silencing. The mind becoming still and quiet, free from distracting patterns of thought, results in silence which is the nature of *atman*, the Self. It is a resolution rather than a destruction. *Manonasha* can also mean understanding that the mind is *mithya*, apparent.

The next question is, do you have a mind? (laughs) I guess you have a mind.

Is that statement meant to trick me into something? (laughs)

No tricks here. There is an idea that enlightened saints don't really think, that they have no mind.

There is no human will and effort. Because there is nothing to achieve there are no choices to make. Like the potter, things happen but you are not the doer. The doer and enjoyer is the *jiva*, the mind, the person. But one who knows the Self as consciousness is a non-doer, a non-enjoyer. The Self is not the doer, all the doing that happens, happens through the non-self. The doing is done by nature, by the non-self. I remain a witness to all the doings; I remain a non-doer.

We are looking at this at a metaphysical level. We say that consciousness is a non-doer, that the Self is a witnessing consciousness. It is not a doer; all doing, enjoying and experiencing belongs to the body-mind-sense complex. The body-mind-sense complex is a doer and an enjoyer, an experiencer. The Self, *atman*, is not an experiencer, it has no experience. To experience, the body-mind-sense complex is required. The body-mind-sense complex can only experience whatever it comes into contact with. It is made up of the five elements and the world is made up of the five elements, so the two can come into contact and there is experience. The skin can feel the touch, the eyes can see the form, the ears can hear sounds. All the doing takes place at the non-self level. Self is not a doer.

We say that saints enjoy the non-doing state of being, and things happen through them. What this means is that they remain detached when doing takes place. If my sense of 'I' is placed in the consciousness, not in the body-mind, then nothing that the body-mind does belongs to me, the Self. That does not mean that the body-mind will not do anything; it will do what it needs to do. But the doing is not owned by the Self, the Self remains a non-doer. Things happen, things get done. I abide in the Self; there is no doing involved here.

I am consciousness. Within consciousness is this body. Within consciousness is the creation. Within consciousness is Arunachala. Within consciousness are the stars. Within consciousness is you. Within consciousness is the earth, the sun, the moon, the planets, the galaxies, the whole. That consciousness is the Self – period, full stop, it ends there. There is no place for doing or being a doer as there is nothing to be done. All the doing belongs to the body-mind complex, which is not the Self, and therefore it is *mithya*, apparent. The Self is *satyam*, the real, the Truth.

What about* vasanas, *the tendencies of the mind? Must these be removed before Self-realisation can become permanent? Is it enough to achieve a* sattvic *(calm and peaceful) state of mind and to know one's* vasanas *so that they no longer bind? How to remove the* vasanas*?

The third prerequisite for the spiritual life, for Self-enquiry, is *nididhyasanam*: meditating on what I know about myself so that my habitual patterns and body identification can be seen as *mithya* in the light of my knowledge of the Self.

Removal of the *vasanas*, working towards a state of mind where the *vasanas* do not disturb, is the third prerequisite. You have just put this differently. *Vasanas* can also remain as long as they don't disturb the quietude of the mind. You are sitting by a lake watching the still waters when suddenly a bubble comes up and pop, it bursts; then again the lake is quiet. After some time another bubble comes up from the bottom and again, pop! If there are things that come up when you sit in your meditation, what do you do? Nothing. You just watch. Be a witness. I don't have to do anything to remove that bubble. It is just putrefied matter that's coming up. Similarly, *vasanas* are the putrefied patterns of behaviour that existed before Self-knowledge. Some of it has not yet gone. It will go only after popping up, so let it pop up. So what? I remain as a witness consciousness to whatever the play of the mind is. I don't judge it, I don't identify with it; I remain a mere witness to it.

But we do identify with them.

Yes.

Most of the time!

We identify, we judge. Oh! I am still thinking like this! Oh, I shouldn't be thinking like this! Oh, why is the mind still disturbed? Look at it. What is it that is disturbing? If you have a wound on your hand which has not healed it draws your attention through pain. If there was no pain you might not take care of the wound. Very soon your hand has to be amputated. Pain is a great blessing, it draws my attention: 'Hey, look here. You need to address this. You are hurting! Please see.'

There is some *vasana*, there is something there from the past and we judge it: 'Hey, why are you there! Pain, you shouldn't be there! After ten years of spiritual practice why are you still there? I will walk away from my *guru*! He didn't work out for me!' You get mad at the teacher: 'You didn't tell me my pain would continue even after ten years of hanging around you! You are a phony!' Poor *guru*. There is nothing to judge. Remain in witness consciousness when *vasanas* bring up issues. Let me see what is there to be looked at, what needs to be worked through.

The* vasana *may be there but it is harmless if we just witness it.

Yes.

But if it is still motivating our actions then we are a victim of it.

Yes. Then we need to look at it, we need to address it. If we are not able to remain as the witness, if we identify with it, if it brings out pain and memories which disturb the quiet of the mind, then we need to come out of the meditation and address it. Look into it, write in your journal, do visualisations, recall the situation. If something arises from your childhood then okay, it happened, but how can I correct the situation now as an adult? What can I do to close that chapter, to clear my debt? Because the mind attracted my attention to that pain, I go through this process. Once I have addressed it then I can go back to the meditation and be more settled. It won't come back.

Would you say that there are sometimes very strong issues or structures which would benefit from some kind of psychological therapy?

Yes. The modern Western world has really come up with some good tools. We have so many methods, such as hypnotic past-life regression. We have healing meditations, like white light and *reiki* (spiritual energy healing). They do wonders. Some of our issues are not necessarily connected to this life alone and something more than counselling is required. Certain patterns, very vulnerable patterns of behaviour, are connected to some core issues from previous lifetimes. You can address them through past-life regression; your inner intelligence brings you back to those situations and helps you to heal.

At the end of his book,* Self-Enquiry, *Sri Ramana says, 'He who is thus endowed with a mind that has become subtle, and who has the experience of the Self is called a* jivanmukta.*' Is this the state that can be called Self-realised?

He goes on, 'And when one is immersed in the ocean of bliss and has become one with it without any differentiated existence, one is called a* videhamukta. *It is the state of* videhamukti *that is referred to as the transcendent* turiya *(state). This is the final goal.' Is this the state that can be called enlightenment?

I will share with you my understanding of these two expressions as the tradition holds. *Jivanmukti* is that state of firm, abiding, clear knowledge of the Self as *satchidananda* (Truth-consciousness-bliss) and as free from *karma* or *punya-papa,* good and bad action. When a *jivanmukta* passes on there is no further relationship with the body, and therefore there is no new embodiment for him. This state of freedom from the cycle of rebirth is called *videhamukti.*

To explain more clearly, understand that the tradition divides the *punya-papa* of a *jiva*, a soul, into three types: the first is called *sancita karma*, which is *karma* accumulated over many births; the second is called *prarabdha karma*, which is the portion of accumulated *karma* that matures in the current human life; the third is called *agami karma*, which is new *punya-papa* being added by the person by doing fresh *karma* in the current human life.

But in the case of a wise person, the self-knowledge has already destroyed the *sancita karma,* all acculumated *karma.* There is no longer the ego, saying I am the doer, I am the enjoyer. Instead there is only the knowledge that I am *satchidananda.* In addition, since the individual nucleus is gone and he is not an individual soul doing *karma*, he does not therefore acquire any fresh *karma.*

Truly speaking, the only *karma* that sustains the wise person is the *prarabdha karma*, the accumulated *karma* that matures in the current human life, giving him the experiences of pain and pleasure during *jivanmukti.* In *jivanmukti* it is not that pain and pleasure experiences go away, they continue to exist. But the difference now is that the wise person recognises that the *prarabdha karma* can only affect the body and not the Self. Once the body has fallen, since there is no more accumulated nor fresh *karma* and the *prarabdha karma* is over with the fall of the body, there is no more rebirth possible for the wise person and so he is said to enjoy *videhamukti.*

***It appears to me essential to meet a* guru *and stay with that* guru. *Who is the* guru? *What is the* guru's *role? How to recognise a true* guru?**

In your one question there are three questions! Okay, let's start with the first one. Who is the *guru*? There is no *guru* in the same way that there is no father or mother. *Guru* is a role a person takes on for another individual who sees himself as a disciple to this person. A *guru* is only a *guru* to a person who sees himself as that individual's disciple. There is no 'the *guru*' as such; this is one thing we need to know.

What do we mean when we talk about the *guru*? *Guru* is a *Sanskrit* word. *Gu* refers to ignorance. *Ru* means removal. The one who is able to remove your ignorance is the *guru*. What ignorance? You can have a dance *guru* or a music *guru*. But *guru* is the word given for one who removes Self-ignorance. The role of a *guru* is to remove Self-ignorance, to guide the person through *shravanam* (listening to the teaching) and *mananam* (reflection of the teaching), the first two components of teaching Self-knowledge.

And how do you recognise a **guru*****?***

Arjuna asked this question of Lord *Krishna* in the *Bhagavad Gita* (classical Hindu scripture). How does he talk? How does he walk? How does he sit? If he walks in slow motion then I can say, 'Ah ha! I caught him!' (laughs) If he walks too fast, 'No, he can't be a *guru*.' Lord *Krishna's* answer to *Arjuna* is very interesting: the one who can remain contented in himself, by himself, with himself, he is a wise man. It also means having given up all desires born of the human mind, not wanting to fulfil any desires. That is, desires do not dictate his happiness. Whether the desires are fulfilled or unfulfilled, he is free from them.

Whether the wise man is your *guru* depends upon whether he chooses to teach you his wisdom. Therefore, truly the question should be who is a wise man, not who is the *guru*. The *guru* is the one who teaches you; his role is defined by the disciple. But the wise man is someone who is connected to wisdom that reflects in his life. He is the one worthy to be asked to teach me, to be my teacher.

Would you say that when the disciple is ready, the **guru** ***appears?***

Yes. That is part of the cosmic justice, that a seeker is never let down. As a seeker, I have given up my normal life, my society, in search of Truth, in search of that deep calling. But I don't know what it is that is calling me. I don't know where I am going. I don't know where my answer will come from. I don't know who will exploit my trust. There are so many unknowns in the journey of a spiritual person. Is it not so? At every stage and at any point I can be taken for a ride. Therefore, the scriptures promise that when I am ready, when I have worked on my prerequisites, when there is true dispassion, discrimination and a commitment to growth, when there is a commitment to forgiveness and prayerfulness, I will never be left hanging in life. I will find my answers. The right person will show up at the right time for me. That has to happen. That is the law.

Would you say that another element is an inner fire or longing?

Yes, because that is the message. It's your core calling out in the universe to send somebody. I'm ready. Come on! Fill me up Lord. I've cut through this so-called 'normal' life. Now give me what it takes to complete my journey. Once that call is declared to the cosmos it cannot fail to be answered because there is cosmic intelligence. Omniscience is in the creation; that call is picked up and the right situations come up and take you to the right soul. One should never have any doubt about this.

Arjuna asked this question in the *Bhagavad Gita*. He had a doubt. We all love *Arjuna* because very often he sounds like us, full of doubts! He asks the Lord: 'If I give up everything and take to this, what if I die? I didn't make it in normal life, what if I don't make it here in the spiritual life because I didn't get the right guide? What will happen to me?' Lord *Krishna* answers, 'You will never lose anything. Even if you die today you will take your next birth and pick up the thread from where you left off.' In the spiritual journey there is no restarting, reinventing the wheel. You have already come this far. There is no going back, it is only one-way traffic.

You just keep piling up the credits.

Yes, that's it.

Sri Ramana's devotees had tremendous devotion to him, and he to Arunachala. Please say something about* bhakti, *devotion, in the pursuit of awakening.

Bhakti is a word which we all understand in our own way. For many people devotion means singing *bhajans* (devotional songs).

There is some element, an invisible bond, between the seeker and the* guru*; is this something to do with devotion?

Yes. I would say there is a similar relationship with the Lord. The relationship of an individual with the total is the fundamental relationship of every human being. Every person has a relationship with the total, in whose laws this birth has taken place. The fundamental relationship of an individual is with the creator, basically the relationship of a devotee, of a created being towards its creator.

Again, like with *karma yoga*, we need to be alert. Devotion is also sometimes looked upon as an activity. Let's have some *bhakti*, sing some *bhajans*, say some prayers, light a candle or a lamp or massage the *guru's* feet. Many think that *bhakti* is an act of worship. It may begin with an act of worship but it doesn't end there. An action is performed simply in order to invoke the spirit behind the action.

You use a symbol to carry your sentiment because sentiments are subtle. Sentiments cannot be carried without a form. That's why many great friends, couples, relationships, fall apart: because they cannot share the basic sentiment that they love each other. They can't talk about it or express it in any form. *Bhakti* as an act of worship is a form used in order to invoke a sentiment. Nowadays I have seen New Age groups light incense, put on soft music and turn down the lights for their meditation. It creates an ambience. It creates the atmosphere that helps me go into myself. Incense is not meditation but it is a facilitator to carry me deeper into myself. *Bhakti* takes the form of certain actions which help express a certain attitude towards the creator, or towards an exalted being like Ramana Maharshi.

When Self-knowledge becomes my main pursuit of life, the Lord is included in my awareness. I remain ever devoted. Knowledge doesn't go away. The sentiment becomes an attitude, not an action, just as *karma yoga* is an attitude, not an action. *Bhakti* is an attitude towards the one to whom you are devoted. In this case we are looking at devotion to the

Lord. The saint is possibly the greatest devotee. One who has Oneness with the Lord is the greatest devotee of the Lord.

Seekers often have curious ideas about the enlightened state. Please describe your typical day and how you perceive the world.

(Laughs) My typical day has nothing to do with what I hold within me. Each day has its own character. It's like a kaleidoscope. Have you ever looked through a kaleidoscope? You can never look at the same design twice. Each moment is a frozen design; it has its own pattern, its own beauty, its own shape and form and colour. You try to re-create it, turning it backwards thinking that the previous design will come back. So there is no typical day. Sorry to disappoint you. (laughs) Each day is new. Each day is fresh. Each day has something to offer that I didn't even know existed the previous day. And I live my life day-to-day, moment to moment.

Thank you.

Radha Ma

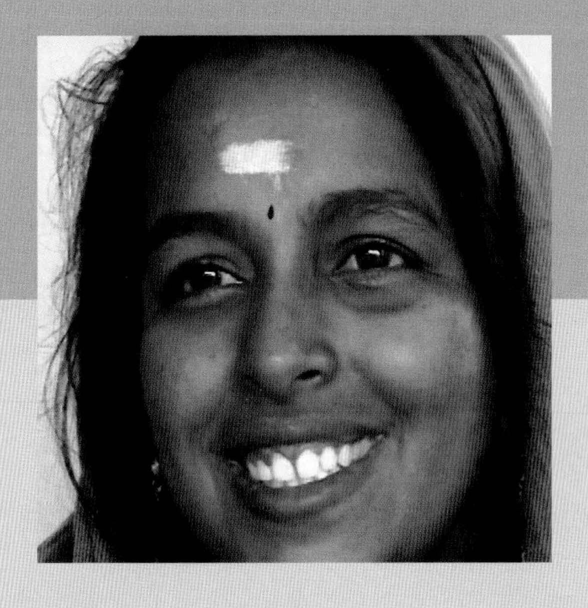

The moment you make a blueprint then you are freezing the moment. The whole awakening is a mystery and the moment you make a blueprint, the beauty is gone. It is different for everybody, a different path and different way, so you can't make a common blueprint.

We are already That,
we are not ignorant to be enlightened.

Radha Ma

Radha Ma

A young woman of unknown age (perhaps early 40s), she originates from Bangalore and she was successfully working for many years in Hyderabad as a chartered accountant. It was here she met her husband and they chose to marry to escape the family marriage pressures. He lives with her now as a devotee. She refuses to see herself as a *guru* or master but many come to her anyway.

Arranging this interview with Radha Ma in 2003 was a delight. She was immediately completely available, saying, 'Why not now?' So we sat together and had lots of fun making the interview. Meeting her again in recent years, there is tremendous love in her presence. The large sign on her gate reads: 'I'm not a guru. *Instead of wasting your time trying to meet me, you can go to Ramanashramam.' I am touched that despite this, she accepts my invitations to speak at the Arunachala Pilgrimage Retreat. Her uncompromising delivery of Truth is lovingly and humorously expressed. A wise woman.*

Radha, I am very pleased to be sitting here with you at your home in the shadow of Arunachala in Tiruvannamalai. Before we start the questions, I understand that you have something to say about this title, Blueprints for Awakening*?*

The moment you make a blueprint then you are freezing it, freezing the moment. You see, the whole awakening is a mystery and the moment you make a blueprint, the beauty is gone. You can't make a blueprint as it is not a common thing for everybody. It is different for everybody, a different path and different way, so you can't make a common blueprint.

I agree with you. By approaching different teachers who have different paths or a different experience or kind of awakening, I am asking them to share that, to share their blueprint.

Oh! I don't have one, I was not awakened. (laughs)

So you don't have any blueprint?

Right, because I was not awakened. Because I never slept.

You were always awake?

Yes. Awakening comes, it is a relative term. The moment you sleep the awakening comes, but to the one who has never slept there is no awakening. So the term awakening is meaningless for me. (laughs)

Sri Ramana proposed the fundamental question 'Who am I?' Who are you?

Yes. Ramana proposed the fundamental question for the *sadhakas*, the spiritual seekers, to control the mind, not for the masters, not for the one who is already awake. The moment you asked me 'Who am I?' that is the moment I started describing myself, and sadly the beauty was gone. I started limiting the unlimited and trying to finite the infinite; do you understand? The moment I start saying that I am this and I am that then it's sadly mixed up and looks so ugly. And it's infinite! I can say that I am consciousness, I am this, I am that, but I am none of these. I am not this, I am not that; I am what I am. So this only goes for the spiritual seekers who are trying to figure out who they are, not for the one who knows who he is. (both laugh)

Are you saying you know who you are, and who you are is this moment?

No, I said 'Who am I?' can't be comprehended. It can't be explained. It's the infinite. People can't understand the infinite, so we start using words like 'I am compassionate', 'I am *Brahman* (absolute reality)', 'I am limitless' and 'I am consciousness'. Suppose you changed the term 'consciousness' to 'stupidity' in the dictionary, then I am stupidity too! Consciousness is a dictionary term, and if it is stupidity then I am stupidity! It's the mind trying to comprehend something that can't be comprehended, so these words are needed for that.

You are just who you are at this moment, right? As it is now in this present moment?

Yes, I am ever and the same; I am changeless. If you talk about time, then I am the same whether it is past or present or future; it's me, it's changeless.

Many Western seekers, like the people coming to your* Satsang *(meeting in Truth), come to India looking for enlightenment as though it is an experience. What is enlightenment?

It's a mind game. It is what you call a mind state. Always this mind wants something higher: if it goes to the material world then it wants to be rich, if it goes to the emotional world then it wants to be loved, and in the spiritual world it wants enlightenment. So, always the higher things in the mind states. There is no such thing as enlightenment, there is no such thing as a spiritual seeker, and you are already That. We are already That, we are not ignorant to be enlightened. Ignorance needs the enlightenment; ignorance is the mind and needs the enlightenment. There is no mind; we are not the mind. It's an ego trip, nothing else. If people are unsatisfied with the material world then they try spirituality, only to find that nothing like enlightenment exists.

So my next question is a bit funny because if there is no enlightenment then there are no qualifications for enlightenment. My question is: Are there any qualifications for enlightenment?

Who is here to qualify anybody? Who can say that you and I are qualified to be enlightened? My enlightenment is given, then where does the qualification come from? It's just gross, just a business.

So is it necessary to do some spiritual practices? Is* sadhana *(spiritual practice) necessary?

It is necessary to know that ultimately it's unreal, that there is no enlightenment required. Enlightenment is an illusion; our mind is an illusion. But *sadhana* alone will not bring you that reality. Spiritual practice is needed to know the Truth and to understand the Truth. Suppose you go to a farmer and tell him he is God, he will never believe you and will laugh at you. He needs a basic *sadhana* to understand the ultimate reality, or rather to accept this reality, that this is real. The spiritual seeker, the *sadhaka*, is real, and to know that he needs a *sadhana*. But he does not need that for anything else, not for enlightenment.

So in a way it is useful to be able to get to know the mind, to see the mind and to know that is not who you are. In that way it is useful?

Yes. To know that ultimately mind is an illusion, to understand that. *Sadhana* is not going to bring you the final cut; through *sadhana* you can never lose identification. But to know that as knowledge, as an understanding, then *sadhana* is required.

Is it also necessary to quieten the mind, to have a* sattvic *(calm and peaceful) mind?

Yes. The mind is an illusion but the moment you say it then people can't accept this. They find that they are struggling and fighting with the mind every day. Spiritual practice is required to make your foe into your friend. All these days you are fighting with your mind, and by doing *sadhana* and doing meditation it is going to become your friend. That's it. But still the mind exists and the illusion exists. That's the Truth.

Whether a friend or foe, it is an illusion. The nightmare becomes a sweet dream, that's all, but the dream is continuous.

Sri Ramana said that Self-enquiry is the most direct route to realising the Self. What do you say about Self-enquiry?

I don't know. I never practised Self-enquiry so I can't comment on this. (both laugh) Seriously, this is correct. I never walked on the path so I can't say whether it is right or not. Ramana never practised Self-enquiry either. There was no need for that.

You see what happens? The moment you start 'Who am I?' maybe it helps initially to control the mind, but after some time it becomes an auto-suggestion. Then when a thought comes you ask 'Who am I?' and the thought subsides, but you never erase the thought. It becomes an auto-suggestion after some time if you don't have a proper understanding.

I think the idea of Self-enquiry is to bring your attention to the part that never changes.

You see, the moment when you reach the final path and you are ready for that awakening, or whatever you call it, then anything will wake you up. It may not be Self-enquiry. It may be surrender, love, devotion; anything will wake you up. Any thought will take you there, once you are ready for that. It is not Self-enquiry alone, it is not the only way.

And when you say 'ready for that', what do you mean?

You do all the *sadhanas* and then you understand this ultimate Truth.

That is what I mean when I ask, 'Are there any qualifications?' I mean is something needed as preparation?

Preparation happens. It need not be this and that, but continuous; it is like beginning college. To get a degree in college, what happens? First you have to go to playschool and go higher and higher and then finally you get your degree. But there is no qualification. No one can decide about the qualification. Nobody can say that somebody from playschool goes directly to college. We are not here to decide it.

We are seeing only one lifetime, only one scene of a movie, and we don't know the rest of the lifetimes, so 'qualifications' is a limited term. You see somebody who meditates for a year and he is enlightened, then you see someone else who has been meditating for forty or fifty years and he didn't get any glimpse of it. So trying to judge the qualifications through this one lifetime is not possible.

In your case you say that you were awakened already?

I never said that I was awakened! (laughs)

You said that you weren't asleep and that you have never been asleep, yes? So you didn't have to awaken. Are you saying this is the result of other parts of your movie, of other lifetimes?

You are trying to make me identify with myself. My last dream is over, I am just awake and you have asked me to identify myself. Which dream shall I identify myself with, the last dream? Or the dream previous to that? I don't have any option and I don't know how to identify myself with any of these things. I am not that, I am not the dream. I am not the dreamer to identify myself with. You are forcing me to tell something about the dreams, but it is all over for me. There is no reason for me to go back and relate myself to any of these dream characters. I am having difficulty can't you see? You are talking about my dream and I don't know which dream I can relate to you.

***Right. Your response is very fresh and innocent. If you continue to teach, and lots of Westerners come, you will have to find a teaching and some techniques and then you will have to write some books! (laughs) Then you will need an* ashram.**

Come on! If you are really in Truth then there is no need for any compromise. All these things you are telling, they are all compromise. There is no need to compromise if you are already in this Truth. Nothing matters, so if I tell the Truth and people believe, let them believe. I can't suggest a false method or a false practice for them. The moment I do that, I compromise the Truth, I fall back from the Truth.

But you must already experience that with Western people. When Indian people come they want to worship you and make you the Divine Mother, and when Western people come they want some technique, right? They want to know about enlightenment.

That's true, but I said that enlightenment doesn't exist. You are already unlimited. You are not ignorant to be enlightened. That is the Truth too. I don't find any difference. If I find that you are sleeping or if I find out that you are ignorant then I ought to find a method for you to wake up. But I find that you and I are the same, there is no difference; you are the divine and I am the divine, everybody is the divine here. So there is no need for me to find a practice to suggest to you. You are pretending you are sleeping; you are not really sleeping. There is no reason for me to compromise with the Truth.

As a Western person I am conditioned to do things. My life is all about doing things. I expect I have to do my enlightenment. Do you see?

Sure. But you are conditioned to do it this way.

You will never be successful as a teacher if you tell them it is simply grace!

Success is such a worldly term. The one who stands in the Truth doesn't care for success or failure. It is for the Truth. The Truth is the Truth. If it is accepted then it is accepted, if it is not then it is not. That's it! I have nothing to do; I have no personal motivation in this Truth. I can't make any personal business out of this Truth. Do you see that?

I understand that. I am just provoking you! (both laugh)

There is no need for me to compromise anywhere. It is not me or the personal 'I' that exists to compromise. It's the Truth and non-truth. The Truth decides and there is no need for me to compromise. I no longer exist for any personal benefit. It is the success or failure of the eternal Truth. If it fails then who cares? Let it fail, then it can't be Truth. If it is not being accepted then it can't be Truth. If it is really Truth, if it is eternal, then it should be accepted. It is not my personal failure or success anyway. I don't want to be a master. I don't want to be a *guru*. To say that I am going to be a successful *guru* or not, it does not matter.

When Sri Ramana was asked, 'When will the realisation of the Self be gained?' he replied, 'When the world which is what-is-seen has been removed, there will be realisation of the Self which is the seer.' What is the true understanding of the world?

It is the mind. It is very simple. The world never exists outside our mind. Our mind is the world. The mind created the world. The moment that you identify that there is no mind, you see yourself – that's it! You have identified all these years with the mind; the moment the mind is gone then the world is gone too! The world, that never exists, is the mind.

And how to remove the world?

Now this is what we call *sadhana* or practice. We come back to all those lengthy procedures. Right?

Right.

All these days you are thinking you are X, right? I am telling you, or everybody is telling you, that you are not X but you are A. So how does this identification fall off? You are a prince on the road but throughout your life you are lost, the lost child of a king. You don't know that you are a prince; you are in beggar's garb.

Then one day the king comes and tells you, 'You are not a beggar, you are the prince. You are my lost son.' In that very moment you become the prince, whether you are in the garb of a beggar or not. In your mind you become the prince immediately the king tells you; the identification of the beggar falls off at the same moment.

So why not this? I am telling you that you are not the mind, you are the Self. So why don't you throw this off? It should happen in the same moment. Realisation is as simple as that.

When you say it is as simple as that, do you mean that actually you don't need thirty years of sitting in meditation or singing* mantras *(sacred sounds)? You can just see this Truth in any moment?

Yes.

That I am the Self?

Yes. *Sadhana* is not necessary. Nothing is necessary to see this Truth, but to accept this Truth needs *sadhana.* Suppose the king comes and says, 'You are my son,' then you will believe it. Suppose somebody else says, 'You are not the beggar, you are the lost child of the king, you are the prince.' You will not accept that. The spiritual practice is needed for the acceptance, not for the Truth. We should accept somebody's words; that needs *sadhana.*

It has been suggested that the mind must be destroyed for liberation to occur. Do you have a mind?

No, no. The mind is illusion. The mind does not exist anymore. I don't know what mind is.

You say that you don't have mind; if you got in a car then you could drive the car, right? When you worked as a tax officer you could work with computers and with figures and calculations, right? So for doing those kinds of things you need a mind.

Sure, also I have a point of view to answer all these questions and I should have a dictionary in my mind to speak all these words, right? But it comes spontaneously from consciousness, from my inner being. It's not through the mind. Mind always manipulates, judges; nothing of this happens here. Before I answer a question I don't have to think whether I am right or wrong, nothing like that. That is the problem with the mind. The mind always calculates and manipulates, but when something comes from spontaneity – the mind never existed here. I don't know whether I am right or wrong from your point of view, I don't care about it either. There is no judgement, nothing. It just happens.

When you say you don't have a mind, do you mean that you don't have the memories, experiences, worries, conditionings and knowledge that society and teachers gave you? Are you saying that you have a mind in the sense you can do things when you need to, to operate your body?

Yes, that has been taken care of, but there have also been so many days that I have lived without food. I am beyond the physical and beyond the mental, the mind cannot be here now. All these emotions and attachments are transcended. I don't want to say that I am different; the moment I say that I don't have mind I feel I am different from you. It feels ugly to say it, but it is true.

Could you say, 'I am not attached to my mind'?

No, there is no mind at all to be attached to! Attachment is a different thing. I don't have a mind at all, it does not exist, it's an illusion. And once you cut off that illusion, where does it come from? There is no mind at all. It is just an illusion.

Are you telling me that since you were very young you never really had a mind? You never really lived in your thoughts?

No. No thoughts. I don't know how to explain it more than that. I didn't have words to explain those stages. I was what I was. Maybe what

I was when I was a child and what I am today are the same. There is no difference in me, I am the same. So what you say about the mind is relative. I don't find that the world or mind exist for me, but as the body is in the world, you think I am in the world. And because I talk, you think that I have mind too. Apparently it looks like that, but it is not.

When you worked in the tax office it looked like you had a mind to do these complicated calculations.

Nothing of the sort. It is being taken care of. In fact I didn't study much about these things. I didn't even study computers. The moment I wanted to learn about computers I went to a hardware training institute. My lecturers objected. They told me, 'You are a tax consultant and don't have any electronics background so we can't teach you. You need some electronics background.'

But after a few days it was as if I knew the subject best in the class. I was even correcting the master; I told him that he was wrong in so many things. He was really shocked and he thought that I had learned it somewhere else and that I was there teasing him. (both laugh) This really happened, I am not joking! Actually they thought that I had learned it somewhere else and was coming to class to annoy these people, but I was not. The moment I had made the decision to learn it, the knowledge came to me.

Then I found that there is no need for me to learn anything. Whether in this world or another world there is no need to learn. Everything is already available. When you use a computer you use a server. I am a client, so I receive whatever record is being sent by the server – that's what happens. The ultimate takes care of that. I don't have anything of my own, just a monitor is enough. So whatever the server sends, the client receives it, that's it! I need not have a CPU (central processing unit) of my own.

When Western people come with their minds, their sufferings, their worries, tensions and fears, can you understand immediately that this is an illusion, that this is not true? What do you say to them?

Whether a person is Western or Indian, all suffering and pain are illusions. You are dreaming and you believe that you are having a nightmare; you dream that a tiger is chasing you, but it is an illusionary tiger and illusionary fear too. Any suffering, whether it is Western or Indian or whatever, is like that; all suffering is illusion. You imagine you suffer, that's it. There is no suffering really. Everything is perfect in you.

Everything is exactly as it should be!

Yes, it is perfect. I can say that you are dreaming. I can say it one hundred and one times but still you dream and still you are frightened of the tiger; you can't help it, because it is perfect and it should be like that.

You yourself will wake up from the dream one day and see that all those times you were chased and frightened by an imaginary tiger! But everything is perfect. It is perfect for you to be afraid now. It is perfect for you to have the nightmare now. We can't say that it is wrong, it is perfect.

Are you saying that you accept whatever comes, whether it be happy or unhappy, sad, angry or blissful?

Mind is illusion, so why are you bothered if mind is angry or not, or whether it is jealous or suspicious? The mind itself is illusory, so why should you be bothered by this negative quality of the mind? Everything is perfect. Mind is like this. Mind can be angry or peaceful, mind can be happy or unhappy. But it is illusion. How to say something is good or something is bad in the illusion? This illusion is illusion, it is still illusion, and it is perfect whatever comes.

What do you say to somebody that comes to you? You tell them that it is an illusion, but still they are suffering and they come every day to see you with this pain. The pain is there from something which they believe so strongly that they can't just throw it away. What do you say to them?

I say the same thing to them: it is all perfect! You suffered, it's perfect. You trusted, it's perfect. So many people seek in the world and then come back. They say, 'We have meditated for ten years and we didn't get it,' and they are frustrated. And this frustration is perfect. I can say that your seeking is a waste, but this is not real for you. My knowledge and my Truth is not real for you, it is not your Truth; you have to find out your own Truth.

So I say this, 'What you are seeking is stupidity, there is no enlightenment,' but still your mind can't accept that. You meditate for one week and there is no enlightenment, so the mind says 'Why should I meditate?' So you stop meditating and then next week the mind comes back and says, 'What you are doing is rubbish. You have to sit and meditate.'

That's what the mind says, so you follow the mind. It is that which is going to give you the happiness, not me! My Truth is mine and your Truth is yours and until you find out the Truth for yourself you have to walk on the path.

Suppose you start off from home and I say that this is your home and that you need not travel anywhere; you can't accept this, you have to travel, you have to get fed up and be frustrated and come back to the same place and realise that this is the home from where you actually started. It's perfect. You have to find out for yourself. It is the mind, that is what the mind is.

But you are also telling the people that it is just grace, that in a way they cannot do anything!

You see there is no other way to tell them, right? Grace is just a word we use. Grace is not outside us, grace is us, we are the grace. They say, 'I waited, what to do?' Or 'Why does grace happen to somebody else and not to me?' I say that it is just like a fruit on a tree: the moment it ripens it falls from the tree and until then you have to wait for that. If you are not falling that means that you are not ripe enough!

Grace is a word and there is no other way to express that waiting. Ultimately everybody is reaching the same place so there is nothing to worry about. It's perfect. Today it's me and tomorrow somebody else. So it doesn't make any difference. It is not through my own effort that I am in this state. It's the Ultimate that is taking care of me, and it takes care of everything. So the Ultimate Reality which is Truth for me is Truth for you too. It takes care of you too.

Even me? (both laugh) Even me with my favourite sufferings? Even me?

Why not you? (both laugh) Why not you?

Because I am not worthy!

Then I am not also. I am a fellow unworthy person.

I think that this sense of unworthiness…

It comes from the mind.

Right, it is just mind. It's a very common thought.

It's a very tricky mind! Suppose you corner it with, 'I am not worthy,' then it will say, 'Oh, no! I am most worthy! I did meditation for so many years. I am most eligible.' If you go positive then the mind will take the negative stand and if you go to the negative it will then take the positive stand. That's it.

I am very glad I brought a video camera because many times you say something and I can feel it in the silence around what you say with words. The way you look, smile, laugh and also the way you do nothing.

What about **vasanas,** ***the tendencies of the mind? Must these be removed before Self-realisation can become permanent?***

Okay, (laughs) when you are talking about *vasanas*, who is having the *vasanas*? The mind is having the *vasanas* and it has nothing to do with

Self-realisation. The mind itself is an illusion, and what are the *vasanas*? They are another part of the illusion. Maybe the moment you know you are the Self and that the mind is an illusion, the *vasanas* never existed.

But there is a certain quality about* vasanas. *I can say from my own experience that for a number of years I haven't had much mind.

There is no 'much mind'. Either you have a mind or you don't have a mind. You can't say that you don't have 'much mind'. It's the wrong word. Either you are in the mind or you are not in the mind. That's it.

Well, I am English so I am rather modest! (both laugh) Okay, I can say that I haven't had a mind for a few years now. But still there are times when the mind is there and when I look I see certain patterns again and again. In my case two strong patterns have been coming up for my whole life. So even though I can say that I don't have a mind, I still can say that I have some kind of mind-storm. Everything is calm and suddenly a* vasana *will come. It will be the conditioning of the mind, it will be some silly pattern that seems to recur, what I am calling a* vasana *or tendency. It has a very persistent quality.

I know a number of people who spent time with Papaji. He had a very powerful energy and many woke up to the Self. They would go away and come back saying, 'I have lost it.' Many of them had this experience with* vasanas *pulling them out of that awakening. Can you say something about* vasanas *in this context?

If *vasanas* still exist that means that you are in the mind, you are not out of the mind. The moment you have lost the true identity, even if you have had a glimpse of it, the moment it is lost, it is lost forever. The moment you find it is illusory, then the mind no longer exists for you. The mere fact that you are saying you still have *vasanas* means you are still in the mind. Maybe you have a much quieter and friendlier mind; maybe the mind is even your slave and you may even be the master of the mind, but still the mind exists for you because *vasanas* exist for you.

Once you get it there is no way of losing it, if truly you got it. You know the mind has created the world; all creation is from the mind so it is easy for the mind to create hundreds of enlightenments too. You get such praise, happiness and feel almost enlightened, but after some time the mind comes back. That's the reason, because it happens in the mind. Some parts of the mind are agitated and very aggressive and angry but some parts are so peaceful, just like the ocean; but still it happens in the mind.

You are saying that you can feel, 'Oh! I am awake,' but the awakening is still in the mind, it is not beyond the mind.

Awakening happens only in the mind because mind is waking and wants awakening. Awakening is a term related to the mind, not to us, not to Self. The moment you say you are awakened it happens in the mind. It's not the Truth. The moment you say you are awakened, that means you were sleeping all those days; it is the mind who sleeps to wake up. If you are really the Truth, and if you lost identification with the mind and know you are the true Self, then there is no awakening and enlightenment for you. This happens in the mind. The moment you talk about *vasanas* it is still happening in the mind. The mind is the one that was born with the *karma* (result of all action); it is an illusion. *Karma* and *vasanas* are total illusion. The moment you talk about it, and it is real to you, then the mind is real to you too.

All those days you have tied yourself with a rope. It's all illusion, you are free. That's it. If you feel that the rope is hurting you here and there, that means that you are bound with an illusionary rope. There is no bondage for the one who is free. The moment you find that the rope is illusion, you cannot find any bruises on your body. So the moment you find that mind is an illusion, then you can't find *vasanas* anymore; *vasanas* are like the bruises.

If you say 'I still have the bruises on my body,' that means that you still have the ropes on your body. You still think that the ropes are real to you. The rope is imaginary!

At the end of his book, Self-Enquiry, *Sri Ramana says, 'He who is thus endowed with a mind that has become subtle and who has the experience of the Self is called a* jivanmukta.*' Is this the state that can be called Self-realised? He goes on, 'And when one is immersed in the ocean of bliss and has become one with it without any differentiated existence, one is called a* videhamukta. *It is this state of* videhamukti *that is referred to as the transcendent* turiya *(state). This is the final goal.' Is this the state that can be called enlightenment?*

I don't believe in enlightenment at all. So this question becomes irrelevant. I don't believe in enlightenment and awakening. The mind was ignorant and needed to be enlightened, right?

Are you saying that there cannot be Self-realisation and enlightenment, there is not even anything?

These are just names given to identify the mind and cross beyond it. These are just words. The moment I say that you are enlightened, or that enlightenment is there, that means I am limiting you, I am saying that you are ignorant and need to be enlightened. The moment I say that you are awake and talk about your awakening, that means that I am limiting you to sleeping now. That is stupidity! You are not sleeping; you are imagining that you are sleeping. You are not sleeping. Do you see the difference? So I don't believe in this enlightenment at all.

So you certainly don't believe in any stages of enlightenment?

No stages. There are no stages; stages always belong to the mind. These stages, procedures, methods, successes and failures, whatever you call them, are relevant to the mind, not to the Self. The Self is beyond all these things. You cannot have a stage in the Self; that's it. How can you put stages in this?

Swami Shivananda from Rishikesh is a famous saint, he has a book where he talks about the seven stages of enlightenment...

Suppose I tell something about a particular place beyond this hill but you can't understand because you see only the hill and not beyond it. So maybe to take you beyond the hill somebody says, 'Okay, you go up this hill and then you can see that.' But if you go up the hill, then they say, 'If you cross the hill, then you can see this.'

This is a way to make you walk. If they say that this is a hundred kilometres from here then you will be fainting. So they say, 'Okay, you should walk twenty kilometres and then you will see a tree and there you will get the guidance.'

You walk that twenty kilometres and then the guidance says you should walk another twenty kilometres and you will find somebody else and that will be the end of it. So you walk the whole hundred kilometres like this. It is a way to make you walk. Don't think about it. All these are just tricks to make you interested in this, to take you beyond this. It is a way to make the people move, it is a practice.

You are saying that because Swami Shivananda had an* ashram *he needed a teaching and then he needed a book? (both laugh)

I don't care what he says. He is a master and he knows what he does. We are trying to find out something that can't be found out. That is the difficulty for all the people, right? You want to comprehend something that is beyond the mind, and through the mind you try to comprehend it. It is beyond the mind and it is very difficult. He is a master in his own right and he knows what he does.

In bookshops you find a whole section of spiritual books and they are full of all these kinds of things, like seven stages of enlightenment. So what you are saying is that all these books are nonsense because they are attempting to say what is on the other side of the mountain?

I know what you are doing. You are trying to fix me up! (laughs) Okay. But I don't believe in these stages. You are That. And who can create stages in the Self? I don't want to ridicule the books or the authors I don't know, but certainly I feel that the Truth to me is that there are no stages. Who fixes the stages? There are no stages. Either you are yourself or you are not; either you are in the mind or you are not in the mind; that's it. Some people say, 'I am so close to that.' There is no close. There is nothing close to the Truth.

You have to promise me that when I come back to interview you in ten years you don't have any stages, okay? (both laugh) I shall come in the back of the crowd and shout out, 'Hey, what about stages?'

Who knows, maybe people will say that I was never in any of the stages. 'She is in playschool and didn't reach any stage,' but I am still going to talk in the same way. They will say, 'She didn't even reach the first stage, and there are a hundred stages!'

Right. They probably will say that.

That's true.

You will need a book I think. Maybe your husband can write it, with stages. (both laugh)

Him write about me? What stupidity! What is he going to write about? The past? It's stupidity! The dream is over so what is the point writing about those dreams? It is all over for me, nothing matters now, nothing. I say that whatever he writes, that it's all false! He can't write about me anyway. (Premananda laughs) That's true. What I experienced he doesn't know. What I am, he doesn't know. He can't write about that, only I can. But the moment I start writing it becomes so ugly and full of falsehood. The moment I start explaining this, all that I am saying to you, and all of your ten questions, it's all false; it's not true. That's it. That's the Truth. The moment I start to explain the unexplainable, the moment I start reducing it into words, then it loses its beauty. It loses its Truth. Truth can't be told.

I completely agree with what you say. That is really true.

But you say you want to write a book. (laughs) You are close to Truth, maybe? Can we say that you are close to Truth? (laughs)

At the beginning of the book we can write, 'This is all rubbish, don't buy this book.'

Now that is the way to sell your book, you are an intelligent businessman now! (laughs) People will become all the more interested the moment you talk about rubbish. If you say that it is all Truth and tell them to buy it, they won't buy it. But the moment you say that it is all rubbish, then they will buy it.

Do you think that is a good technique?

Yes! (both laugh)

I think this will be a bestseller because your answers are very spontaneous and fresh. It is very beautiful.

So you think that after ten years I will lose my freshness?

***Possibly, possibly. We will see. I will come and knock on the door of your* ashram...**

Oh come on, I don't think I will have one.

No?

Ashrams are like cages, limiting the masters. I am a free bird and I don't want to limit myself anymore. So the moment I have an *ashram* I have to compromise the Truth, and I have to find some practice to teach people, to earn money.

Right, you will need a big practice hall, and then you will need some practices.

Yes, the way to enlightenment; I will have to teach them in ten stages! (both laugh)

You could become famous by saying that there is no enlightenment, there are no steps and there are certainly no stages!

I don't want to become famous like that. It is the Truth that I feel. Maybe I will become famous too, but who cares about it?

In fact it is a good book title. After this book I can do a new one called **No Enlightenment, No Stages, No Anything.**

No mind first.

Somebody talked to me today about killing the ego. I said that is illusion. It is the ego that says, 'Kill me!' It's one of the ego-trips too. It is a new phrase that the ego likes. Ego itself is illusion.

So now here is a perfect question for you. It appears essential to meet a **guru** ***and to stay with that*** **guru.** ***Who is the*** **guru** ***and what is the*** **guru's** ***role? How to recognise a true*** **guru?**

I never had a *guru* so I don't know how to answer this. And also I am not a *guru* either.

Do you think that it is important to have a **guru?**

Yes and no. It all depends. Some people are like children and they need the physical presence of a *guru*. But people who are already strong and independent enough don't need a *guru*. So I can't say whether you need a *guru* or you don't need a *guru* as it all depends on the individual's growth and strength. It can be *karma* too. This question depends on the individual and there is no common answer for this.

If you are really seeking a *guru*, the moment you meet your *guru* you know that he is your *guru*, that's it. The *guru* is the one who never identifies himself as the *guru*. The *guru* doesn't say, 'I am a great master and I am here to teach you.' No true *guru* will say that. The moment that you meet a true *guru* and you become a disciple there is a difference, right? You make the difference. It's all the same because a *guru* never finds anybody else. There are no others for him.

When you stop your seeking and go to your *guru* and say, 'I am in ignorance, enlighten me,' the *guru* never finds that you are in ignorance. He knows that you just have the illusion that you are ignorant. So he never says, 'I am your *guru* and I am here to save you.' No true *guru* will say that. He never finds anybody else in the world; it is he who exists everywhere.

So the moment you make a *guru*-disciple relationship, it is always the disciple who makes the relationship, not the *guru*. For the *guru* there is no relationship because he never thinks of himself as the *guru*. The moment I say that I am the *guru* and you are the disciple, the Truth has vanished. The moment I say, 'I have the capacity to teach,' then the Truth has gone.

What I understand from talking with you is that it is just this moment now, it is just this very fresh moment. I can say that my whole experience of meeting you is like this.

I turned up at your house, you came out and then after a few minutes I said, 'How about an interview and a video?' and you said yes. It was so uncomplicated. Everything is simple. That is what I experience with you. It is simple and easy and you just decided in the moment. I was ready to come next week but now is the moment. You just do it now. And in the end it is just like that.

I don't know how it happened. It is happening, that is all.

Seekers often have curious ideas about the enlightened state. Please describe your typical day and how you perceive the world.

I never existed, I exist everywhere. Who is sitting in front of me and asking questions? There are no others here, only I exist here. Nobody else. If you want more humility, then I can say that God exists. If you don't like the term 'I', then we can say you are God and everything is God here. This I is very confusing for most people. They ask if it is a small I or a big I. (laughs) So we use the word God. God exists here, there is nothing else. It is single, there are not many here. This God exists here and that is it. You are God and I am God, rays of the same source. There is no difference at all. I don't find any difference.

I experience that you are mostly in peace. Are there also times when you feel very sad or angry or experience any other kinds of feelings?

I don't think that any of these strong feelings exist for me. I am laughing when I am scolding or am angry with someone else; that is the Truth, I enjoy that. But there is no real anger in that. This real anger I don't get unless someone really needs it. It is just a way of correcting people that need it, that's it. There is nothing there to be angry with. Everything is perfect so I don't feel any of these strong emotions. Everything I enjoy, being angry too. It's fine.

What about the* leela*, the divine play? Is your life a kind of* leela*?

It is a divine play, a *leela* only. It's only fun.

Only fun, whether you are having fun with anger or with bliss?

Fun itself is bliss. Bliss is fun. Realise nothing but the bliss.

Anger is also fun?

Anger is what those people perceive. So I say something harshly, change the tone, and they say that I am angry. It is not that I am angry. It is not an emotion. There is no anger.

If I talk like this (speaking softly) then the world interprets that I am talking softly and gently, but the moment I raise my voice then they say, 'Yes, she is angry.' It is what you perceive, it is not my actions. It is your idea, it is your reaction to my action, but there is no real anger. If

I am talking in a loud voice then you say, 'Oh! She is angry.' It is not Truth. It never happens because I don't want to talk in a loud voice. I know people who do that. No others exist for me but still they have a mind, so I can't be harsh to them. No other strong emotions for me, except fun. My whole life was full of this so many times. I found it a real problem for others. Maybe for my husband too!

All the time I was having fun. Nothing was serious in my life. The *leela*, as you call it, is so much in my life. (both laugh) Everything is fun.

Before we finish, is there anything else you would like to add?

Now you have all the answers maybe you would have prepared different questions! (both laugh) Am I not right?

Would you like me to find some other questions for you? Is there something we missed?

No. Did we miss something? Only you know.

Thank you.

Thank you too!

Samdarshi

It's not easy to be near the master, not easy. Only those come who really want to finish, to burn. Very few people come. They know: 'He is fire, he is death and if I come closer I will be finished.' But they want to finish, therefore they love him, they want to be with him. This can only happen with a living master.

There is only one desire that will finish all other desires: 'I want to know myself.'

Samdarshi

Samdarshi

Samdarshi was born in 1961 in Kanpur, northern India, as the oldest son of a cloth merchant. His spiritual search began at the age of twenty-one, triggered by the sudden death of his grandfather. In 1983 he took *sannyas* at Osho's *ashram* in Pune, India. After seven years of intense meditation and searching he became fully awakened. He has an *ashram* that attracts seekers from around the world to his Osho meditations and his Seven Steps to Enlightenment programme.

In the final moments, as this book was receiving its last touches on the beach in Goa, Samdarshi appeared and agreed to be included. I knew his master was Osho and that many of Osho's disciples spent time with him at his* ashram *in Manali.

Sri Ramana proposed the fundamental question, 'Who am I?' Who are you?

I would like to begin my answer by telling you how my inner journey began. I was a normal twenty-one year old boy, having everything, going to the movies, drinking. I had my own business, a clothes shop. Then one weekend, while I was visiting my parents, my grandfather had a heart attack and died.

When I was told he had left the body at first I felt I didn't have much attachment. In India we have a tradition. The body lies in the house and friends and relatives come. There was crying and much sadness, and all day, from eight in the morning till four in the afternoon, I was looking at this body. We bathed the body with curd, milk and water and I was looking very curiously and wondering, 'What is happening?'

Suddenly a very big shout came, 'Where is he going?' Everyone was quiet, wondering what was happening. Somebody said, 'Stop, Stop.' But I went on crying and crying. Then we took the body to the burning *ghat* (cremation ground), and, as we were preparing to burn the body, a question came, 'Hey, yesterday I met him in the evening and now he is finished and soon we will be burning him. Where did he go? I am now twenty-one years old and will die some day – so where will I go? What is this? I have heard we are consciousness, we are soul, we are part of God but I don't know anything. Who was I before? What was I? Who am I?'

These questions came, and for the next three days and nights I could not sleep. 'Who am I? Who am I? I want to know. What will happen when I die? What about before my birth? Where was I? Who was I?' These questions were very strong in me.

There was an Osho disciple renting a room in my house. He gave me a book which suggested doing one hour of meditation every day – only one hour – for fifteen days. On the sixteenth day you can do it or not, as you want. Just one hour for fifteen days, this I can do; it's no big thing. So I found a meditation centre. I was alone with the leader and he said, 'Just relax the body, relax the body.' And then something started happening here, started touching the third eye … a big roaring came and then after that, crying and crying.

Every day I was crying. After that I met Osho as my master. For eight years I asked this question and then Osho left the body. Just two and a half months later, the answer came. Then I knew what death is, what happens after death, what death means. When you know what death is, you know everything. You know who you are and that what you are cannot finish; it is always here, it will never go away, even after death. This can't be spoken about. There are no words which can catch it. There is only the experience; it is your nature. After this happened I went back to a normal life – family, business, shop.

Can you explain at all this knowing?

Knowingness at that moment happened. I left the body for maybe thirty minutes and then again I was back in the body – I came back. As I came back into the body, suddenly knowledge came about *Krishna*, about *Shiva*, about everyone – all the masters, what they are. These visions went on all night for six months.

After two years people slowly started coming to me. We held a three month camp in Kerala and from there we went to Arunachala for one week. I had not so much connection with Ramana Maharshi in the past, but as I sat in his cave I felt him. He just came. His presence. His essence – not presence – essence, what he is. Every master that I connect with came to me, *Krishna*, *Shiva*, Ramana.

The essence of* Krishna, *of* Shiva, *of Ramana – is it the same essence?

Yes, the same essence, same consciousness – consciousness is One. The body, the teaching, the way of talking can be different but the essence is One.

Many Western seekers come to India looking for enlightenment as if it is an experience. What is enlightenment?

Enlightenment is coming back to your nature. How do we go away from our nature? The mind creates emotional mind games and many thoughts. Society creates in us a false ego: 'You are a man. You are a woman. You are a doctor, an Indian, a Christian.' Slowly, slowly, one more identification and we begin to understand that this is what we are. All our identifications are from the outside; they are all false. This is ego. We don't really know ourselves, so nobody can be satisfied, relaxed. When we really want to know who we are, what we are really about, when the question 'Who am I?' comes like an arrow to the heart, then there is no rest, no relaxation.

Then you want to know: 'Yes, I am – but who?' When this question comes, then the real search has begun, and the day when the answer comes, that day we know everything; there are no more questions left. That is real satisfaction and relaxation. Then there is nobody to know. So this is what I call enlightenment. Be with yourself, come back to your nature. Your nature is just being present, being in this moment.

No mind – mind is finished. No movement. No future and no past. Whoever lives in the present comes to meditation. Meditation means being present, no mind. Living in this space, existence sees that you are ready, you are ripe, then one day it happens and then this beyond, this opening, starts.

Are there any qualifications for enlightenment? It seems you are suggesting that the qualification is to come into a still mind, no mind, and then you are ready for enlightenment.

When there is no mind you are almost enlightened. Almost. You are bliss – there is no mind, no ego. But still something is there: 'I've finished, ego is finished…' and this has to be finished also. One type of ego is *sabija,* which means 'with seed'. Bliss comes, but the seed of the mind and the ego is still there and can grow again. While the seed is still there it can grow and shrink again. So one more step is needed. *Nirbija* means 'without seed'. When one knows the Truth, then this seed goes out of the body and is burnt in space. Finished! This person never comes back.

Is* sadhana *(spiritual practice) necessary and if so, what form do you advise?

Sadhana is necessary because if you want to get somewhere, you have to take the inner journey. *Sadhana* has many forms: meditation, or, as Ramana suggested, asking 'Who is angry?' 'Who is happy?' Then slowly, slowly emptiness comes. Devotion and prayer are also techniques. Different types of pupils prefer different paths. It doesn't matter which path you take: all paths reach the peak of the mountain.

Everything is moving towards consciousness, even those who are not conscious, who never go to the temple, never meditate or pray or never take a master; even the trees and the rocks – they have a long, long journey. Those who are coming near to their centre are becoming more conscious about it – they do their *sadhana* journey and they start searching for it.

Sri Ramana said that Self-enquiry is the most direct route to realising the Self. What do you say about Self-enquiry? How to conduct Self-enquiry?

All *sadhana* is Self-enquiry. This question comes, 'Who am I?' I don't know, we don't know. 'Who am I?' This is enquiry. And for this, just remembrance is needed, always. If we can remember all the time, whatever we are doing, whatever is happening, just remember, watching, looking, watching it … then it is going right. Self-enquiry – all techniques, all *sadhana*, all paths – only one thing is important – Self remembering.

How can we remember? Through Self-enquiry you will remember, remembrance is coming. It doesn't matter which path you take, but all things, all inner journeys, all inner *sadhana*, have to depend on Self-rememberance. When remembrance is there, enquiry is not necessary. We only need to remember. That is already there, only we forget it because we are always outside, looking out. Nobody is telling us to look inside; nobody wants to look inside.

So, when someone is getting interested, slowly, he comes to Self-remembering. Be aware about it. The body is always present, so if we connect to the body and look at every action then we become very, very present. Whenever body energy and mind energy meet there will be a showering of joy that will be felt in the body as joy and bliss. This is a master technique to bring you to rememberance. Be fully with your body the whole day. Watch the body walking, working, eating, sleeping, everything. You will very, very quickly become present.

You told your own story, about standing at the gate of Osho's* ashram *and asking yourself, 'What do I really want?' And you told us, 'What I really want is to know who I am.' Could you say something about priority?

Yes. When you really want to know, and this 'Who am I?' question goes into your heart like an arrow, there is no relaxing. So it is a good thing, when you are going into *sadhana*, to always be satisfied with your circumstances on the outside. But never be satisfied inside until you are finished. When you make this your priority, 'I want to know myself,' no matter what you are doing on the outside, then the journey will happen very strongly. Always focus on *om* (sound of universal consciousness).

Having a master helps with making this a priority. His work is only to break your sleep – nothing else. He wants you to wake up and won't allow you to sleep. With a master also comes a *sangha*, people on the journey together – much easier. If your priority is to your inner search, then automatically your old friendships, based on outside pursuits, will drop away. The atmosphere around you is important and you will find friends with the same priorities.

What you were saying about being aware of the body through the whole day, whatever the activity, suggests that a spiritual journey can also happen in the ordinary life.

Yes, the ordinary life.

It doesn't have to be a special, spiritual journey?

No. As I said before, everyone, even those who don't know it, are on an inner search. Things happen more consciously to those who come near. Those who still have a very long journey are not conscious about it; they are busy with other things and even telling those who are going on this journey, 'You are crazy, you are wasting your time.' But those who are conscious and coming near, they are not listening to anyone. They are going on with it. Even if the whole world is saying to them, 'You are wrong, you are bad, you are wasting your time, you are crazy,' they don't listen.

I always say, 'Whatever you have, whatever you are doing, go on with it. Don't give up your family, don't lose your work, don't drop it, just go with you, but, be aware. Just remember yourself, remember what you are doing.' If you can take one or two hours every day to taste this rememberance, through Self-enquiry, then the taste will stay with you the whole day. Then there is no need to leave anything, no need to drop anything, no reason to run away from anything. Just go with whatever existence provides. Wherever you have to be, you be there and just go on with Self-enquiry, then automatically there will be remembrance.

When Sri Ramana was asked, 'When will the realisation of the Self be gained?' he replied, 'When the world which is what-is-seen has been removed, there will be realisation of the Self which is the seer.' What is the true understanding of the world? How to remove the world?

For anyone who has Self-remembering, anyone who is awakened, the world is nothing. They will say, 'When I close my eyes, the world is finished; when I open my eyes, I look in the world and the world is there.' But for them the world is finished because they don't have any mind, no relations, no emotions, nowhere to go, no attachment.

The world only exists for people because they have attachment. When you are attached to your wife, she is everything to you. When attachment goes, she is there, but your energy is not going there; it is finished. When someone is awakened, they don't have any attachment. They say, 'This world is like a dream, it is false. It is a drama, and in the next sixty years I will play many roles. I will be a husband, a father, a warrior, a child, a mother, and, like an actor in the movies, when the shooting is finished, the role is finished – no father, no mother, no warrior.'

When we realise, we know who we are. We know 'I am not the body, I am not the mind.' With this knowledge, how can I see the body as 'mine'? How can my wife be 'mine'? How can my husband be 'mine'? We are just playing roles. An awakened person knows 'I am not this,' so he can play the roles perfectly – father, husband, businessman, anything! He is just playful. Whatever existence provides, wherever he has to go, whatever he has to do, whatever his body has to do, he goes and plays – whenever he closes his eyes, nobody is there.

We only see the world when mind arises. When energy, attachment and greed are there, the world comes. But as the mind gets less, then the world goes; when mind is not there the world is totally finished. This does not mean you will not be in the world or in the room.

It has been suggested that the mind must be destroyed for liberation to occur. Do you have a mind? Sri Ramana used the term* manonasha *to describe the state of liberation, meaning destroyed mind. How to destroy the mind?

When enlightenment happens, the energy fully, one hundred percent, wakes up. How much capacity, how much power, has the mind? Its power is like one star in the sky, and consciousness or awareness is like the whole sky. So when the sky opens, when you become the sky, become the awareness, then the mind just blows, finished. Now, mind is everything, but when awareness comes, when consciousness happens totally, then the mind is like one tiny star in one little, little corner in the sky, and the sky is full of millions and millions of stars. Millions and millions of people in the world, millions of minds.

Mano means mind, *nasha* means finished, destroyed. Destroy the mind. You can ask: 'How can you talk, how can you work without a mind? You cannot even move the fingers; you need the mind. So what does it mean?' When there is awareness, the mind is like a star. Before, a star was everything; now, the sky is everything, unlimited, it is me, and the star, the mind, is very, very tiny. The mind works, but I am not the mind. I am very, very much more. So, when the mind is tiny, we say that the mind is almost finished. It has no power any more as it has been destroyed.

What about* vasanas, *the tendencies of the mind? Must these be removed before Self-realisation can become permanent? Is it enough to achieve a* sattvic *(calm and peaceful) state of mind and to know one's* vasanas *so that they no longer bind? How to remove the* vasanas*?

Vasanas means desires. The mind is a machine that produces desires, endless desires. But when we go on our inner journey, doing *sadhana*, slowly, slowly the mind goes and we become more and more conscious. As this happens, the desires become less. When desires are becoming less, automatically life becomes more *sattvic*. More Truth, more purification will come. When purification comes then you eat as much as you need, you know how much sleep you need, how much you need to talk, to work. You know. Everything becomes systematic, perfect. Disorder is finished. Life is happening, *sadhana* is happening.

There is only one desire that will finish all other desires: 'I want to know myself.' *Vasanas*, desires; it is their nature never to be fulfilled. Automatically, when you have the desire, 'I want to be more conscious,' other desires will finish. As this desire becomes stronger, other desires become less and less. Your mind is like the wax of a candle, the wick inside like your inner Self. When you want to burn yourself, burn your mind, the master comes and lights the wick. He will set you on fire. Now you have to burn. This fire, this flame, slowly burns the wax – the desires – and the candle grows smaller and smaller until the last moment when the wax is totally finished. The wax is finished, the wick is finished, the flame also is finished. Everything is finished.

So the *vasanas* go away and gradually your life becomes *sattvic*, pure. Pureness comes into your work, your behaviour, your eating. And then one day it happens: everything is pure and the flame is finished. The one who wants to know is also finished. Nobody is there to say, 'I am enlightened.' Nobody is there to be enlightened. Many people nowadays are saying, 'I want to be enlightened.' They think that wanting to be enlightened means something. You might want to be the president, or a hero, or an actor, but enlightenment is totally another thing. Instead of saying 'I want to be enlightened,' say 'I want to finish. I want to die.' Then you are on the right path and then you will not stop until the end.

Otherwise, when you have a little blessing or something good happening, you might say, 'Yes, I got it. I am finished.' So, whatever comes, remember, 'Not this, nor this, nor this.' Go on until nobody is there to say, 'Not this.' Then it's right! With this, much purification is coming, and with this purification negative energy becomes positive. One day, this positivity becomes total.

At the end of his book,* Self-Enquiry, *Sri Ramana says, 'He who is thus endowed with a mind that has become subtle, and who has the experience of the Self is called a* jivanmukta.*' Is this the state that can be called Self-realised?

He goes on, 'And when one is immersed in the ocean of bliss and has become one with it without any differentiated existence, one is called a* videhamukta. *It is the state of* videhamukti *that is referred to as the transcendental* turiya *(state). This is the final goal.' Is this the state that can be called enlightenment?

Yes.

Good. (laughs) There is some confusion as to whether enlightenment is one, or if in fact there are stages of enlightenment.

There are not stages of enlightenment. The body has seven *chakras* (energy centres). The fourth *chakra* is the heart *chakra*. After the fourth *chakra*, the blessings start, going out of the body starts. So if anybody reaches the fifth *chakra* he is blessed, fully blessed. He knows himself, Self is there. At this stage, he knows the mind is finished; no mind, no ego, no me, no I. But there is still a tiny seed which has the capacity to again become ego.

In the sixth *chakra*, the third eye is open. Here, one's vision is open and the Truth is known. Enlightenment happens in the sixth *chakra*. Someone in the sixth *chakra* is saying he is finished, but there is still a little bit more to go. People in these two *chakras* are cosmic, universal; they know everything. They are in the bliss body. A sixth *chakra* person can come back one more time if he wants, if he has a strong desire to share and give something to the world.

Reaching the seventh *chakra*, *nirvana* (I-less state), is very, very rare. If someone jumps directly from the heart *chakra* to *nirvana*, they cannot come back! Perhaps they have already been in the fifth and sixth *chakras* in a previous life. This is called enlightenment; really nothing is there.

At the end of his life, Osho was talking about beyond enlightenment.

Enlightenment will also be finished; nobody is there to say, 'I am enlightened.' This is really the stage of *nirvana*. And this one never comes back. So living in these three stages, *chakras*, is living at the same peak. All are the bliss body but their way of working, their quality, is different. One who is in the bliss body doesn't go to people, he just sits there and those who want, come, those who don't want don't come.

We've been discussing meditation, Self-enquiry – doing something that brings me to a moment of knowing. I think that after some point there's nothing to do.* Nirvana *comes or it doesn't come. Is that right?

After the heart *chakra*, doing is finished. Doing only works up until the fourth *chakra*, where there is still mind. After that there is nothing in your hands. You will be bliss, like an *avatar* (incarnated god) or a *bodhisattva* (enlightened being), or you will be a very big master; nobody can know. When the third eye is open, one slowly, slowly, automatically, goes to *nirvana*.

Only grace is working.

Grace is working. It is all written in your seed. Perhaps the seed will grow into a small plant or perhaps it will be a very big tree and many people will come to take shade. Everything is written in your blueprint.

The title of this book is* Blueprints for Awakening. *Are you saying that this blueprint is in our seed?

Yes, it is written there, which type of flower will come, which type of tree will come, how big it will be. When we started our journey it was already written. Enlightenment is when this seed is open. The seed knows, 'I'm the seed.' It doesn't know what it has inside, how much will happen when it breaks open. As long as the mind is saying; 'Yes, I am this, I am that, I am doing this,' doing is still there. As the seed opens, as the mind is finished, reality is experienced, then nobody can say what will happen. This is totally existential; it is written in the seed what has to happen to you. Those who understand this are very relaxed because they know there is no doer. Automatically things happen. Whatever happens, they enjoy.

If we want to put some names to the highest level, this* nirvana*, we can easily agree on Buddha, Jesus, Lao Tzu. If we look more recently, say to the last hundred years, which names would you suggest?

In the last one or two hundred years there was Sri Ramana Maharshi. Just a few years before him was Shirdi Sai Baba, not the Sai Baba who is still living, but the one who has left the body.

And what about Ramakrishna?

Ramakrishna also. Five hundred years before there were many, such as Kabir and Farid.

And do you put Osho there?

Osho is surely there, fully there. After my opening I knew what Osho was, how he took care, because at that moment you are like a new baby. Actually he is not doing anything, but existentially he will totally take care.

Do you think there are unknown people living in* nirvana*, living in the forests and on the mountainsides, alone?

Yes, very possible. It has happened. Sometime you might see a beggar lying on the road. His clothes are dirty and torn, and his body smells. It is very difficult for him to move, even to open his eyes. We call these people *paramhamsa*. They have a thousand suns shining inside. They have no mind. Even to open the eyes you need a mind. This can happen but it is very rare.

It appears essential to meet a* guru *and surrender to that* guru*. Who is the* guru*? What is the* guru*'s role? How to recognise a true* guru*?

As I said before, we have seven *chakras*. The *guru* can happen in every *chakra*. If someone has awakened in the third *chakra*, he will attract people who have only reached the third *chakra*. Every *chakra* has masters; whichever *chakra* we are in tune with, we will find the right master. The ego can only dissolve with one whose ego is finished, whose mind has totally disappeared. Your heart will say: 'Yes, I am at the right place, I am at the perfect place.' Where the ego is melted, where you feel totally relaxed, the mind is going to stop. Automatically, we find the right master.

Would you say that when you are ready the* guru *comes?

The *guru* comes to you or you come to the *guru*; both are happening. The master appears if you are ready! The master is already here, but you are not ready for him. When you are thirsty the rain will start. The master, the *guru* is always here – the disciple has only to open the eyes and look. As much as you are ready for, you get – no more, no less. Existence is very just.

There is a story about a man who told his family: 'I want to meet a master, I am going now to search for a master.' As he crossed his village he came to a big tree and an old man was sitting there. He asked, 'You are very old and have knowledge, how can I recognise a real master?'

The old man told him the master would have a beard and long hair and would be wearing a certain type of clothes. He explained everything. So the man said, 'Thank you,' and went travelling.

Thirty years after he comes back and he sees this man. He has the same hair, same beard, same clothes and then he looks: 'This is my village, this is the same tree,' but this man is looking different, older. Then he is a bit angry with him and he says, 'You are my master.'

'Yes, I am your master.'

'But why didn't you tell me this thirty years ago when I asked you the question?'

He said, 'I told you everything; I told you "He has a beard like this, he has clothes like this, he has eyes like this, he talks like this." I spoke about myself, but your eyes were looking somewhere else. You were not ready. So, at last I said, "You follow your nose," and you took thirty years to recognise me.'

And the man said, 'You have wasted thirty years of my life.'

'You are talking about your thirty years, what about my thirty years? At that time I was sixty years old and now I am ninety years old and I was only waiting for you to come back!' (all laugh)

What is the* guru's *role?

The real *guru* is awakened; his ego has gone and he has only one role. Only one work is happening through him; to wake everyone up. Those who want to wake up come to him; they want to be with him and they enjoy him. Then the work starts. We cannot have any ideas about how the master should be: 'He should do this, he should not speak like this, he should not eat this, he should work like this.' He wants to break all our ideas and conditioning because this is how he breaks the mind. Naturally, when this starts, the mind freaks out and judgement comes. But the master is only doing his job. Existence is giving its message through him, and through the *guru* people can recognise and remember themselves. They remember existence.

Here in India there is a clear tradition of coming to the* guru*, but in the West people have been told, 'You can be your own* guru.*' They have a different kind of mind and they have the strong idea, 'I can do it myself. I am my own* guru.*'

Yes, this is very strong conditioning. From childhood they are taught 'I, I, I'. The spiritual journey is to finish the 'I'. As I said before, the ego can only melt with one whose ego is already finished. In India, the conditioning is, 'Without a master, it's impossible. Who can take me there?' Without a master it is impossible. At a certain level your ego keeps coming back. To stop the ego a master is needed.

In India the conditioning is to bow down to anybody. Germans, for example, who have no conditioning for this, would fight it: 'No, I don't accept this, I don't want to do it.' So if a German were to touch the feet, then it is very genuine. When this surrender happens it is real surrender.

Is it important to have a living master?

It is very important to have a living master, then fire is there. Something happens in his aura, in his energy field; it's very strong. If you want to go on this journey, you have to follow him, if you trust him. With him, your conditioning no longer works. But without him, nobody is there to break the ideas, the *samskara*, the conditioning. A living master is like an oven in a room. The fire is burning and making you warm, producing heat. A picture of a master cannot give you this heat. This is the master's love. He is saying, 'I am the love, I am the fire, I am the death. You just be with me.'

It's not easy to be near the master, not easy. Only those come who really want to finish, to burn. Very few people come. They know: 'He is fire, he is death and if I come closer I will be finished.' But they want to finish, therefore they love him, they want to be with him. This can only happen with a living master. So always, wherever consciousness is, wherever the flame is burning, just go, at any cost. Whatever you have to pay, pay it, but be there.

Ramana's devotees had tremendous devotion to him and he to Arunachala. Please say something about* bhakti, *devotion, in the pursuit of awakening.

Most masters, both Eastern and Western, say 'Follow me, drink me, eat me, be with me, open your heart.' The drinking and eating only happen as much as the heart is open to him. The closer you are to him, the more open you will be to him. So, when you are open, this *bhakti* way, the way of devotion, is the most easy way. No need to do anything, just be with the master. Be with him, follow him and be open to him. When you are open, this energy is coming, this light is coming, his light is coming to you. *Tantra* (path of uniting masculine and feminine) says, 'When all meditation is finished, where meditation ends, there surrender begins.' All meditation, all effort, is to come to this surrender. Heart people take the path of devotion, mind people take the path of *sadhana*: searching, searching, searching. Both have to be developed.

Your heart has to be open and your mind has to be awakened also. Then the right journey happens.

Devotion is a very beautiful path. Ramana Maharshi's devotees knew only devotion. At the peak of devotion you can feel the master. It is not you looking, it is the master looking through you; you are not walking, it is the master walking; when you eat, it is him eating. So, devotion is very easy. I work with Westerners and Indians. If Indians don't cry they feel nothing is happening. They want to cry and bow down. For a Westerner it is difficult to cry. They even feel crying means something is not okay.

Everybody wants devotion, but everybody has mind. When we are in the mind it is 'I, I, I' and when we are in devotion it is 'you, you, you'. Some people are more heart and some more mind and everybody also has both. In the mind: I don't need anything; I am my own master; I can do everything. In the heart: I cannot do anything; I want to follow someone who can show me. Be like a child – always playful, nothing to worry about, everything happening moment to moment. As mind comes there is more feeling of responsibility, more 'I' feeling, more seriousness.

Seekers often have curious ideas about the enlightened state. Please describe your typical day and how you perceive the world.

Yes, people have many, many ideas; an enlightened person should walk like this, talk like this, work like this. But these are only their ideas; they don't know. They only understand when someone touches their heart. When someone opens your heart then all ideas are finished. A person must be open before the master can begin his real work with them. So before he begins cutting away the conditioning he first says, 'Come, come,' and he supports their ideas. As they become open he can clean the slate, ready for writing. Sometimes an opening will happen, sometimes not.

Could you say anything about sex? Is it possible for enlightened people to have sex?

For them, everything is possible. But why would an enlightened person want sex? Orgasm is desirable because at that moment there is no time, no mind, no ego. Everybody wants to go there. Inside, in the *hara* (energetic body-centre), just above the sex centre, there is *kundalini*, the life energy. Everyone is living in the mind and when we have sex we slowly, slowly come down. When we reach orgasm we pass and just touch the *hara*, just touch our centre. Just a little touch, a little shake and we feel so much joy that we want it again. This is why there is so much desire for sex. An enlightened person's *hara* is totally open and awakened. So twenty-four hours a day they are at this peak with no time, no mind, no ego. If they are there they have no need for sex and so they don't go there.

It is possible; they can do it. *Krishna* was born enlightened, born like a god, but he married and had two sons; *Shiva* also had two sons. Kabir was enlightened and he married an enlightened woman. They married because they wanted to live together and this is difficult without being married. They had a son and a daughter who were also enlightened. The whole family was enlightened.

Enlightenment means 'flying like a bird'. Having sex means coming to the body, back to the ground. The enlightened person knows, 'If I come to the ground then I touch all the emotions.' With sex comes greed, jealousy, anger. So they don't want to come to the ground in the body, they come in the heart. Heart to being. Sex is totally first *chakra*. Usually they only come as far as the fourth *chakra*, the heart *chakra*. They don't want to touch the emotions so they don't leave their space for sex.

You have given us a profound discourse on awakening. When you meet someone with a passion for awakening, what would be your short advice?

If one has a passion and is ready, it is a different thing from just having a passion. Passion says: 'I want, I want in a hurry.' My advice to someone with passion is, 'Okay, sit down and be here. You will get it. But don't be in a hurry. You have to be more relaxed, more present because when you are in a hurry you are not present.' Mind is always looking to the future: 'When I get…'

For someone who is very ready there is no advice. He doesn't even ask your advice; he just says, 'I am with you. What will happen will happen.' For him it will surely happen. However open one is, this much they will receive. Whatever each needs, they get. Everybody is different. Everyone has the same question but there is no ready-made answer. The answer will depend on what each person needs. I don't know what answer will come in the moment.

Just ten days ago a man in *Satsang* (meeting in Truth) had a *satori*, a glimpse of consciousness. He asked me, 'Can you give me this, show me this?' So I said, 'Okay, just sit, come every day and sit. Be patient. Accept whatever happens without complaint. Say, "If it is not happening yet, I am not ready yet."' It will happen when you are ready. It cannot be late!

Is there anything you wish to add?

It was a wonderful conversation – good questions, good answers. I enjoyed it very much.

Thank you, thank you. (laughs)

Swami

Satchidananda

Ramana wants us to find out who we really are. His question, 'Who am I?' is to clarify that we are not the body, mind, intellect and senses, but the Self.
If we realise that, we have realised everything.

We are eternal; we are deathless and we are birthless.

Swami Satchidananda

Swami Satchidananda

After a period of trials and struggles in his early life, Satchidananda met Papa Ramdas when he was thirty. He became a *sannyasin* and, having served Papa Ramdas until he left his body, he assisted Mataji Krishnabai in running Ananda Ashram in North Kerala. In 1989, when Mataji left the body, Satchidananda inherited the mantle of running the *ashram*. True to the divine wish of beloved Papa and Mataji, Swamiji, with his exemplary qualities, has become the guiding spirit of the *ashram*.

Swami Satchidananda is a man of unconditional love. We met one quiet evening in 2003 and spent a beautifully intimate time together making this interview. In the years that followed, I have brought many to meet him and all have been touched by his grace. Despite a stroke, he has continued to live an inspiring life. I am profoundly touched that it was he who gave me the name Premananda – unconditional love.

Swami, Sri Ramana proposed the fundamental question, 'Who Am I?' Can I ask you, who are you?

I am not sure if I am capable of dealing with Ramana Maharshi's teachings, all the same I shall try. Ramana Maharshi's approach is direct. He always puts the question, 'Who am I?' This answers all the questions. If we understand what we are, we have nothing more to ask.

We identify ourselves with the body, mind, intellect and senses; that is a wrong identification. Actually we are the Self, that which controls all these things. Ramana wants us to find out who we really are. His question, 'Who am I?' is to clarify that we are not the body, mind, intellect and senses, but the Self. If we realise that, we have realised everything.

Can I ask who you are?

I am That. (both laugh)

That is the correct answer, thank you! Many Western seekers come to India looking for enlightenment as if it is an experience. What is enlightenment?

Enlightenment: we can call it the realisation of the Self. We are in a state of darkness, we are groping in darkness, we want to see light. How to get into this light? We are actually light ourselves, only we have forgotten what we really are. Self-enquiry will lead us to that light. To know ourselves is enlightenment.

Are there any qualifications for enlightenement?

The qualification for enlightenment is absolute purity of the mind. When the mind becomes absolutely pure, the mind as such does not exist. Then enlightenment comes. The mind, with all its dirt, thoughts and *vasanas* (tendencies of the mind), is standing in the way of our knowing what we really are. If the mind is made perfectly pure then we are face-to-face with the Truth, or rather we are one with the Truth.

Would you suggest a period of* sadhana *(spiritual practice) to purify the mind?

Of course. There are various methods and various *sadhanas*. Our master, Ramdas, and other teachers say that if we take up chanting the name of God it will gradually cleanse the mind of all its dirt and make it pure. With the pure mind we can see the light of God. When we first take up this chanting we feel that God is separate from us, we give Him a separate personality and we consider ourselves as His children, His servants, or something different from Him.

This type of devotion, solely to Him, will purify the mind. We consider Him as our mother or our master, we serve Him and dedicate our life entirely to Him, and we think about Him day and night. Whatever we do, we do for His sake, and whatever we think it must be about Him. Moreover we consider that everything is Him in different forms, this way we will be immersed in thoughts of Him only. This constant thinking of Him will perfectly purify our mind and prepare us for His revealing Himself in us. That is the easiest and safest *sadhana*, as prescribed by our master.

In fact, he did that* sadhana *himself for a number of years.

Yes. I just put it in a simple way, but the chanting of God's name gradually makes us feel His presence within us and without us, everywhere. You start feeling His presence everywhere, that He alone is in every action and that His power is absolute. That will help us understand that anything happening in the universe, through this body or that body or any other body, is happening by His will alone; it is a perfect surrender to His will. Master used to say that constant remembrance of God and perfect surrender to His will creates God-realisation.

So the ego, in the sense that it is separate, simply melts away?

That's right. The ego has no place there. When God is in the picture, ego disappears. As long as we are in intense remembrance of God, ego cannot enter, it disappears through the back door. But when we stop remembering Him it enters again. (both laugh)

Would you say that a spiritual ego eradicates the ordinary ego?

In the final stage we can say that it is the spiritual ego, but in the other stages it is the troublesome ego which is an obstruction to our realising God. But the spiritual ego also has to disappear when our mind is perfectly purified and when we don't want it anymore.

Having realised our oneness with God we do maintain a sort of ego, our individuality, but it is perfectly purified and absolutely harmless. It is purely for the sake of playing this game, this *leela* (divine play) of God.

After realisation you know your position as a child, look upon God as your mother and happily engage yourself in day-to-day activities.

Hearing you say this, I feel very blessed in deciding to make this project – meeting and speaking with great masters. I find that each one is expressing God, and yet each does it in their own very individual way. It's the same Truth but experienced and described in different, unique ways.

That's true, because God is infinite. He is a diamond of many facets. We only see Him through one facet and we can only explain about this one facet. People experience Him in different ways and express these different experiences in their own language. And nobody can say that we have understood Him completely because He is infinite.

You mention* leela*, divine playfulness. Could you say something more about* leela*?

That is the way devotees look at the world. They do not consider the world as an illusion or non-existent, they consider the world to be God playing His eternal drama. He has assumed innumerable forms to play this drama: He Himself is every player. And in the innumerable parts that He has taken, He has assumed individuality in every form. He forgets that He is Himself in these different forms, because of *maya* (illusion of the conditional world), His own illusionary power. So He plays this eternal drama taking innumerable parts Himself. And who is the witness to this great drama? He Himself is the witness, and His drama goes on eternally. That is the way that devotees look upon it.

We see before us concrete forms and we cannot deny that they exist; we have to deal with them. So we appreciate what the devotees say about the *leela* of God. But *jnanis* (ones who have realised the Self), those who have been following the path of Self-enquiry, say that He doesn't exist at all, that He is just a creation of the mind.

The game is ever changing, what happens this minute is different to what happens the next minute. It is an eternally changing game.

Would you say that the world is a war between good and evil, and the divine* leela *plays through both?

It is the divine *leela* only. In the divine *leela* everything is permitted. In the drama we have tragedies and comedies and we appreciate every part played. If one person plays the part of a robber and he does it well, when he comes out of the drama we can congratulate him, 'Oh! You have done your part very well!' In this *leela* everything is possible and everything is necessary.

The question will arise: Why should there be suffering in the world? And the answer is: Who is suffering? If we find out who we are then there is no suffering. Say someone is playing the part of a robber and a policeman comes along and shoots him, the robber falls down on the stage; is he really dying? It affects only the external body, not his soul.

We are eternal; we are deathless and we are birthless. We have taken a body which has a birth and grows, which becomes a corpse and decays. What happens? The body doesn't affect us really, this is why it is called the eternal *leela* of God.

There are different answers about the existence of the world. Some call it illusion and some call it a manifestation of God. God Himself manifests in different forms. They say the forms are consciousness solidified. Like an iceberg. What is an iceberg? It is water in a different form, solidified. This is called ice; it is not different.

So the universe of names and forms is not different from the Self, or Truth or reality. He Himself appears as names and forms, the names and forms are not different from Him just as the ice is not different from water. That is why they say that everything is God. In the scriptures they say, *sarvam kavitam brahman*, everything is *Brahman* (absolute reality), there is nothing but *Brahman*. Because of ignorance we see them as diverse things, but when our vision is purified, we see them as forms of God Himself.

Sri Ramana said that Self-enquiry is the most direct method to realise the Self. What do you say about Self-enquiry? I understand that here in your* ashram *the focus is on devotion.

Self-enquiry is one approach, it is a direct approach, but there are other methods too, like the path of devotion. There are many types of devotion. In our case we chant the names of God. We say *Om Sri Ram, Jay Ram, Jay Jay Ram. Ram* stands for the Supreme Being, *Om* is the Supreme Being that is everything and beyond everything. *Ram* is the substratum for this manifestation and *Sri* is the manifestation itself, the power of manifestation. So *Om Sri Ram* covers everything: the Supreme Being, the sub-stratum for the manifestation and the manifestation itself.

When we are chanting *Ram Ram*, we are thinking of the Supreme Being and all that is beyond everything. When we keep thinking that, our mind is taken away from all wordly thoughts and becomes perfectly purified. The purpose of our spiritual practice is only for purifying our mind, taking away all the dirt that has been accumulated over the ages.

So when a person chants sincerely does there come a time when the mind empties and becomes* sattvic *(calm and peaceful)?

Yes, yes. They should do it with concentration, that is important you see. The chanting alone is not sufficient, they must do it with love, devotion and concentration. We chant the name but our mind may be thinking of something else. That is why they say that when you are chanting the name you must keep the mind fixed on the attributes of God. That He is all-pervading, that He has become the entire universe, that He transcends everything and that He is seated in everybody's heart; these are the attributes of God. We can also say that He is all love, all compassion and all mercy.

These things must be working in our minds so that our minds do not stray from the path or think about material things. If this is done the progress will be very fast and the mind will become very pure.

And when somebody stops doing the chanting, does their mind come back?

It comes back until it is perfectly purified. When it is perfectly purified then it has nothing to think of and it can stay quiet for quite a long time. We are all trying to attain this stillness of the mind, it is in the still mind that God reveals Himself.

When Sri Ramana was asked, 'When will the realisation of the Self be gained?' he replied, 'When the world which is what-is-seen has been removed, there will be realisation of the Self which is the seer.' What is the true understanding of the world?

The world we see now is full of diversity. We must practise seeing the unifying force, the unifying spirit that is the substratum for this entire manifestation. That is the Self, the reality, God, or whatever name you may give it. Just like in the cinema the wide screen is the substratum for this manifestation, and what is going on here in this universe is the film, the moving picture. It is always moving but the screen is permanent, just as the substratum is permanent.

If we know that what we see in the world is moving and if we find that which is not moving, then we have realised the Truth and we do not see the world as such. We see it only as a moving thing within the unmoving or immutable existence. Then the world has a different shape for us, we don't see it as diversity, we see it as one.

Jnanis do not say that they don't see the world. They are moving, they are seeing, they are talking, they are talking to others, they cannot say that they don't see the world at all. They see the world but they don't see it as the world. They see it as moving names and forms on the immutable existence. Devotees use another language: they see the world as God Himself.

Our master, Ramdas, wrote a book; he called it *World is God*. Others see the world as world, but saints see the world as God.

How to remove the world?

We don't remove the world. We see the substratum, which we see is God, and we see the world as God. The world as world is removed and the world as God remains. The world does not change. Except of course when we sit in sacred *samadhi* (absorption in the Self). When we sit in meditation we lose our body consciousness and merge with the unmanifest aspect of God for a short while. We merge with our own Self. There the world does not exist for us. But when we come back to world consciousness we see the world, and at that same time we maintain that stillness and peace absolute. This is the state of all the saints. The world does not run away from us, the world is still very much with us but in a different form.

This is a very important statement because it has been suggested that the mind must be destroyed for liberation to occur.

It is not destroying the mind, it is purifying the mind. When the mind is purified of all the dirt, the tendencies and the desires, it is *atman* (the individual aspect of the Self) itself.

Can I ask you, do you have a mind?

I have not become a *jivanmukta* (liberated soul in this life) yet. (both laugh)

Nobody here will believe you.

It's a fact! When the thoughts completely disappear and the mind is completely immersed in God, then we can say that we have realised the Truth. But until then we have no authority to say that.

How to destroy the mind? Self-enquiry is one of the best spiritual practices prescribed, or we can chant the name of God. With this practice, purification takes place: all the thought waves disappear and the mind becomes perfectly pure. It is not destroying the mind, it is purifying the mind.

What about* vasanas, *the tendencies of the mind?

They all have to go before we can realise the Truth, they are the dirt accumulated during the ages.

Do you mean that these* vasanas *have come with us into this life?

We must have accumulated them for ages. We come with all those *vasanas* and we may add some more and carry them forward, and it goes on until the whole thing is destroyed.

And how to destroy the* vasanas*?

When we have made the mind pure and realised that we are one with absolute Truth, then the *vasanas* are all destroyed. This is the only way.

So in a sense it is a constant purification?

Yes, it is a constant struggle to keep the mind perfectly pure.

At the end of his book,* Self-Enquiry, *Sri Ramana says, 'He who is thus endowed with a mind that has become subtle and who has the experience of the Self is called a* jivanmukta.*' Is this the state that can be called Self-realised?

That's right, it's called Self-realised.

He goes on 'And when one is immersed in the ocean of bliss and has become one with it without any differentiated existence one is called a* videhamukta.*'

As far as I understand, they say *jivanmukta* is a soul realised while in the body and *videhamukta* is a soul realised at the time of leaving the body. I may be right or I may be wrong, but as far as I understand this is the difference.

Death alone does not liberate. Death of this particular body does not give us liberation; what has to die is the ego. The physical form, the mind, intellect and senses, all these bodies must go, and only then are we fully liberated. But when this physical body dies we carry the other bodies with us; the astral body, the mind and the intellect. We are not completely dead, we have only dropped one part of our body, so we are not liberated souls.

And then we take up another body?

Until we take up another body we remain as the subtle body, the astral body. Then we come back as a child and bring back with us all that we have accumulated in previous births; we grow up and work these things out in our life.

How can we tell who is a* jivanmukta *and who is not a* jivanmukta*?

It is difficult for others to understand, it is difficult for us.

We would all say that you are a* jivanmukta *yet you say you are not.

That's right. It is difficult for others to understand. We ourselves don't know if this is the case or not the case.

Can you give some guidelines for this state of* jivanmukti*?

The guidelines are these: when we know that we are the all-pervading reality and we are one with everything in the universe, when we are no longer bound by the ego, then we have become *jivanmukta*s and we are realised souls. But when we see another person as different to us, 'Oh! I am nothing to do with him!' then we are in the small self, the ego-controlled life. That is not *mukti* or *jivanmukti*, that is ignorance.

We have to get out of ignorance, break out of the small self and embrace the entire universe and beyond as our own. We can know ourselves, it is not difficult. A bird in a cage knows that he is in a cage, but when the cage is open he flies about and enjoys freedom. This we can enjoy.

As I have been travelling to make these interviews the teachers I meet seem to have some common attributes. There is availability, a stillness

and peacefulness, even a playfulness, a* leela *about them which seems to set them aside from other people.

Yes. This is naturally so when they are one with the entire universe; these teachers are not bound by the ego and all the pairs of opposites that had been troubling them. They are not affected by the play of God in the universe, so they take everything easy. Suppose you come and abuse me, why should your words affect me? I am unaffected by all these things. I am not burned by fire, water cannot wet me. I am the Self.

They say that Buddha had so much patience that when somebody started abusing him, using filthy language, he just continued smiling. And when his abuser's vocabulary was exhausted, Buddha said:

'My dear friend, suppose you offer me an apple and I don't accept it, where will it be?'

'The apple will remain with me.'

Buddha said, 'So whatever you have said, I do not accept it.'

They have that much patience. They don't feel that abuse, or anything else, in any way affects them because they are identifying themselves with the Self only, whereas we are identifying ourselves with the body. That is the only difference.

So when you see me sitting here, do you see me as the Self?

We see the body plus the substratum. We see that everything in the universe is based on the substratum that is Self. So when we are progressing on the path our vision gradually changes, and when we are finally established in the Self we are completely changed.

Are you saying there is a gradual movement into the depth of the Self?

That's right, according to the purification of our mind. When we wear very dark glasses everything we see is dark. As the tint becomes gradually less and less, slowly we see everything clearer. When our vision is perfectly clear we realise the Truth and we see everything as it really is.

I always thought that there was an 'Aha!' moment when this realisation comes. But you are saying that it is a gradual process.

It is a gradual process but when you finally get it, it is sudden – 'Oh! I am That.' You are still the same thing, and appear to be the same thing as before, only before you did not know that you are That. That is with us but we don't know that it is with us, and we don't know that we are peace and bliss-absolute ourselves. When the dirt is removed, we see we are That and we have been That always.

It is just like a man who has a heavy purse in his pocket but has forgotten all about it.

He says, 'I have no money at all. I am a beggar.'

Someone comes to him and says, 'You forgot about all those coins in your pocket.'

He puts his hand in his pocket, 'Oh! I have a lot of money, I am a wealthy man!'

That is what we are doing now. We are bliss itself and we are pretending that we are miserable creatures in this world. The *guru* comes and tells us we are not miserable, we are peace and bliss-absolute; we have just forgotten. Meditate on That and you will be able to realise your own Self, which is absolute immortal peace and bliss.

Are you saying that if we have purified the mind and we are ready, when the* guru *comes and tells us who we are, then there is this 'Aha!' moment, which is recognition of Truth?

That's correct.

And after that moment of recognition we see clearly but there is still a deepening of the realisation?

One who has realised the Truth and his oneness with the all-pervading reality can say, 'I am bliss myself.' But there is still another state. He has not accepted the entire universe as the form of God or as his own manifestation.

When you are in the state beyond body consciousness and you are immersed in the Self, you have the most blissful experience, oblivious to external things. This is called *nirvikalpa samadhi*. When you come out of it you are once more mixing with the world. You have not accepted the world as the form of God and as the form of your own Self, so the mind is disturbed and wants to go back to that stillness. But after further spiritual practices you realise that the manifestation is your own, and it is not different from you. You can live and move in the world accepting everything as God Himself. That is *sahaja samadhi*, absorbed in natural being. When you are fully established in it you are full of peace, whether you are active or still.

So are you saying that the 'Aha!' moment is Self-realisation and full establishment in the Self is enlightenment? Are you saying that they are two different states?

You accept the entire universe as the manifestation of God and you become established in That.

You would call that enlightenment?

That is full enlightenment. Those who have realised the Truth, but have not accepted the universe as the manifestation of their own Self, as God, they still can be called *jivanmuktas* for they are liberated souls. When their ego has merged in the *paramatman* (supreme soul) or the *parabrahman* (supreme universal Truth) and there are no more rebirths, they can be called realised souls. But the fullest realisation is to accept the universe as the manifestation of God. Then they live as free, liberated souls, though apparently they are like ordinary people. You cannot find any difference in them except that they are always blissful. That is the *sahaja samadhi.*

And that is the natural state of a human being?

That is the natural state.

So there is nothing really special in this?

There is absolutely no effort for fully realised souls. Whatever they do is spontaneous. They have completely eradicated the ego, it is gone! God alone is working through them. There is no 'I' there. The small 'I' has gone completely.

And would you say that this is very rare and that there are very few people who achieve this?

Very, very rare. It is the highest attainment and very few persons are that. I know of two. I had the great privilege to live with them for some time – Ramdas and Mother Krishnabai.

Can you suggest some other people who come into this category?

It is very difficult, it is not easy to recognise them. The only way to recognise them is if many people go to them for advice, help and peace. When we go to them and sit at their feet, somehow our mind becomes still and all the waves disappear because of their influence. When someone has that experience and endless peace is dawning in them, then we can say that this is a *jivanmukta*, a realised soul, and he is in *sahaja samadhi*; he is absorbed in natural being. That is the only way we can find out.

So is it possible that there are many others that we don't know about, who are just living very simple ordinary lives and not attracting attention?

There may be, unknown to the world. But where there is a drop of honey, there are ants.

We are the ants! (laughs)

They cannot avoid it.

***It appears essential to meet a* guru *and stay with that* guru. *Who is the* guru? *What is the* guru's *role? How to recognise a* guru?**

It is essential for people on the path to get real guidance from a realised person. He is called the *guru*. But to find the *guru*, as I told you, it is not easy. We may see many people approaching him and adoring him, so we can also go there and sit at his feet in all humility. Then we will experience peace and bliss radiating from him and we can say that he is the one that can be trusted and who can guide us. I can then say I will accept him as my *guru* and serve him and love him and take guidance from him.

But we should not stay with him too long. When we stay with him too long we start finding faults. First we consider him divine, but if we stay with him for too long we start seeing faults, and then we see him only as a human being. That is not good for the spiritual aspirant. So stay with the *guru* for some time and then go away and practise independently, alone somewhere. That is more beneficial. But come to the *guru* often for guidance.

You are not suggesting going to another* guru, *you are suggesting spending time alone?

Staying alone, that's better. Even if you have to go to another *guru* you should look upon him as a manifestation of the same *guru*, the same Truth. The *guru* is only one, only the forms are different. The *guru* is God Himself and that is the way we should look upon him.

What tends to happen is that a devotee stays with one teacher until either the devotee sees faults in the teacher or the teacher shows the devotee something he doesn't like. Then perhaps he moves to another teacher. It happens many times. For the spiritual aspirant it is a fall, and he has to get up from it. It will take some time, it can waste time and energy. Sometimes one lifetime is wasted.

So it is important to stay with one teacher? It is a waste of time going from teacher to teacher?

Stay with one teacher. Cling to one teacher. Do *sadhana* independently, sincerely, perfectly, as guided by him. Somebody wrote to our master Ramdas, 'I was told about you and your greatness. I took initiation from another saint ten years ago. As I find no improvement I am thinking of coming to you and requesting initiation from you.' He also added, 'I have asked my *guru* for permission to come to you.' His *guru* wrote back to him saying, 'It is all right for you to go and get initiation from Swami Ramdas if it is going to help you. But one thing, if you had followed the instructions I gave you at the time of your initiation you would have felt no need to go anywhere else.'

So Swami Ramdas wrote back to him, 'Your *guru* has said correctly that if you had followed his teachings perfectly you would not find the need to go in the search of another. Even if you take initiation from Swami Ramdas and do not follow the instructions, nothing is going to happen and you are not going to benefit in any way.'

So what is required on the part of the spiritual aspirant is to sincerely follow the instructions of the *guru*, and intense *sadhana* is essential. Without that, nothing can be gained.

So what you are saying is that whatever the practice, devotion to the **guru** ***is needed?***

Devotion is needed.

And you are saying that it is important for the devotee to find the right **guru*****?***

Yes.

It has been said that when the student is ready, the master appears. Is that your experience?

That's right.

So it is not really necessary to search for a teacher?

You may be seeking a teacher, but when you pray sincerely to God, 'Oh! God guide me to a teacher who will give me directions so that I may reach You,' then it is God's responsibility either to bring the *guru* to the disciple or bring the disciple to the *guru*. Somehow you meet up, you accept him as your *guru* and your spiritual practice begins. God arranges everything if we are sincere.

By sincere, you mean a single-pointed desire for liberation?

That's right. When we are groping in darkness we don't know how to open the door because it is so dark. So we pray.

Sri Ramana's devotees had tremendous devotion to him and he to Arunachala. Please say something about* bhakti, *devotion, in the pursuit of awakening.

If the devotees are sincere, if they are one hundred percent devoted to the *guru*, they must look upon the *guru* as God Himself. They must serve him, think about him day and night, and dedicate their life to him. Naturally the *guru* also watches over all of the devotees, this comes automatically.

On the devotional path, the path of *bhakti*, the devotees praise the *guru*. Sometimes a devotee comes to him and asks, 'What service can I do for you?' The *guru* doesn't need any service, he says, 'Do your *sadhana* properly, think of God constantly, that itself is sufficient to make me happy.' That is what the *guru* really wants, he does not want any other service.

What does the* guru *want from the disciple?

The *guru* wants him to find true devotion to God. When I am devoted to God I think of God always, I love everybody and I serve everybody as well as possible. Only then will the *guru* be pleased. To say, 'I am devoted to God, but I don't like my neighbour, I don't like my brother,' that is not devotion. A real devotee loves everybody.

Because he sees God in everybody?

Yes. And not just in everybody but in every creature.

Is there a danger that the devotee will become too attached to the form of the teacher?

That is also a danger but from the very beginning the *guru* hammers it into the disciple that he should be looked upon not as the body but as the Self. They always say don't get attached to this body, this body will perish one day or another and then you will feel bad about it. But be attached to the Truth within this body, cling to the Truth and not this body.

In spite of all this, some devotees become attached to the* guru's *form and naturally they feel the separation when the* guru *drops the body. When Sri Ramana was about to leave his body his disciples were very upset and begging him, 'Don't leave, don't leave.' He said, 'Where could I go…'

'… I am here only; I am in your own heart.'

So the true devotee will understand this, and it will be his experience?

Right.

Seekers often have curious ideas about the enlightened state. Can you tell us how the enlightened one sees and acts in the world?

I cannot say that they see nothing in the world. They see the world, they see the names and forms, and they know that they are all the forms of God. God Himself has taken different forms and God Himself is playing this eternal drama. That is their vision. They are conscious of the physical part of the universe as well as the spiritual substratum, they are conscious of both.

They are always in bliss but emotions are still coming and going?

They are established in their own Self, but when they see something wrong then they feel bad about it, when they see something good then they will be happy about it. This is part of their nature and they are witnesses of what is happening in this nature. They don't identify themselves with the universe or with the nature, but they remain as witnesses. At the same time, when bad things happen they will feel sorrow.

For example, Papa Ramdas might say, 'Ramdas is sorry to hear about the passing of your father.' I would ask him, 'Why do you feel sorry when you know the Truth that everything passes?' 'Oh, even sorrow is all right, it belongs to nature, it is part of the play, and it is all false.' So these expressions of different feelings are also possible in realised souls, but at the same time they remain perfectly safe in their own Self, always peaceful and blissful.

Can they be angry also?

They can be angry. But their anger is righteous indignation. It is harmless and it is only to set others right. When Mother was seriously ill, before she passed away, they would ask her, 'Mother, how are you?' She would say, 'The body is suffering a lot but I am perfectly peaceful and happy.' The realised soul knows they are not the body. Ignorant people only have the body, nothing more than that.

You have given us a profound discourse on awakening. When you meet someone with a passion for awakening, what would your short advice be?

We have to tell him that he has to work for enlightenment, he has to purify his mind and pass through a course of *sadhana* prescribed for him for that purpose. He should take the advice of some saint, get initiation, then he will be able to get enlightenment. This is how I would guide him.

When you say initiation, do you mean become a* sannyasin *(renunciate)?

Not necessary. Initiation is when a disciple goes before a saint and asks for spiritual help. The saint gives him a particular name of God to repeat always, for the purification of his mind. To become a *sannyasin* is also an initiation but this is at a later stage. If he has purified his mind to a certain extent he is initiated into an order of *sannyas*, if he is fit for it.

Before you go I would like to read you one paragraph from Master (Ramdas) about what a saint is:

> A saint is he who has attained the eternal, lives in the eternal and has realised the eternal. Call the great reality by any name, the eternal, God or Truth. Such a saint is a veritable blessing upon this earth. By his contact thousands are saved from the clutches of doubt, sorrow and death. He lives what he preaches and preaches what he lives. He exerts a wonderful influence and creates in the hearts of ignorant men a consciousness of their inherent divinity. He awakens the sleeping soul into the awareness of their immortal soul and all-blissful nature. By his very presence he lifts the hearts of people out of their brazen and unbridled passions. The faithful derive the greatest benefit by communion with him.

I think that you have amply done that tonight. Thank you, it has been very beautiful to talk with you. It is all very clear and very heartful. Thank you.

Om Sri Ram Jay Ram, Jay, Jay, Ram.

Ma Souris

If you have faith then it will come to you in a minute. But who has that faith? You don't want to have your personality annihilated. For realisation there has to be tremendous desire, a longing, a passion, a fire. I used to cry, I had to cry.

When you are ready, the guru will be with you.

Ma Souris

Ma Souris

Ma Souris came to Sri Ramana in May, 1938. Her father, Gudipati Venkata Chalam, was a well known writer, artist and admirer of women who advocated freedom for women. He was a disciple of Sri Ramana, later becoming a disciple of his daughter, Souris. He lived his last years at Arunachala. Ma Souris's story can be found in her book, *A Memory*. She left the body in 2004 or 2005. Very little is known about her.

I met Ma Souris in 2003 when she was in her late eighties. She lived simply with a small group of devotees in the north of Andrah Pradesh. I was impressed with her beautiful singing voice. Each morning she sat and arranged vases of cut flowers for the shrines and pujas *(devotional ceremonies). She seemed rather formidable during the interview but later on, during an excursion to the beach, a lighter, naughty little girl was revealed.*

Sri Ramana proposed the fundamental question 'Who am I?' Who are you?

I don't know. I really don't know.

Many Western seekers come to India looking for enlightenment as if it is an experience. What is enlightenment?

There is nothing like enlightenment at all. You just become nothing.

Can you explain what you mean?

When you come to the end you will find that you have not done any *sadhana* (spiritual practice), and that it was only imagination, nothing else.

And when you say the end, do you mean awakening?

I mean the end of my *sadhana*, not the end of everything.

Many people are searching for enlightenment, awakening. Can you say something about this?

They have to seek for themselves, only the *guru* can help them. Through the *guru*, who is the Self, they can awaken, but without the *guru* nobody can awaken.

You are saying that a* guru *is necessary?

Of course.

Who is the* guru*?

The *guru* is yourself. Until you see this you need an outer *guru*, a physical *guru*, like Bhagavan Sri Ramana Maharshi.

And what is the* guru's *role?

Only the *guru* knows. Who can say?

How to recognise a* guru*? How can I find a true* guru*?

How can you find him? A baby knows its own mother, 'You are my mother.' It is natural, just like that. When you are in the presence of your *guru* you know that he is your *guru*. He doesn't come and talk about being your *guru*. Bhagavan Ramana Maharshi never said, 'I am your *guru*,' to anybody.

So recognition of the* guru *just happens?

Yes, it is a realisation. The first realisation is to know that you are in the presence of your *guru*.

Is* sadhana *necessary for an awakening?

It was necessary for me, I don't know about other people. Somebody could awaken all of a sudden without any *sadhana*.

***Sri Ramana Maharshi didn't do any* sadhana.**

Right, he didn't have a *guru* and he didn't do any *sadhana*. It came to him, but for me it was not like that.

What type of* sadhana *did you do?

The proper sort: 'Who Am I?' I began at the age of fourteen.

You did Self-enquiry?

Yes, Self-enquiry. I had read some books and then my father returned from visiting Ramana Ashram and told me that Bhagavan had said that you must realise yourself. We began to do this Self-enquiry. One cannot do anything without it, you cannot quell the thoughts, they will come like the waves of the ocean. Then suddenly I saw Bhagavan before me. I had never seen him before, but I had wanted to. I saw his presence in a flash; that was the *guru's* grace. From then on my *sadhana* began to progress.

Did you visit him?

I went to visit him one year after the vision and I realised it's all the same thing, that's all!

***Sri Ramana said that Self-enquiry is the most direct* sadhana?**

Yes. But you see, in the book, *Upadesa Saram*, he explains step-by-step how to do *puja*, *japam* (chanting of God's names), concentration on a picture and then Self-enquiry. He goes step-by-step. You may do these things if it is your inclination. Ramana never said to do only Self-enquiry, it's up to you. If you can manage it, it is quite right for you, but if you can't then you may do *japam* or the other practices he suggests.

But in your case you did Self-enquiry from the beginning?

Self-enquiry, yes.

Could you explain how to do Self-enquiry?

I don't tell anybody to do it. The people who come here come with devotion. They don't ask for instruction. A few people come here and ask me questions and I give answers according to the individuals.

But could you explain for other people how to do Self-enquiry?

No, I don't give any messages like that! It is an individual thing. You can't teach it to the masses.

Could you explain it for me?

Have you read the book on Self-enquiry, *Who Am I?*

Yes.

It has every step in it, that's the way. You are not the body or the mind so you should go deep within yourself. The enquiry is not an intellectual question. When you ask 'Who am I?' it doesn't take you to the mind, it takes you to yourself.

You must watch the thoughts which enter your mind, and ask, 'Who is thinking? To whom do these thoughts arise?' It is not a question; you have to go deep inside to search for the source of the thoughts. That's how I did it.

So it is looking for the source of thought?

Yes.

Beyond the thoughts?

Yes.

Could I say that the answer to this question is a deep stillness?

There is no answer, (Premananda laughs) you never come to any conclusion! If you get an answer, nothing further will happen, you will never move on. I have seen so many people in Tiruvannamalai getting small experiences, thinking they are the source. It's really an illusion!

So we should continue to ask this question until something happens? Or until nothing happens?

Nothing happens. But you have to go through all this *sadhana* to realise that you have not done any *sadhana*. You thought you did, that's it. That is what you realise.

So are you saying it is necessary to do some years of* sadhana *in order to come to the point where you see that this is nothing?

This is my experience. It is not for everybody to know.

And at the end of this enquiry, when you see that nothing happened and you see that there is no answer, can you call this enlightenment?

I don't call it anything! There is nothing in me to name anything. You see, everything has gone.

There is no question of enlightenment or non-enlightenment?

You will not get anything. If you get anything it means that your mind is still working. If there is nothing, then who is there to know whether they are enlightened or not? I don't always feel that I am enlightened. When people come, only very rarely do I give answers. You come with questions about Self-enquiry and everything else, so I give answers. These answers are for you, but I will give different answers to another.

When Sri Ramana was asked, 'When will the realisation of the Self be gained?' he replied, 'When the world which is what-is-seen has been removed, there will be realisation of the Self which is the seer.' What is the true understanding of the world?

When you are sleeping are you aware of the world?

When I am sleeping, no.

No? Then where is the world? When you are sleeping and there is no awareness, then where is the world? When you wake up in the morning the first thought is, 'I have awoken and I must do my work.' The thoughts begin to arise. There are no thoughts at all in sleep.

So you are saying that the world is caused by my thoughts?

Yes, by you.

So to remove the world I remove the thoughts?

Yes. What is there? If you are not here and I am not here, then there is no world. It is our thoughts which motivate us to live and act, which create desire. Without thoughts we have no needs or desires.

It has been suggested that the mind must be destroyed for liberation to occur.

No. If you are immersed in yourself there is nothing to destroy. When you realise that there is no mind, the mind is not animated; it is just merged within yourself.

So it is not a question of destroying the mind, but a matter of finding the Self? I find the Self and then the thoughts go away?

No. When the thoughts go away the only thing that remains is the Self. First you must watch the thoughts; where do they come from?

This is Self-enquiry?

That is how I did my *sadhana*. I don't recommend everybody to do it.

If we ask where the thoughts come from we see that they come from the Self?

We don't see, we just feel. There is nothing to see.

When you say that there is nothing to see, is that because the Self is emptiness, stillness, nothingness?

No, Self is everything. Self is everything: the world, and you and me; it is everything you see!

I will give you an illustration. You see, the waves fall upon the shore and they leave behind a pool: that is the mind. When the waves dash back upon the shore, where is the pool? The pool is submerged into the ocean. That is what happens. There is nothing separate. There is nothing which is called mind; it is just a bundle of thoughts. If you have no thoughts then there is no mind, and if there is no mind then there is no world.

Do you have a mind?

I don't know if I have or not. I don't question anything.

But, for example, to eat, to talk, to move your body, to walk, you need a mind.

I just use the mind for my existence.

So there is a mind but you are not the mind?

There is a mind. The mind means the thoughts; I must use the thoughts to do things for my existence.

And do you sometimes experience thoughts arising?

Nothing now. I feel like everybody else. I don't think I am a realised soul or anything. I play with the people who come, and talk with them. (both laugh) And sometimes I am very naughty.

You are naughty?

Yes. They like it very much. (both laugh) Even in the car I go on singing and making jokes. I am a good singer. I have recorded myself singing.

At lunchtime I was lucky enough to hear a recording of you singing. Your singing is extraordinary, it comes from very deep inside and is very beautiful and very strong. Could I say that you are not singing, you are not the singer, and the singing is just appearing?

You may say whatever you wish. When I am singing I am immersed in the song, I forget myself.

Can you say something about* vasanas, *the tendencies of the mind? Must* vasanas *be removed before Self-realisation can become permanent?

It depends upon your *guru*. It is he who is the remover, not you. That is a function of the *guru*, to remove the *vasanas*. *Vasanas* are there and without the *guru's* grace you cannot do any *sadhana* or anything.

I understand that some of the people who were devoted to Sri Ramana Maharshi for many years did not realise themselves. Apparently they had some* vasanas *and these kept them from realising. Is this your understanding?

You see, people don't like to hear that we are all realised. When Buddha's disciples said, 'There is so much misery, why don't you just give realisation?' he answered, 'If I went from door to door and asked if people wanted realisation, nobody would accept. They don't want realisation.'

But some of these devotees were with Sri Ramana Maharshi for thirty or forty years.

Because there was such a peaceful atmosphere there. That is why they were attracted, they just liked the peace!

Are you saying that, even in the case of these devotees, they didn't have enough desire for liberation?

If you have faith then it will come to you in a minute. But who has that faith? You don't want to have your personality annihilated. For realisation there has to be tremendous desire, a longing, a passion, a fire. I used to cry, I had to cry.

I understand that in your case you achieved this realisation before your father?

Yes, before my father. (laughs) And after that I became his *guru*.

Did you awaken first because your fire and longing were stronger than your father's?

My father had so many longings, particularly for women. He was a great author and had written many books. He began to question whether there is realisation or not. When I was young we had a discussion. He said, 'You are just following Ramana like an opium-eater, there is no bliss or anything.' He said that Self-enquiry was just auto-suggestion. I told him strongly that I felt I was progressing and that I was feeling bliss.

So your father had some doubts?

Always he was questioning, he was always a doubter! If you question anything you can never know.

You mentioned also that your father liked women. Did these kinds of worldly things also have to be dropped?

He was an artist, he had an eye for beauty and he liked sex.

Do you mean that he was interested in beauty and sex because he was an artist?

Yes.

And this came in the way of his realisation?

He wanted a woman to lead him, to have a romance, but how could that be? I said that can never be. When they are entangled, how can they free themselves?

Because of their expectations of each other?

I am only telling you that my father had entanglement and attachment. How can he have realisation through women and through romance?

In the Indian spiritual tradition there is* tantra *(path of uniting masculine and feminine).

That is a different thing; *tantra* is a *sadhana*.

Can sexuality as a* sadhana *lead to liberation?

Yes, if you take anything as your *sadhana* it will lead you there. Even motherhood can be *sadhana*. If you deeply think that it is the Truth then everything will be a *sadhana*, a realisation.

I have seen ancient statues from Tibet showing the Buddha sitting with the* yogini *(female* yogi*) in a sexual embrace. Is this* tantra*?

Yes that is *tantra*. They want to liberate through sex; even without sex they need a woman by their side.

You said that in order to remove the* vasanas *you need a* guru*. Is it possible that I can remove my own* vasanas*?

Only a *guru* can do this, you cannot do it.

So a* guru *is very important.

For me, but not for everybody.

Are you saying that Sri Ramana Maharshi removed your* vasanas*?

I'm not saying anything; I just surrendered to him when I was twenty-one and I never questioned him at all, whatever he might do! Surrender must happen automatically, without thinking, 'I must surrender.' Until then I never knew what a *guru* was or was not, because my life was quite different from the spiritual.

You were completely devoted to Sri Ramana Maharshi. Could you explain what you mean by* bhakti*, devotion?

Loving him with all my heart. That is *bhakti*. Not coming and going.

Would you say* bhakti *and Self-enquiry together are important?

Jnana marga, the path of knowledge, without *bhakti marga*, the path of devotion, cannot achieve anything. You need *bhakti*.

You need* bhakti *in order to surrender to the* guru*?

Yes, to whom can you surrender without *bhakti*?

***This is a very important point for Western people; they have difficulty with surrender. It is not so easy for a Westerner to take a* guru.**

When you are ready, the *guru* will be with you.

The* guru *will just come?

Yes, of course. And also the outer *guru* will disappear when the time comes.

When you say that Sri Ramana came to you in your dreams, was this as a vision or more like an inner voice?

He used to appear in my dreams and give me guidance. I knew nothing about *sadhana* or anything.

You never spoke directly to him? You just sat in his presence?

Yes, I just sat in his presence. If I had any doubts, somebody else would ask him the right question and my doubts would be cleared by his answers. For so many people it happened like this.

Many people got their answers in his silence?

Yes.

Seekers often have curious ideas about the enlightened state. Please describe your typical day and how you perceive the world.

Yes, I know! I have seen so many people in Tiruvannamalai who think that they are realised souls.

What is your short advice for somebody who has a passion for awakening?

I don't say anything to them. People don't ask me such questions when they come to me. It is not advice I give; I show them how to proceed. Many come just with devotion and don't ask me anything; they just want the benefits and not realisation. Whatever they ask, it happens for them.

And if they came sincerely wanting realisation what would you say?

Some *sadhus* (wandering ascetics) came from Sri Lanka and they said, 'Our *sadhana* is saying, "Be quiet, shut up," to the mind.' That is a powerful *sadhana*.

My* guru, *Papaji, always said, 'Be quiet!'

Yes, be quiet, shut up! (laughs) That is the easiest and most powerful *sadhana*. Did you see him alive?

Yes, I spent five years with him.

So many people came to me from Poonjaji (Papaji) after he had passed away.

I spent five years living with him in Lucknow. I asked him three questions in the first three meetings. In the third meeting something happened. Since that time I have no more questions. I didn't want to leave him, so I just stayed for nearly five years. It is ten years ago now, and I still have no questions.

That's good.

It is very beautiful to meet you because when I am sitting quietly I can feel a deep melting in this silence.

That's the most sensible thing to do, to be quiet.

Is there anything else you would like to say to people?

I have no people, only friends. If they want anything, then I do anything I can do for them. If they need money, I give them money. If they say they are hungry, then I feed them.

You have had a wonderful life.

Of course, from my childhood. I had a wonderful father.

***I find it extraordinary that you were his* guru.**

Yes. He accepted me as his *guru* because I was his daughter. After that he never thought of me as his daughter.

He must have been a very unusual father.

Yes, he was a dare-devil, experimenting with everything! Since you are interested I will tell you more.

My aunt, my father and my aunt's mother, a doctor, used to live together. When I was ten years old they told me, 'We have no plans for tomorrow, we don't want to keep money for you or land or anything. You will have to look after yourself.' I said, 'That's good, if you want to do anything for me put some cash in the bank. I don't want any land.'

So you lived a life of trust, trusting in everything?

Yes, I came here without anything, without a *paisa* (Indian penny). Everything just came, and I don't know how it came.

I have read your life story. At one point it says, 'Mother (Ma Souris) told Iswara *(the Lord) that she wanted to realise the Absolute.* Iswara *replied that, when she was ready for it, the mind would disappear and she would indeed realise herself as the formless, absolute being.'*

Does this mean manonasha*: that the mind is destroyed? That in the moment of realising the absolute being your mind is completely gone?*

Yes.

A little later you talk about consciousness descending into the heart, the source of all. Could you explain what you mean by the heart?

Heart is here. (points to the right side of her chest)

Sri Ramana Maharshi talked about the right side of the chest as the resting place, the spiritual heart. Is that also your experience?

Yes, of course.

How do you know that this conciousness is coming to the heart?

You feel it. The *Yoga Sastra* describes six *chakras* (body energy centres): *muladhara* (base *chakra* at the end of the spine), *svadhisthana* (pelvis *chakra*), *manipura* (navel *chakra*), *anahata* (heart *chakra*), *ajna* (third eye *chakra*), and *sahasrara* (crown *chakra*). From the crown *chakra* the energy of spirit descends back into the heart and the lotus of the heart then opens. There is a brilliant light and after this the mind must merge into the light, the heart, *anahata*. Then there are vibrations of light and sound; it is called the *omkara* (sound of universal consciousness).

You say that twenty years later Iswara *appeared and said, 'Now seven veils are going to unfold.' And with your inner eye you saw seven subtle layers unfold within, and you heard a voice saying, 'I am dead.' And the world receded to the outer fringe of the vast and unlimited space of consciousness.*

Until then I was in a state of bliss, but even the bliss disappears. There was no one to experience the bliss so the seven veils themselves disappeared. They unfolded, and after that I just felt that I couldn't see them.

You had this experience of consciousness going to your heart and your mind merging into the heart. So who experienced the seven veils?

You just see them as a witness.

You said before that you still have thoughts because you need some for day-to-day life, like walking and eating.

Yes, I use them for my purposes, but they are subtle, like clouds in the sky. They don't attach me to anything.

I still have thoughts arising but I don't get caught up in them.

Previously I had that stage, but now there are no thoughts at all and everything comes to me automatically. Now there is nothing.

The way you are describing this is as if there is Self-realisation and then later there is enlightenment. Are there two different stages?

There are not two stages. *Iswara* told me: 'I am keeping the power within you, otherwise you would be dead from the unfolding.' So I had to wait twenty years after, and then it happened.

Was there some kind of dissolving during those twenty years?

Yes, of course. I was always in bliss but even that disappears; there is no mind to record or experience the bliss.

Over the ten years since my experience with Papaji I can describe a kind of dissolving. Day-by-day there is a lot of stillness and peace and very few thoughts that disturb me. Could you comment on this?

I can't say anything about other people's experiences. Bhagavan realised in one hour.

I experience no big problems in my life anymore, just a kind of surrender to life. But really I don't know; I don't really know what this is. When I asked, 'Who are you?' you said, 'I don't know.'

Of course.

This is a very honest answer.

So now it is time for food.

Yes. Thank you very much for our talk.

Swami

Suddhananda

Where is happiness? It is in your Self. So what are you looking for in life, happiness or Self? It is your Self. When you find your Self, you find your happiness. That is what every person is looking for.

SUDDHANANDA

A person who learns from his own experience is smart,
but the person who learns from others' experience is even smarter.

Swami Suddhananda

Swami Suddhananda

Swami Suddhananda, now in his early fifties, studied the *Vedic* scriptures under Swami Chinmayananda and Swami Dayanananda Saraswati at Sandeepani Sadhanalaya, Mumbai. Swamiji says, 'I was thirsty and went for a drop of water and found that I am the water.' He travels widely in the world teaching *Vedanta* and was a delegate at the United Nations' Millennium Peace Conference held in New York in August 2000.

Swami is an unusually humorous and Self-illuminating teacher. He has a fine sense for art and architecture. It has been a pleasure for me to meet him because, while being well versed in* Vedanta, *he has travelled in the world enough to understand the ways of the human mind. Our first meeting was under a huge tree and later we met in his new house built with traditional architectural elements.

Sri Ramana proposed the fundamental question, 'Who am I?' Who are you?

To really answer the question I should keep quiet. You might misinterpret the silence and think that I don't know anything. But I don't say anything because who I am is a nameless entity. It is as simple as that.

It is not only who I am, but anything for that matter. Let's take an example, a *mala* (prayer beads). Somebody asks you, 'What is this?' You'll say, 'It's a bead.' It's not a bead. It 'has' a name: bead. What it 'is' is nameless. It doesn't depend on a name for its existence. In the same way, 'I' is my name, but who I am is a nameless entity whom I call 'I'. And it is the same pronoun for everybody. Once I understand clearly about this then I know who I am, I know who you are, I know who everybody is – the same 'I' because that is the universal first name. When you ask somebody, 'Who are you?' everybody has to begin with the word 'I'. What you 'have' and what I 'have' are different, but who we 'are' is the same.

I am giving such an elaborate description. I should have kept quiet! But the occasion demands me to say something. Suppose I go to the embassy for a visa and the man asks me who I am. If I say, 'I am the nameless,' there will be no visa. I have to say who I am, in whatever language the other person understands. I know who I am, but while communicating with people I talk to them in the language that they understand. If I take it for granted that you know the Truth, I don't have to say anything.

Many Western seekers come to India looking for enlightenment as if it is an experience. What is enlightenment?

That's a very interesting question. Most of the time people think enlightenment means something to do with the light. So most people start looking for red light, white light and yellow light, depending on their imagination. It is not the mistake of the seeker. One who is seeking is never at fault because he is ignorant. An ignorant man has the full right to be stupid. It is the mistake of the teacher, the *guru*, the person who is guiding, if the seeker equates enlightenment with an experience.

People equate some type of experience with enlightenment. If you see a red light, you are enlightened; if you see a yellow light, you are enlightened; if there is no thought you are enlightened; if there is this particular thought, it is enlightenment; if your body starts reeling and rolling, it is enlightenment. Extraordinary, uncommon, bizarre feelings, almost to the point of insanity. The person who is seeking doesn't know what he is looking for. Everybody is desperate. When somebody is desperately looking for enlightenment and he is told that he should see an inner light and that is enlightenment, he sits down, closes his eyes, and starts imagining some light. He may be told that this light is at the tip of the nose, or between his eyebrows, or the top of his head, or the bottom of his spine.

In fact, these are beautiful points for concentration, but this has a different purpose altogether. If he succeeds in imagining this light, it doesn't last. So then he is told that it will happen in the Himalayas, or Arunachala, or the Swiss Alps as though no other place has the possibility for enlightenment. It's not the mistake of the people seeking; this is what they have been told. It is really a tragedy in the name of spirituality.

Enlightenment is your Self, so there is no question of your going someplace. It can be recognised anytime, anywhere, because it is yourself. You can take the example of Ramana Maharshi. He didn't come to Tiruvannamalai for enlightenment, he was already enlightened before coming here. But now people think that by visiting Tiruvannamalai they will become enlightened. They must learn about themselves wherever they are! People are very honest. They are all looking for somebody who can direct them. But first of all they must know what it is they are looking for, then it becomes very easy.

So what is it?

Exactly! Suppose I am in Germany and I meet you and say, 'Premananda, please tell me which way to go.' What can you do? You'll ask, 'Swamiji, where do you want to go?' I say, 'I don't know! You tell me which way.' Now what will you say? For you to give me a direction I must know the destination! For a teacher to tell students where to go, first he must know what is the destination. The student must know what he wants in life. If he doesn't know what he wants, then the teacher's first job is to awaken him to what he wants. The next step is to tell him how to get there.

If you ask anybody: What do you want in life? Immediately the person may say I want an education, or I want money, or I want a job. Why do you want education? You get an education, but once the education is over you still don't know what to do. Then you look for a job. Only then you say, 'Oh my God! I didn't want education for education's sake, I was really looking for a job.' You get a job. Next you ask how much is the pay. You don't want a job for the job's sake, you want the job for the money.

I say, 'Okay, I will give you money. How much do you want?'

'Five hundred million.'

'It's yours, but you can't spend it. It's all in a Swiss bank account.'

You wanted it. But you don't want money for money's sake. You want that money so you can have houses, cars, planes, all these things. You don't want money, you want things.

'Okay, you should have told me. I will give you things; houses, cars, everything is yours. But you can't live in that house, drive that car, fly that plane.'

'So who wants it?'

'You wanted it. It's all yours. Legally it is all yours.'

'No Swamiji, I want to live in that house, drive the car, fly the plane, swim in the pool, so that I can be happy.'

Aha! So ultimately you do know what you want. Everybody wants happiness in life. Another person might say, 'No, no, I am not a materialist. I don't want a house, a car, all these things, I want God.' Why do you want God? Have you ever got a phone call from God saying, 'Hi, how are you doing?' Why do you want God? He doesn't want you. Do you know why most people want God? What one person gets by hard work, this fellow wants to get by grace and prayer. That is why people chase God. Nobody wants God for God's sake. Again, it's for things. Why do you want things? For happiness' sake.

So everybody wants happiness in life. Once that is clearly seen, the next thing is, where is it? If you want education, go to college. If you want a job, go to a company. If you want money, go to a bank. If you want things you can go to a supermarket. But where do you go for happiness? Where is it? The secular society will tell you that if you get educated you will be happy, get money you will be happy, get a job you will be happy, get married you will be happy. With everything at your disposal you will be very, very comfortable. But at no time must you equate comfort with happiness because you can have a very comfortable air conditioned nightmare. None of these things work. Why? If you get educated, you are educated but not happy; if you get money, you are rich but not happy.

This is the point where religion jumps in and says, 'None of these things will bring you happiness. You follow my God, my religion, my faith, my practice, then you shall be happy.' Secular persons will say indulgence is happiness. Both religion and society are pointing to the wrong address because if we say that happiness is a thing, we shall be unhappy. Why? In the absence of that thing, what shall we do?

If my happiness has a reason, then when the reason is withdrawn the happiness is gone. Somebody can shatter your faith, time can snatch your husband or wife, your wealth, your job. You can't stand it. That is why most of the people do not like to expose themselves to thinking. So where do they go? Somebody will tell you that happiness is inside. So your search moves from outside to inside. The search never ends. But when somebody says happiness is your Self, this is not just a statement; you can see it from your own experience. In any moment of happiness you are with your Self.

Let us talk for one moment of unhappiness. Suppose I want a car. I am really miserable about the car and missing the car. I am unhappy because the thought of the car is bugging me. Somebody says, 'This car is for you.' 'Oh! How sweet!' Immediately you are so happy because the car came. Now please tell me what was bugging you; was it really the absence of the car, or was it the presence of the thought of the car? It was the presence of the thought of the car. When you get the car, what gives you relief? The presence of the car or the absence of the thought? If the presence of the car gives you happiness, then the car dealer will be the happiest man because he has a thousand cars.

That is where you make another mistake, to conclude that the absence of thought is happiness. Then everybody wants to remove their thoughts, but it's not the absence of thought that gives you happiness, it is the presence of your Self that gives you happiness. Whenever you are happy, you are with your Self. So what you are looking for in life is happiness. Where is happiness? It is in your Self. So what are you looking for in life, happiness or Self? It is your Self. When you find your Self, you find your happiness. That is what every person is looking for.

Are there any qualifications for enlightenment? Is* sadhana *(spiritual practice) necessary?

The biggest qualification is that you must look for it. This means you must be sure of what you are looking for in life, because nobody can tell you that. If you are looking for a cricket bat and I tell you that happiness is your Self, you think I am nuts. The person must look for it; that's very important. In *Sanskrit* (language of ancient Indian scriptures) they say *mumukshu. Mumukshutwa* means the desire to be free. Let me be free. Let me be happy once and for all, free once and for all. There is no question of happiness for some time – sometimes happy and sometimes miserable. You know this type of little passing comfort. No, I must be happy once and for all – free now, once and for all. That is everything I want in life.

When you look for that you see that suddenly everything falls apart because there is no relationship, no object, nothing that can fulfill this expectation. Everything in your life will fall apart. At that time you discover that you really can't blame objects, because when did the objects promise you happiness? Please tell me, when did the gold say, 'Take me home, I'll make you happy'? When did the diamonds say, 'Take me home, I'll make you happy'? We impose onto these objects.

If you give a five hundred euro note to an Indian cow she will chew it and not even burp. (both laugh) She won't say, 'Oh man! A five hundred euro dinner, oooh!' It's a stupid little piece of paper, but people will kill each other for that. This is conditioning; woman gives me happiness, man gives me happiness, things give me pleasure. No! They don't. Don't blame the world for it. I have imposed happiness on the world, that is why I am in trouble. Society does that. And if secularism says that happiness is in objects, religion will say there is no happiness in objects. *Samsara* (circle of rebirth), *dukha* (sorrow), the whole world is pain. What nonsense! You can impose neither pain nor pleasure on the object.

The person who is running towards the world seeking happiness is as stupid as the person running away from the world thinking that the world is unhappiness. You can't run. You have to be yourself. Not many people will recognise this by themselves. A mature person may recognise this from his experience: 'My God! I have done everything I wanted to do, education, money, job. What now?'

The person doesn't understand his confusion, so this is where the teacher comes in and gives him direction. 'Ah! Your frustration is natural. Go into yourself.' The teacher knows. Most of the people in the world, when they are frustrated, try to experiment with drugs, sex and liquor. There is no guidance. A person who is frustrated in life is an ideal student. The *Upanishadic rishi* (seer of the *Upanishads*), the sage, will be happy when a frustrated person comes to him. 'Good! At last this one is ready.'

Could we call this a moment of becoming hopeless?

You can say it how you wish, but that is what it is; he can now come home to Truth. You have come to India many times so you must know there are so many holy places in India, especially riverbanks. Do you know why? Wherever the river takes a turn towards the source, that becomes a holy place symbolising each incident in your life that helps you to take a turn towards yourself – a very holy incident. It may be the death of your father, it may be the collapse of your business, it may be parting from your lover; if that suddenly takes you towards yourself it becomes a very auspicious moment. If it takes you to liquor or to suicide, that is a misdirection. When a person is frustrated he can go into enlightenment or into depression, but when the teacher is there, he can be directed towards himself.

Yes, I have seen many times that it takes a strong situation on the outside to bring somebody to really look at themselves.

True. There are two types of people. There are some people who learn from their own experience; they need that heavy kick to understand this stuff. They need to be frustrated, they need to lose their business, they need to lose their people, they need to lose everything. 'No! Oh my God! It doesn't work!' They are intelligent because there are many people who don't learn from experience. So a person who learns from his own experience is smart, but the person who learns from others' experience is even smarter. (both laugh)

You travel a lot in the West so you probably see how busy Western people are with relationships. When this relationship story collapses there is a choice. You can move towards a new husband or a new wife, or you can move towards your Self.

Yes, one hundred percent true. This kind of story is everywhere, but in Western countries it happens more because of the freedom people enjoy. We say Westernised or Easternised but I personally don't like that much because we are all human beings. Human experiences are the same everywhere. There is no Western emotion and Eastern emotion, there is no Western pain and Eastern pain. It's a human thing.

The Western world was not always like this. Fifty years back, a hundred years back, your father or your great grandfather were living exactly as people are living in the East now. There were arranged marriages, there were also communities and there was not so much migration. I have been to France and have seen many of those medieval villages. So beautiful, almost like my own home, my own village, where my family has been living for hundreds of years. Now, what has happened in the West is happening in the East, our generation is slowly moving out.

This migration is inevitable, partly because you now have to look for your love and affection elsewhere. It's a big investment. People sometimes ask me, 'Swamiji, what do you like about arranged marriage?' It's very simple. Arranged marriage has advantages and disadvantages, just as love marriage has advantages and disadvantages.

The most abused statement in the whole world's literature and speech is 'I love you'. It's the biggest mistake, the biggest lie. Make a list of whom you love. Of course everybody has a list. The priorities change, but everybody has a list: I love my father, my mother, my husband, my wife, my money, my dog, my car, my job. Everybody is lying because they have been trained to lie. 'How am I lying?' It's a simple thing. You have got a gold watch which you love.

A gunman comes up to you and says, 'Give me your watch or else you are dead.'

Will you say, 'Leave my watch, kill me'? (both laugh) Most definitely not.

You will say, 'Take this. Not just mine. You want me to collect the watches from the others too? I'll collect the others.' Why? If I am the only one to lose my watch I will be unhappy. If everybody loses their watch, I am comfortable. (both laugh) So do I love my gold watch or myself?

Now, in the same way, you can look at anything: I love my husband, I love my wife. Okay then, why do you divorce? As long as she gives me security, gives me happiness, I love her; as long as he gives me security, gives me happiness, I love him. The moment he or she becomes the cause of insecurity or pain, I give them up. So do I love myself or the person? I love myself. Please understand, this idea must change around; it is very important. People think that loving yourself is selfishness. There is no more misunderstood statement. Only when you love yourself can you love everybody in this world. This is because you will not be insecure.

If you love yourself, only then can the other person be loved. But when I am depending on somebody to love me, that means I need that person to make me complete. When that person makes me complete I sometimes feel exploited; maybe she is asking for something because of this need, maybe he is asking because he fulfils me. So you are frightened all the time. That is why, by the time the relationship ends, you are totally shattered.

You find the happiness in yourself because it is the simplest thing; your object of love is the source of happiness. If I love myself, I love the source of happiness. Because you are the source of happiness, you love yourself. You can't escape this, everybody must love himself. It's an injunction; either you do it or you live your life at your peril.

How about spiritual practice? Does that help us?

'Love yourself' is spiritual practice. This is exactly what spiritual practice is all about. When you are happy with yourself you are happy with everybody else. You are kind, compassionate, and you don't exploit anybody. I don't have to exploit anybody in this world because I am happy with myself. Who exploits? When you feel miserable you will exploit people, you cannot stop exploiting. As long as you feel hurt you cannot stop hurting people. If you don't feel hurt you'll never hurt anybody. If I love myself, you can't offend me. When I am so sure of myself, why should I get angry with you?

The ultimate spirituality is you are seen as That. This is what is needed for the world. All of us, each person, must love himself, then other things in your life are simply decided by circumstance: don't ask an Eskimo to be vegetarian; he can't cultivate rice and cauliflower on the ice. He has to eat meat and drink blood; there's no choice. But in a country where vegetables are plentiful, so much sun, so much rain, there's no reason to kill an animal.

Sri Ramana said Self-enquiry is the most direct route to realising the Self. What do you say about Self-enquiry?

This is an ancient tradition. It's not what any one person said. It's like saying *Shankara* gave us *Advaita* (non-dual teaching). If you asked *Shankara*, 'What is your contribution to *Advaita*?' he would say, 'Nothing.' What is his reason? It was already there; it is in the *Upanishads* and the *Vedas* (ancient Indian *Sanskrit* texts). He commented and wrote to facilitate an easy understanding because of his brilliant mind. He wrote many works, but the original vision, the approach to Oneness, was already there. When *Shankara* says *atman*, the Self, what does he mean? He means who am I? What is *atman*? *Atman* is who I am. So this enquiry has already been there for thousands of years.

Ramana Maharshi had an experience in Madurai. He had a question for himself and he got it. That's beautiful! Afterwards he related this experience to the holy scriptures, the *Bhagavatam*, the *Periya Purana*. Self-enquiry has always been there. Ramana Maharshi's life gave it a fresh thrust.

In *Upanishadic* tradition, no *guru's* name is mentioned, because the *guru* is not a personal thing. The teaching is continuously passed down.

In the *Upanishads*, a student asks the teacher, 'Who told you this, that you are the I of the I, the mind of the mind, ultimate, nameless, who you are? Who told you this?' The teacher says, 'This is how we have heard it from the scripures.' 'And who is the *guru* there?' The teacher answers, 'No name.' So ultimately it goes like that.

If you ask me what practice we should do, this is what we should do. We should understand this word 'I'. This is very important. If I ask a simple question, 'Do I have a fear of death?' my answer is yes. I ask, 'Who is afraid? Is the body afraid or am I afraid?' The body is not afraid of death. The body is not afraid of old age. The body is not afraid of anything. I am. Who is this 'I'? The method of teaching is to know that 'I'. That is the complete tradition, what we call *guru shishya parampara*, the tradition of teaching.

Enquiry does not mean simply repeating, 'Who am I? Who am I?' By simply repeating a question, can anybody find an answer? If you say, 'What is Swamiji's father's name? What is Swamiji's father's name?' you can repeat it for a million years, no answer will come. By repeating a question nobody finds an answer. Also the other way around. Suppose somebody repeats an answer. Some people repeat *so ham, so ham*, I am That, I am That. By repeating an answer you will not know how to arrive at it. That is the reason for the tradition of teaching – somebody reveals it to you. That is *guru shishya parampara* – a teacher is needed.

When Sri Ramana was asked, 'When will the realisation of the Self be gained?' he replied, 'When the world which is what-is-seen has been removed, there will be realisation of the Self which is the seer.' What is the true understanding of the world and how to remove the world?

The trouble with this type of question is that you are referring to a particular person, and what I say is sometimes different. It may look like disrespect.

If we start thinking logically, the removal of the world means the removal of my body too. Can I remove the world without removing my body? What are you asking me? You are asking that I should be dead, right? If enlightenment means disappearance of the world, that will include my body because I can't make the world disappear without my body disappearing. If my body disappears, then what is this understanding for? Why would I learn to drive and then sell my car?

The personal reference makes it a little delicate for me to give a statement. Ultimately, it doesn't matter whether the world is there or not, because it is not a problem. Is it a problem that the body is there? No, it is not a problem that the body is there. I am hungry; it is not a problem that the body is hungry. That the body is dying is not the body's problem either.

So you're saying that the real problem is how we see the world.

Exactly! You must see yourself, understand your nature, who you are, then just let the world continue. Why should the world disappear? Does it matter? Why should thoughts disappear? Why should anything disappear? Understand the sense of 'I', know what this word 'I' means. This word is the most important word. The *Upanishads*, *Sanskrit* and all the *Vedas* talk about this. All austerities are undertaken to understand this, to enquire about the Absolute, this one word. This one word is *om*. *Om* or *aham*, they are both the same. *Aham* means I, *om* means the truth of the word 'I'. It's all technical, but all the words mean the same thing. That's why, if you understand this one word, all the words simultaneously explode and everything is understood.

You asked me in your first question: Swamiji, who are you? I have to begin my answer with the word 'I'. If I ask you who you are, you will begin with 'I'. Ask five billion people: Who are you? Everybody has to start their answer with 'I'. So I is the universal first name. If I understand this one word, I understand everything.

The Truth in me, the Truth in you, the Truth in all, is one and the same. But what I have, what you have, is different. My body is fifty years old, your body is sixty years old, somebody else's is thirty years old. I have five million, you have fifteen million. What we 'have' varies, but who we 'are' is invariable. What you have, I don't have. What she has, I don't have, but together we have everything. In a movie they are all actors, but each has a different role. Somebody is a king, somebody is a policeman, somebody is a musician, somebody is an electrician, somebody is putting out the chairs. Now who is better? Everybody is the same, but they also have different roles. Who is more important? Nobody. It needs all of us to have a beautiful show.

Anyone can sabotage the whole thing. Hundreds of people are needed for a plane to take off but one single person can sabotage the whole flight. Trillions of cells are required for the body to function but one cell goes cancerous and you are unhealthy. It is the same thing in your mind. Hundreds of roles make you who you are. One role can destroy you – husband is affected, wife is affected, then your entire personality collapses. When you know yourself you are the best player in and through every role. That is why you don't have to throw away your roles, you don't have to change your body, you don't have to change your religion, you don't have to change your belief, you don't have to change anything. You are of this world. Let it be exactly as it is.

It has been suggested that the mind must be destroyed for liberation to occur. Do you have a mind? Sri Ramana used the term* manonasha *to describe the state of liberation, meaning destroyed mind. How to destroy the mind?

You see, it is really difficult to comment because if you attribute a statement to a person and I don't agree, it will be seen as disrespectful to that person, and the people who are holding onto that statement as sacred will say I must be an idiot.

But do you have a mind?

Of course I have a mind! How else am I going to function? How am I listening to you, and how am I talking to you? These are the functions of the mind.

But there is a strong spiritual idea that the mind must be destroyed. For example, thousands of Buddhist monks are sitting every day in meditation trying to attain no-mind.

You must first know what exactly you are talking about. I will give a simple example. When you see a bead for the very first time (holding a bead on his *mala*), some thought takes place. When the thought takes place, naturally you have a mind. The thought is taking place in you. That thought is knowledge. First, your mind will throw you the thought 'What is this?' because there is no information on it. Just like a computer it will say 'Data not found.' I tell you it's a bead so you now name that thought as 'bead'. That is knowledge. Previously, if somebody had said 'bead', that thought would not have come to your head, but now when somebody says 'bead', the thought comes to your head. That is not a problem.

Do you know when problems begin? When I say, 'I want that bead!' A simple thought becomes a desire. When the thought of the object is converted into a desire, the object of thought becomes desirable. Then the struggle begins. Who should have it? Because ten people want it, the price goes up. Okay? So now you are in deep trouble. You have to have it! You have a very strong desire to have this bead. Other people will make you very angry because they are not helping you to satisfy your desire. So now, from desire, comes your anger. You are destroyed.

Who created this desire, anger or hatred? Who converted the thought into a desire? 'I' did. Now if you want to remove the desire, which one should you remove: the object, the thought of the object, or the one who is converting the thought to desire, this 'I'? What are you destroying the thought for? What are you destroying the mind for? What are you destroying the object for? What are you destroying the world for? You don't even have to destroy the 'I' either. Just understand what this 'I' is. Then it becomes a functional 'I'.

When water is flowing we call it a river. When there is just water which is not flowing, is that water a river? Water is not a river, but flowing water is a river. Consciousness is your Self, a flow in consciousness is the mind. You can see the water in the river. You can see the water as it is or you can see the flow. We need both. Be your Self, the changeless, and enjoy the changes, use the changes! This type of idea, 'the mind should not be there, thoughts should not be there' puts people into such a huge mess because you end up trying to destroy something which is natural. People must learn how to think, not 'not' think at all. Thought is needed. How are you going to know you are hungry and how will you satisfy your hunger? Very little will be possible if we don't know how to think. When you start analysing statements like that they do not stand up to the test.

But it is quite common to hear that saints or sages have no mind.

As a figure of speech it is fine, perhaps, but if you take it literally you are in trouble.

Let's say you are a billionaire and you have everything at your disposal. A poor man comes to you and says, 'Sir, today I had a very nice piece of bread and a little cheese as well.' Do you say to him, 'What a stupid fool you are, eating bread and cheese! You should have a five-star breakfast.' No. If that is what he had, it's fine. 'Oh, that is very nice! I am so happy you enjoyed it.' Same thing with knowledge. When you are happy and comfortable in yourself, you don't have to dismiss anybody's standpoint. If a person is using his mind, don't tell him, 'You should not use your mind.' If he doesn't use it then what does he do? Who you are is not a state of mind.

So you are actually pointing to an understanding that is needed, not a practice. This image of spiritual life with monks sitting for hours trying to destroy the mind, it's not what you are suggesting?

No, no. I don't want to suggest or not suggest. Please see what I am saying. The moment we get into that it will be like I am dismissing something. Okay, let me say I'm giving you a statement for yourself. You look out for yourself. Let anyone else who is reading this think for him or herself.

First observe what the problem is, then go to a solution. If your tyre has a puncture they pump it up and put it in water. Wherever the tyre goes 'ssss', that's the point they patch.

Now, what is the point in your life where everything is leaking out? Where is the emptiness, where does it come from? Your body is not a problem, the world is not a problem, your perception is not a problem. Isolate this 'I' and see what it means. When you are trying to see yourself, that is the time that other thoughts keep coming up. That is where different practices are suggested, like how to make your mind slow down. When you learn to drive, you don't start at a hundred kilometres per hour. You learn driving at ten kilometres per hour, but the purpose is not to drive ten kilometres per hour for the rest of your life.

Like that, when you want to understand yourself, slowing down the mind is needed. So you can sit down quietly, you can listen to music, you can do a practice, anything that slows down the mind. But simply slowing down the mind does not solve the problem. Simply removing thought does not solve the problem. It is to help the person recognise himself, know himself. That is the teaching: the person must know him or herself. Most spiritual people will talk as if this is the ultimate: (blissfully) 'Oh there is nothing.' In deep sleep your mind is suspended for eight hours. Do you wake up enlightened? So how do you think by suspending your thought for half an hour you will be enlightened?

You sleep for eight long hours but nothing changes, and still you wake up ignorant. You sit down quietly, maybe the mind goes away somewhere, and thoughts don't happen. Somebody must be there to instruct you. That is where the teacher comes in, somebody who helps you to understand. No teacher can 'give' it to you because it is already yours; it is already you! I wouldn't say, 'I don't need a *guru*.' No. That's not right. You have learnt nothing in your life by yourself. Think about this – nothing. In everything that you know, somebody knows better. You have a house, but your architect knows better than you about your house. Your doctor knows better than you about your body. Same thing with your mind. You have a mind, you have all the thoughts. Yes, you know your thoughts better than anybody, but you don't know how to think.

There is a difference between thought and thinking. This is a weak point until it is understood. I can give you a thought, but you don't know how to think. Most religions and most secular studies give us thoughts, but they don't teach us thinking. Why is science so beautiful? Because it gives us thoughts and helps us to use the thoughts and experiment with them. Painting and music are like this too. But most religious thoughts are unquestioned thoughts. This is the root of fanaticism: you have a thought and you have to defend your thought instead of the thought defending you. This is the right thought! Who said? Somebody has told you that you have no right to question it. Wonderful! When you are given the thought 'no thoughts should be there', naturally you try to fulfill that promise. What a headache!

And what about* vasanas, *(laughing) the tendencies of the mind? Must these be removed before Self-realisation can become permanent?

Same question, same thing. Nothing must be removed. To say that 'I', the infinity, is so incapable of handling a few thoughts that every thought must be removed for me to see myself; what kind of idea is that? It is like saying that all the waves must be stopped so that the water can be seen. Nothing needs to be removed. If anything needs to be removed at all, it is these types of thoughts. (both laugh)

The mind is not a small house. Today we have a fantastic example. On your computer you have one hundred gigabytes of memory, so you can file everything. What is the capacity of the brain computer? A trillion gigabytes? So why should we remove anything? Let it be there. That there is a thought is not a problem, that you misuse the thought is a problem. When you are happy with yourself, what can be the problem? Why should I remove any thought?

***It appears essential to meet a* guru *and stay with that* guru. *Who is the* guru, *what is the* guru's *role, how to recognise a true* guru?**

This is a very beautiful thing. The first thing is, *guru* is not a title, *guru* is not a role. The other day somebody asked me this question straight, 'Swamiji, are you a *guru*?' I said, 'Are you my student? If you are my student, I am your *guru*.' If he says he is not my student, then I am not a *guru*. The *guru* is not a person. Are you looking for a *guru* or are you looking for happiness? Everybody looks for happiness in life, but you don't know where to find it. Whoever gives you the right address is a *guru*, and that brings you fulfillment in life.

***How to know who is a true* guru?**

It's all in you. You can find it out for yourself. You might not be a good cook, but you could give a certificate for taste, 'Oh this tastes good!' No *guru*, nobody, can talk about a Truth which is not already in you. When I speak I may not say where the Truth is, but when I listen I know. In the process of listening, are you becoming independent or are you becoming dependent? If you are becoming independent, go with it.

If you are becoming dependent on a person, a practice, a word, a thought or an idea, you had better run out of that place, or else you will be a clone; you will be a part of a cult, you will be destroyed. Why? Truth is not something. It is not a man, an idea, a thought, a concept or a name or a word. Nothing. It is your Self. I'm not the only one who is the Truth. Everybody is the same Truth. There is nothing special about the *guru*; he is as much the Truth as any other person. The only difference is that the teacher knows this; the student is yet to know this. The *guru* doesn't have to make a big deal out of himself, 'I'm the only guy who knows.' Not everyone can be a scientist, but everybody can be themselves. It's no big deal.

Sri Ramana's devotees had tremendous devotion to him and he to Arunachala. Please say something about* bhakti, *devotion, in the pursuit of awakening.

You see, true devotion comes out of knowledge, whether it is devotion to a tree or a house or a person. Like love; you can't love somebody you don't know. Suppose I say that person is very nice, you cannot know that just because I said so. But the more you know that person – that he is kind, sensitive, doesn't exploit, helps everybody – the more you know about him, the more you admire him. Same thing with God, the Truth. The more you know about it – the more you know that I am the Truth, the Absolute – the more your admiration automatically goes there and the more you know that this body is a part of the total body, this micro is part of the macro, that I don't stand apart, just as a tiny cell in the body is taken care of by the whole body. And where is He? Everywhere. Which mountain? Every mountain. Which river? Every river. Which leaf? Every leaf. Which human being? Every human being. Which moment? Every moment.

So what is your devotion to? Is there a specific place to be devoted to? A specific person to be devoted to? No. You are devotion itself. As God is, everyone is. He alone is existing. It's natural. Don't say, 'This is the only mountain, this is the only place. This is the vibration.' People are killing each other because they say that this is the only place on the earth which is absolutely holy, and the rest of the places are useless. I went to Israel the other day and I saw a little church, the Jewish cathedral, Jewish monument, the temple, the Wailing Wall and then the Muslim mosque. The most precious real estate in the world, and what is going on? Such a beautiful place; the place has no problem. The people have a big problem all around the world. It is the same thing everywhere.

Seekers often have curious ideas about the enlightened state. Please describe your typical day and how you perceive the world.

Seekers have curious ideas because some teachers have allowed it. I can give you a simple example. In the *Bhagavad Gita* (classical Hindu scripture) *Arjuna* asked *Krishna* what you are asking me now: 'Oh Lord, what is the description of a wise man?' (Verse 54, chapter 2) If he walks, how does he walk? If he speaks, what does he speak? If he sits down, how does he sit down? If he moves, how does he move? You know, *Krishna* completely ignored the question. You know why? Because if he said that a wise man speaks *Sanskrit* very slowly, five billion people would be speaking *Sanskrit* very slowly. If he said the wise man sits in lotus, then everybody sits in lotus. Does he move? Yes, very fast. Everybody would be walking fast. It's like Gandhi's *kadhar* (cotton garment) – anybody putting on a *khadar*, can he become a Gandhi? A wise man may sit down in a particular way, walk in a particular way, but a particular way of sitting down, walking, speaking, living, doesn't make you wise. The wise man can choose a lifestyle, but there is no lifestyle of the wise. Be wise and choose your lifestyle.

There is no wise man's lifestyle. Just be wise and do whatever the situation demands; get up in the morning, maybe go for a walk, come back, have a class, have a little breakfast, have a little lunch, have another class, meet people. Suppose you take on the responsibility of a factory, a company, what does it matter? Once you are wise you can choose any role in life. You are happy; a happy father, a happy husband, happy wife, happy child, happy executive, happily teaching, happily moving, happily doing everything. To be a wise man doesn't mean you just teach and nothing else. You can take any role happily, just like an actor. They don't give Oscars to the roles. They give Oscars to the actors.

You have given us a profound discourse on awakening. When you meet someone with a passion for awakening, what would your short advice be?

If such a person was here now I would say to keep that passion going until he sees himself. He must, because that is a great blessing! Like a river that has taken a turn, the person begins looking at himself, looking for himself. If the person is available we do whatever we can to help him, because that is the time he is vulnerable – like the snake when he is removing his skin, it is a very vulnerable time. A person who is changing his lifestyle, looking for a direction, is very vulnerable. If he meets the wrong people, he can be destroyed. The wrong people are those with wrong ideas. He is suggestible because he is vulnerable, he is desperate. That is why you must never ever sacrifice your intelligence. Once you are convinced the teaching is right, okay, that's fine. But if you say, 'Oh, I don't question anything,' you don't know how many sharks are there to gobble you up. It is the same in any other field of knowledge. Not every doctor is a wonderful person. Some cure, some kill. It is the same thing in the spiritual field. So you have to be extremely careful, very cautious. In the process, am I becoming independent or dependent? That is the big thing. So if you are becoming independent, okay, move on. Ultimately, when you truly say, 'I am free,' listen, there is no reason.

'Are you a happy woman?'

'Yes, because my husband loves me.' Your husband leaves you, you are finished.

'Are you a happy man?'

'Yes.'

'Why?'

'I am happiness itself.' Whoa! Nobody beats it.

Thank you. (laughs)

Thuli Baba

Everything is One. We are that One. You are also that One. There is nothing other than that One. In the ocean there are bubbles and waves, yet the substratum is only water. There are millions of species in creation but for all, the substratum is only One. The One manifests in many different forms.

When you listen to a realised person it's always authentic.

Thuli Baba

Thuli Baba

Thuli Baba was born in 1930 in Tirumandiram Nagar, South India. As a child, Thuli Baba was completely absorbed in spiritual life. His father, Sri Vadivel Swami (Sri Gurudev), destroyed the bond of attachment and sense of 'me' and 'mine' in childhood and later went on to become his *satguru*. When Thuli Baba was sixteen years old he followed the instructions of Sri Gurudev and never used the words 'I' or 'mine' or implied personal identification when referring to himself, but rather uses 'This', 'we', 'our' or 'us'.

His chuckles and dreadlocks make him sound and look like a wizard. Almost naked, he manages to appear as a child and a wise man at the same time. We have met very often and are now so familiar that I am welcomed with a slap on the back! Living in a small, intimate **ashram** ***with around a dozen devotees, he touches deeply with his grace, simplicity and presence.***

Sri Ramana proposed the fundamental question, 'Who am I?' Who are you?

Everything is One. We are that One. You are also that One. There is nothing other than that One, *Brahman* – absolute reality. In the ocean there are bubbles and waves, yet the substratum is only water. There are eighty-four *lakhs* (one hundred thousand) of species in creation but for all, the substratum is only One. The One manifests in many different forms.

Many Western seekers come to India searching for enlightenment as if it is an experience. What is enlightenment?

All people want enlightenment. All of us are That only, but because of our ignorance we don't know who we are. That is veiled by ignorance, so when the ignorance goes away we come to know that we are That. Even in the presence of ignorance we are That only. It is not a question of reaching something or gaining something; we are That. We only have to remove the veil.

Great beings tell us that there are two main obstructions to realising our Self. One is the desire for worldly things like money and gold and other possessions, and the other is the desire for pleasure with the opposite sex. These two things are obstructing the path of realisation. You should gradually reduce all desires for money and for the opposite sex. Then it will definitely be possible to realise the Self.

So enlightenment is not something to be obtained from the outside.

No, no, no, no! Inside! You are That! It's not an object that you can receive; no *guru* can give it to the disciple, nor can the disciple receive it. It's not such an object. You need not go any distance to achieve this. It's not like that.

Sometimes during the rainy season clouds completely veil the sun, so there is no sunshine upon the earth. After the monsoon season is over there is very good sunshine. Like this, ignorance is veiling the Self. The *guru* is only removing the ignorance and attachment to worldly things; he's not doing anything.

How to remove the ignorance?

Gradually, the *guru* removes the desires for worldly things and for the opposite sex; he must do it gradually, he cannot do it suddenly. If you stop these suddenly they will come again in different names and forms. If you gradually release these two, then automatically the experience of the Self will happen.

The Lord is One; there is only one God, for everybody. Leave everything to Him, have faith in Him. Either you believe in the Lord or you believe the *guru*, in whichever form.

***So it's essential to have a* guru.**

There are sixteen arts. Out of these, fifteen are different types of worldly activities, like medicine, dance, music, martial arts. All of these are related to the senses. The sixteenth art is knowledge of the Self. For all the other arts a *guru* may or may not be necessary; that we cannot say. But without the guidance of the *guru* it is not possible to attain Self-realisation.

And who is the* guru*? (laughs)

The *guru* is the Self. The *guru* is the support of everything. Everything is in his hand.

What is the* guru's *role?

There are two types of *gurus* in this world: ordinary *gurus* and the *satguru*. *Satguru* means one who is able to make others realise the Self, the true *guru*. The ordinary *guru* will give you more and more *karmas* (results of all actions). He will say you should first enjoy the world and then practise. The *satguru* will not say this. He will gradually reduce all of the activities and guide you to contemplate, 'I am That, we are That.' He will give you *jnanam*, the method of enquiry, and he will take care of your mind and guide you to Reality. You need some time in the presence of the *satguru* so that you can study yourself. Later you can come and go. Only ordinary *gurus* are available in this world. It is rare to find a *satguru* in the world.

And how to recognise the* satguru*?

If you have an intense desire to realise the Self, if you have taken birth only to realise the Self, then automatically you will meet and recognise the *guru*.

We cannot find the real *satguru*, we have no capacity. He appears like an ordinary human being, he eats, he wears clothes, he looks like all other people. So we cannot recognise him. It is the all-pervading Self who sends the *satguru* to the ripe disciple, the ripe soul.

One should completely surrender to the Lord or to the *guru*. 'I am nothing, I am nobody, I cannot get anything without your help.' One should believe and totally depend upon the *guru*. The *satguru* works like this. First, from his experience, he will teach about non-duality. Here he is like the mother cat raising the kitten. Then, after receiving the teachings from the *satguru*, the disciple has to follow the teachings of the *satguru* as sincerely as the small baby monkey clings to his mother's body.

It is necessary to surrender to the guru*?*

Full surrender is required. The individual has no capacity to recognise the *satguru*, so he should pray to the Almighty, the all-pervading Self, to have compassion and come to him as the *satguru*. It is only the all-pervading Self, *Brahman*, who is guiding and taking care of the disciple.

Are there any qualifications for enlightenment? Is sadhana *(spiritual practice) necessary? If yes, what form do you advise?*

The One appears in different names and forms; the mind is hooked on these names and forms. When the mind is attached to names and forms then interaction takes place. Once you know that these are names and forms, then it is clear that the substratum is One. Only through knowledge does this take place.

Do you suggest a particular sadhana *to clear away this ignorance?*

The One is timeless, to reach the timeless you have to go beyond time. That is why patience is very important. Without patience you cannot reach it. *Sadhana* is one hundred percent patience. There are four types of discipline: *viveka* (discrimination), *vairagya* (renunciation), dispassion, and *shradda* (trust). It is important to reduce worldly activities. The more your mind is engaged with activities, the more extroverted the mind will become. With discipline you should regulate your mind, and through dispassion try to eliminate unnecessary, unwanted jobs and interactions. You should also have an immense desire to be free.

Do you mean to be desireless?

Yes, but there should be no hankering to be desireless. There should be *shradda*, which means to have complete and total acceptance of the scriptures and the *guru's* words. Whatever the *guru* says, you should accept. You cannot witness That with the five sense organs; it is beyond them. Therefore, tremendous faith and a concentrated mind are necessary. There should be a reduction of thoughts. Don't talk too much; don't waste your energy. It is important to control both the eating and speaking tongue. These are the basic disciplines. You should also have an immense capacity for patience. If you have done many years of *sadhana* and nothing has happened, you should not become impatient.

Are you suggesting doing* sadhana *to reduce thoughts and bring the mind into a* sattvic *(calm and peaceful) state?

Yes.

Do you have a particular* sadhana *in mind?

Only one method: total surrender. Everything belongs to God; this is the meaning of surrender. We did not create anything. He has given us everything, including our body and mind, and the whole world. Everything is given by Him. Whatever you have, always think that it all belongs to Him, I don't have anything. Then there will be no 'I' and 'mine', and ego (*ahamkara*) and possessiveness (*mamakara*) will not be there; only total surrender. It is the easiest way.

When you practise in this way everything belongs to Him, and the delusion goes away. When it becomes 'I' and 'mine' we get angry at all the problems that come. When everything belongs to Him, *Bhagavan*, God, then nothing will shake us. With total surrender to God you can even get rid of anger. Delusion and anger go away, resulting in tranquillity of the mind.

There is only one thing, one Truth, the supreme, taking on different names and forms, but it doesn't actually have any existence. You cannot reach it through *sadhana*, it is already there. Because we cannot live in the world without interacting, you should be aware every moment that everything belongs to God and everything is God. When you think like that, no problem will come; anger, desire, all those things will not come.

Self-enquiry brings you to the understanding that I am nothing, that everything is God. Is this the same?

People are now writing books interpreting what Ramana said. What Ramana really means is 'be with That'. You cannot reach That by doing enquiry, you must first negate what is not That. You negate everything else and the remainder is you. You will be That. Truth cannot be explained through words. Be with That and let all your words, everything, subside. No more asking 'Who am I?' Stop everything. All names and forms belong to *Bhagavan*. In this way you reduce interactions.

Ramana Maharshi's words have been misunderstood. Many ask 'Who am I?' They say 'I am so and so', 'I am five feet two inches tall' and 'I am this and that.' You are already That. This is the state of being, this is you. Follow the way of total surrender; surrender what is not That.

You surrender what is not essential?

Yes. These are all just manifestations and they come and go. What is real doesn't come and go.

When Sri Ramana was asked, 'When will the realisation of the Self be gained?' he replied, 'When the world which is what-is-seen has been removed, there will be realisation of the Self which is the seer.' What does it mean to remove the world?

The world doesn't have any real existence. It is like the snake and the rope. Due to ignorance and circumstance someone may see a rope but understand it to be a snake. A snake appears to exist, but it doesn't have any real existence. It is the same way for a *jnani*, one who has realised the Self. For an *ajnani*, an ignorant one, the snake is real, but for people who have awoken, they know this world only appears like the snake. It doesn't have any real existence but at this moment it appears to exist.

It is not necessary to remove anything, only to change the vision. Before awakening there are so many attachments that everything appears real. After awakening you will still be in the midst of objects but you know that they don't have any real existence at all, that they only apparently exist.

When we are writing something or counting money the whole of our attention is on this work. Even if a snake came and bit us we would not be aware of it. Wherever our attention is, the other part of us doesn't pay attention. When you pay attention like this to the One Truth, then, even in the midst of the world, you are there but it has no reality to you. It will be there; it cannot be removed. After gaining the knowledge, only your vision changes. You no longer give importance to the world.

The way to remove the world is to focus on the Self, to know the Self?

There must be understanding also. You cannot focus immediately on the Self. First you must negate what you are not. The Self is there when you interact in the midst of names and forms. You know that the names and forms only apparently exist. When you don't pay attention to the names and forms, automatically your mind remains in That, it becomes silent in That. Your attention automatically goes to the Self, the names and forms just come and go.

Are you talking about the Self when you refer to 'That'?

Yes. When the mind and everything withdraws, then you remain in That: your Self. We are the Self only. Enquire into the nature of all these names and forms. The substratum is your Self.

It may take thirty, forty or fifty years, but if you remain in your being, this state is beyond time. Everything just disappears because you are timeless. Whatever you see, hear, smell, touch or taste through the five sense organs, it is as though everything is non-existent. You will be eating, but only for hunger's sake. You will be listening, but just for the sake of listening. There will be no hook anywhere. Your mind will rest only in your being: the Self.

This is *swaroopa ananda*, always remaining in your Self; it is not experiential pleasure. It doesn't give you the experience of happiness. When you are established in that Self, then there will be no seeking, no *sadhana*, nothing; everything just goes.

It has been suggested that the mind must be destroyed for liberation to occur. Sri Ramana uses the term* manonasha, *meaning destroyed mind, to describe the state of liberation. Is this necessary?

There are two factors, *manolayam* and *manonasha*. *Manolayam* is mind suppressed through meditation or *yoga*. Mind becomes temporarily inactive, but this doesn't help you. It may come up again.

Enquire into what is true, *satyam*, and what is not true, *mithya*. When you enquire, you know that all names and forms are temporary, *mithya*, only apparently existing. When the mind no longer goes into names and forms, this is called *satyam dhyanam* (absorption in Truth). The real *vasthu* (nature) is only Self, our Self, *atman*, That, Being. When your mind stays there, naturally mind is destroyed: *manonasha*.

You say that the supreme Truth is flowing through you, but do you still have a mind?

Yes, it is only through the mind that we can speak together, it is the mind that is attuned to the Truth. Here, the mind becomes wisdom.

Could you say that it is not about preventing thoughts arising, it is about not being attached to thoughts when they arise?

A *jnani* (one who knows) does not have mind but he has wisdom. In order to clarify the doubts or to interact with people, he comes down to the witness state (divine state, form of wisdom) from the Undivided State. The individual soul has mind which binds him. On the other hand, a *jnani* has wisdom which does not oscillate like the mind.

Jnanis do not see which country you come from or if you are male or female. They see the *chaitanya*, the conciousness alone, and that it is the name and form that is asking the questions. There are thoughts, but they don't give reality to them in the way an ignorant person gives them reality. Without thoughts how can they interact with the world?

This is important because many believe that a realised person has no thoughts.

Because this body exists we have hunger, we feel heat and cold and all these things. But we act without giving importance or reality to these things. We are detached, these things do not touch us. If the cloth is dry, the dirt can just be shaken away.

There are many who spend twenty or thirty years of their lives trying to kill their minds with meditation.

It is not a question of *yoga*, meditation, or any other thing. It is necessary to proceed through Self-knowledge and enquiry.

Vedanta (*Vedic* philosophy) says *tat tvam asi. Tat* means That, *tvam* means you: you are That. You are That Almighty. The ocean is vast and almost all-pervasive compared to other objects. Imagine there is a big pot and a small pot in the ocean. Both are full of seawater but the small one has a seal over the top.

The water in the big pot mixes freely with that of the ocean around it. In the same way, if you place the all-pervasive, omnipotent, omniscient *vasthu* in a vessel, it takes the form of God. You can give it different names, Jesus or *Shiva*, but it doesn't have any seal over it. So that water from the pot can mix with the ocean. But the small pot of water has a seal over it, so it cannot mix with the ocean. This is like the *jiva*, the individual soul. The seal is iron mind, *ahamkara*. When *ahamkara* and *mamakara* (possessivness) are removed, everything is yours.

With true *bhavana* (development) you remove the iron mind seal and possessiveness. The small pot of water mixes with the ocean. This is *tat tvam asi*. The *Vedas* (ancient Indian *Sanskrit* texts) state that every *jiva* is that Truth. *Aham brahmasi* means I am that *Brahman*, absolute reality. Because of the iron mind seal we believe that we are a limited *jiva*, and that we are not the unlimited. If you want to become the unlimited, all-pervasive *tat*, the Self, you have to remove the seal.

***What about* vasanas, *the tendencies of the mind? Must they be dealt with, or is it enough to achieve a* sattvic *mind and to be familiar with the* vasanas *so they no longer bind? How to remove the* vasanas?**

Through enquiry of Truth all your old tendencies go away. Most people give importance to names and forms, they don't see Truth. Only those who seek the Truth say that names and forms only apparently exist. *Vasana nakshya* means destruction of your habitual thinking. Through enquiry into Truth your habitual error is removed, and there is *manonasha*. But realistically speaking, you do not completely remove your mind; you may still be interacting in the world but you know the names and forms are false, *mithya*.

When you are helpless, first you seek the help of an almighty. Everybody starts with some *Bhagavan* or some God, and through that grace you will meet a *satguru*. Without the help of the *satguru*, ignorance cannot be removed. Your *vasanas* can easily be eliminated with the help of your *satguru*. He knows the problems you have in your mind. The *satguru* tackles your *vasanas* in a subtle way without you knowing. You should have trust and dispassion. Only then can he show you how to practise.

***Is it impossible to become Self-realised without the help of a* guru?**

Yes. A living *guru* is very important. Dead *gurus* cannot help you because they cannot answer your questions. Only flesh and blood *gurus* can solve your problem. Dead *gurus* cannot give you *jnanam*, the method of enquiry.

This is very important. People follow dead* gurus *because it is much easier as they don't tell you things you don't want to hear. Living* gurus *can tell you things you don't want to hear!

That's the truth! (laughs)

Are there any stages of enlightenment?

If there are a lot of *vasanas*, there must be stages. Each person has many *vasanas*: anger, greed, lust, vengeance. Contemplating on 'We are That, That we are', will gradually reduce all the mental qualities. Everyone has to experience this stage. Years before starting our *sadhana* we used to react immediately, we would get angry quickly, we had a short temper. Now we are doing *sadhana* we can see that everything is the Lord, everything is done by His action, everything is His property. So we can see the world in a peaceful manner. All the unhelpful qualities will gradually reduce. Finally, all the *vasanas* will disappear and we will realise the Self. These are the only stages. But you must make a lot of effort; it will take a lot of work and it will take many years.

Sri Ramana Maharshi said Self-enquiry is the most direct route to realising the Self. What do you have to say about Self-enquiry?

We have no experience of Ramana's Self-enquiry so we cannot speak about it. All great beings have separate paths to realise the Self.

What practice do you suggest?

There are two methods. The first is to firmly believe I am That; there is no world at all, no name and no form. If you constantly contemplate 'We are That, That we are,' and that it is only due to mind that we see the world, then you will realise the Self.

The second method is to negate everything: this is false, that is false. Then you will realise the Self. If you firmly believe I am That, gradually the false will drop away. If you negate the false, only the Truth remains.

Traditionally, devotees had tremendous devotion,* bhakti, *to the master. Please say something about* bhakti *in the pursuit of awakening.

Traditionally, devotees had full faith in the Lord as name and form. So they fully devoted their lives to Him. This way, all *karmas* will eventually vanish. After devotion, the *guru* can remove the ignorance. This is like green leaves dried in the sunlight. Green leaves do not burn so we dry them in the sunlight. The *guru* is like a lens focussing the sun's rays on the dry leaves, then they burn up. In previous centuries most followed the path of *bhakti* only. [This is the path Thuli followed. He was devoted to Lord *Krishna*, then his father became his *guru*.]

Western people cannot accept *bhakti*. They don't have a concept of the Lord or anything like that, so they cannot accept it. For them we have to say, 'You believe that the Almighty is the all-pervading Self.' In that way we have to guide Western people. They cannot accept the Lord as name and form. If they cannot even accept Jesus Christ, how can they have devotion?

Do you see a difference between Eastern people and Western people?

The paths are somewhat different. Those from Eastern countries like India traditionally have strong *bhakti*. Eventually there is desire to enjoy the world, so they take their next birth in the West. They fulfill their desires and become dissatisfied. Whatever is so far enjoyed in the world is false, it will not bring peace or bliss. It is a cycle of happiness then sorrow. So then they come to India in search of permanent peace, the ultimate Truth, the ultimate happiness, bliss. They progress on the path of Self-knowledge and become realised.

So really, the reason the Westerners are not taking the path of devotion is because they have already completed that in previous births.

In this birth you contemplate 'We are That, That we are' ceaselessly, like a continuous flow of oil. This alone is sufficient; there is no need to go back to devotion.

Here at Anbin Kudil (Abode of Love) there are Indian swamis and Western swamis living together. Do you see a difference in the progress of the Western people, or do you see them all now as Indians?

Each has their own way, their own *sadhana*, their own attitudes. The goal is One, but the attitudes are different. The Western people cannot follow the path of devotion, but they have full faith in the *satguru*. That is their mission, full faith in the master.

You also are completing your *sadhana*, and now you are sitting here. You cannot go back. You cannot go back to Germany.

Do you mean me? (laughs) I can't go back to Germany?

Stay some days, some months or some years, and then your journey will be finished.

This is why I only come for one day! (all laugh)

If you are truly interested in the spiritual path, the path of devotion and realisation, then your mind will not go back into Western culture. That culture cannot accept *bhakti*.

I was with Osho for fifteen years and with Papaji for five years. I have been visiting India for thirty years and lived in India for a total of ten years. You see, it hasn't worked!

A woodcutter wants to cut a tree. He cuts many trees in the forest but he leaves without cutting any one tree completely. In this way you have been meeting many different things in India. Visiting many saints and getting more information means the mind cannot settle. You are not staying with any one master so you cannot become one-pointed.

Your mind is only on the external activities of the teachers, you are not going within. You have to practise what you have learned from the masters. Nothing is going into the heart. What is the use? Instead of knowing many things from many masters and many saints you should learn only that one thing, and contemplate on that one point, one instruction, one teaching. You should stay with one master and fully observe all the teachings from that one master.

Suppose you purchase one or two acres of land and you want to dig a well to get water. You are digging down when someone comes along and says, 'Don't dig here, the water is over there.' So you go and dig there. Then another person comes along and says, 'You won't get water here. Dig over there.' This goes on all day; you dig and dig but you never finish a well. (laughs) In this way your lifetime is completely wasted. You should not go on getting more and more teachings. You should have only one teaching. You should pray to the Almighty: 'Please show your compassion. I want to go deep into the teachings, I want to observe all the teachings. Let me have my own experience.'

If you go on digging in many places you will never get water. Pray to the Lord and dig only one well. Then you can quench your thirst.

Oh dear, perhaps I should reincarnate as an Indian next time.

No, no! Don't think that you have to take another birth! There is no need! This birth is the last birth. If you gradually reduce all your questions, and gradually finish seeing other masters, then you will definitely be a *jivanmukta* (liberated soul in this life). Reduce your questions.

I only have one more question. (both laugh) Seekers often have curious ideas about the enlightened state. Please describe your typical day and how you perceive the world.

We have no halo, we just sit quietly by ourself. In Tamil we call it *summa iru*, just being by yourself. And we see ourself in everything. There is no difference, no low or high, no discrimination. We see everybody in the same way. Everything is that supreme One.

Is there anything you would like to add?

Jnanis always speak the Truth; with a few words they explain the *dharma*, the path of Truth. When the disciple writes it down, the words arise from his mind and he will add his *vasanas* to it. When you listen to a realised person it's always authentic.

In the Indian tradition, the *Vedas* and the *rishis* (seers of the *Vedas*) are available all the time. Those who have mastered their sense organs become an instrument to that Truth. It does not come from study or imagination. *Jnanis* are like an instrument, they don't add anything to it. They allow the supreme Truth to flow through this instrument.

Who Am I?
Nan Yar

Nan Yar – Who Am I? is the standard introduction to the teachings of Bhagavan Sri Ramana Maharshi. Originally, these answers were written by Sri Ramana in the sand of Arunachala in 1901, when he would have been twenty-one years old. They were given in response to questions asked by Sivaprakasam Pillai. The original work was rewritten in the 1920s by Sri Ramana and is one of the few texts edited and approved by him.

All living beings desire to be happy always, without any misery. In everyone there is observed supreme love for oneself. And happiness alone is the cause of love. In order therefore, to gain that happiness which is one's nature and which is experienced in the state of deep sleep, where there is no mind, one should know oneself. To achieve this, the Path of Knowledge, the enquiry in the form of 'Who am I?' is the principal means.

1. Who am I?

The gross body which is composed of the seven humours (*dhatus*), I am not; the five cognitive sense organs, viz., the senses of hearing, touch, sight, taste and smell, which apprehend their respective objects, viz. sound, touch, colour, taste and odour, I am not; the five cognitive sense organs, viz., the organs of speech, locomotion, grasping, excreting and enjoying, I am not; the five vital airs, *prana*, etc., which perform respectively the five functions of in-breathing, etc., I am not; even the mind which thinks, I am not; the nescience too, which is endowed only with the residual impressions of objects and in which there are no objects and no functions, I am not.

2. If I am none of these, then who am I?
After negating all of the above mentioned as 'not this', 'not this', this Awareness which alone remains – that I am.

3. What is the nature of Awareness?
The nature of Awareness is Existence-Consciousness-Bliss.

4. When will the realisation of the Self be gained?
When the world which is what-is-seen has been removed, there will be realisation of the Self which is the Seer.

5. Will there not be realisation of the Self even while the world is there (taken as real)?
There will not be.

6. Why?
The seer and the object seen are like the rope and the snake. Just as the knowledge of the rope which is the substratum will not arise unless the false knowledge of the illusory serpent goes, so the realisation of the Self which is the substratum will not be gained unless the belief that the world is real is removed.

7. When will the world which is the object seen be removed?
When the mind, which is the cause of all cognition and of all actions, becomes quiescent, the world will disappear.

8. What is the nature of the mind?
What is called 'mind' is a wondrous power residing in the Self. It causes all thoughts to arise. Apart from thoughts, there is no such thing as mind. Therefore, thought is the nature of mind. Apart from thoughts, there is no independent entity called the world. In deep sleep there are no thoughts, and there is no world. In the states of waking and dream, there are thoughts, and there is a world also. Just as the spider emits the thread (of the web) out of itself and again withdraws it into itself, likewise the mind projects the world out of itself and again resolves it into itself.

When the mind comes out of the Self, the world appears. Therefore, when the world appears (to be real), the Self does not appear; and when the Self appears (shines) the world does not appear. When one persistently inquires into the nature of the mind, the mind will end leaving the Self (as the residue). What is referred to as the Self is the *Atman*. The mind always exists only in dependence on something gross; it cannot stay alone. It is the mind that is called the subtle body or the soul (*jiva*).

9. What is the path of inquiry for understanding the nature of the mind?
That which rises as 'I' in this body is the mind. If one inquires as to where in the body the thought 'I' rises first, one would discover that it rises in the heart. That is the place of the mind's origin. Even if one thinks constantly 'I-I', one will be led to that place. Of all the thoughts that arise in the mind, the 'I'-thought is the first. It is only after the rise of this that the other thoughts arise. It is after the appearance of the first personal pronoun that the second and the third personal pronouns appear; without the first personal pronoun there will not be the second and the third.

10. How will the mind become quiescent?
By the inquiry 'Who am I?' The thought 'Who am I?' will destroy all other thoughts, and like the stick used for stirring the burning pyre, it will itself in the end get destroyed. Then, there will arise Self-realisation.

11. What is the means for constantly holding on to the thought 'Who am I?'
When other thoughts arise, one should not pursue them, but should inquire: 'To whom do they arise?' It does not matter how many thoughts arise. As each thought arises, one should inquire with diligence, 'To whom has this thought arisen?' The answer that would emerge would be 'to me'. Thereupon if one inquires 'Who am I?', the mind will go back to its source; and the thought that arose will become quiescent. With repeated practice in this manner, the mind will develop the skill to stay in its source. When the mind that is subtle goes out through the brain and the sense-organs, the gross names and forms appear; when it stays in

the heart, the names and forms disappear. Not letting the mind go out, but retaining it in the Heart is what is called 'inwardness' (*antarmukha*). Letting the mind go out of the Heart is known as 'externalisation' (*bahirmukha*). Thus, when the mind stays in the Heart, the 'I', which is the source of all thoughts will go, and the Self which ever exists will shine. Whatever one does, one should do without the egoity 'I'. If one acts in that way, all will appear as of the nature of *Shiva* (God).

12. Are there no other means for making the mind quiescent?

Other than inquiry, there are no adequate means. If through other means it is sought to control the mind, the mind will appear to be controlled, but will again go forth. Through the control of breath also, the mind will become quiescent; but it will be quiescent only so long as the breath remains controlled, and when the breath resumes the mind also will again start moving and will wander as impelled by residual impressions. The source is the same for both mind and breath. Thought, indeed, is the nature of the mind. The thought 'I' is the first thought of the mind; and that is egoity. It is from that whence egoity originates that breath also originates. Therefore, when the mind becomes quiescent, the breath is controlled, and when the breath is controlled the mind becomes quiescent. But in deep sleep, although the mind becomes quiescent, the breath does not stop. This is because of the will of God, so that the body may be preserved and other people may not be under the impression that it is dead. In the state of waking and in *samadhi*, when the mind becomes quiescent the breath is controlled. Breath is the gross form of the mind. Till the time of death, the mind keeps breath in the body; and when the body dies, the mind takes the breath along with it. Therefore, the exercise of breath control is only an aid for rendering the mind quiescent (*manonigra*); it will not destroy the mind (*manonasha*). Like the practice of breath control, meditation on the forms of God, repetition of *mantras*, restriction on food, etc., are but aids for rendering the mind quiescent.

Through meditation on the forms of God and through repetition of mantras, the mind becomes one-pointed. The mind will always be wandering. Just as when a chain is given to an elephant to hold in its trunk it will go along grasping the chain and nothing else, so also when the mind is occupied with a name or form it will grasp that alone. When the mind expands in the form of countless thoughts, each thought becomes weak; but as thoughts get resolved the mind becomes one-pointed and strong; for such a mind Self-inquiry will become easy. Of all the restrictive rules, that relating to the taking of *sattvic* food in moderate quantities is the best; by observing this rule, the *sattvic* quality of mind will increase, and that will be helpful to Self-inquiry.

13. The residual impressions (thoughts) of objects appear unending like the waves of an ocean. When will all of them get destroyed?
As the meditation on the Self rises higher and higher, the thoughts will get destroyed.

14. Is it possible for the residual impressions of objects that come from beginningless time, as it were, to be resolved, and for one to remain as the pure Self?
Without yielding to the doubt 'Is it possible, or not?' one should persistently hold on to the meditation on the Self. Even if one be a great sinner, one should not worry and weep 'O! I am a sinner, how can I be saved?' One should completely renounce the thought 'I am a sinner' and concentrate keenly on mediation on the Self alone; then, one would surely succeed. There are not two minds – one good and the other evil; the mind is only one. It is the residual impressions that are of two kinds – auspicious and inauspicious. When the mind is under the influence of auspicious impressions it is called good; and when it is under the influence of inauspicious impressions it is regarded as evil.
The mind should not be allowed to wander towards worldly objects and what concerns other people. However bad other people may be, one should bear no hatred for them. Both desire and hatred should be eschewed. All that one gives to others one gives to one's self. If this truth is understood who will not give to others? When one's self arises all arises; when one's self becomes quiescent all becomes quiescent. To the extent we behave with humility, to that extent there will result good. If the mind is rendered quiescent, one may live anywhere.

15. How long should inquiry be practised?
As long as there are impressions of objects in the mind, so long the inquiry 'Who am I?' is required. As thoughts arise they should be destroyed then and there in the very place of their origin, through inquiry. If one resorts to contemplation of the Self unintermittently, until the Self is gained, that alone would do. As long as there are enemies within the fortress, they will continue to sally forth; if they are destroyed as they emerge, the fortress will fall into our hands.

16. What is the nature of the Self?
What exists is the Self alone. The world, the individual soul and God are appearances in it, like silver in mother-of-pearl; these three appear at the same time and disappear at the same time.
The Self is that where there is absolutely no 'I'-thought. That is called 'Silence'. The Self itself is the world; the Self itself is 'I'; the Self itself is God; all is *Shiva*, the Self.

17. Is not everything the work of God?
Without desire, resolve, or effort, the sun rises; and in its mere presence, the sun-stone emits fire, the lotus blooms, water evaporates, people perform their various functions and then rest. Just as in the presence of the magnet the needle moves, it is by virtue of the mere presence of God that the souls governed by the three (cosmic) functions or the fivefold divine activity perform their actions and then rest, in accordance with their respective *karmas*. God has no resolve; no *karma* attaches itself to Him. That is like worldly actions not affecting the sun, or like the merits and demerits of the other four elements not affecting all-pervading space.

18. Of the devotees, who is the greatest?
He who gives himself up to the Self that is God is the most excellent devotee. Giving one's self up to God means remaining constantly in the Self without giving room for the rise of any thoughts other than that of the Self.
Whatever burdens are thrown on God, He bears them. Since the supreme power of God makes all things move, why should we, without

submitting ourselves to it, constantly worry ourselves with thoughts as to what should be done and how, and what should not be done and how not? We know that the train carries all loads, so after getting on it why should we carry our small luggage on our head to our discomfort, instead of putting it down in the train and feeling at ease?

19. What is non-attachment?
As thoughts arise, destroying them utterly without any residue in the very place of their origin is non-attachment. Just as the pearl-diver ties a stone to his waist, sinks to the bottom of the sea and there takes the pearls, so each one of us should be endowed with non-attachment, dive within oneself and obtain the Self-Pearl.

20. Is it possible for God and the **Guru** *to effect the liberation of a soul?*
God and the *Guru* will only show the way to liberation; they will not by themselves take the soul to the state of liberation.
In truth, God and the *Guru* are not different. Just as the prey which has fallen into the jaws of a tiger has no escape, so those who have come within the ambit of the *Guru's* gracious look will be saved by the *Guru* and will not get lost; yet, each one should, by his own effort pursue the path shown by God or *Guru* and gain liberation. One can know oneself only with one's own eye of knowledge, and not with somebody else's. Does he who is Rama require the help of a mirror to know that he is Rama?

*21. Is it necessary for one who longs for liberation to inquire into the nature of categories (***tattvas***)?*
Just as one who wants to throw away garbage has no need to analyse it and see what it is, so one who wants to know the Self has no need to count the number of categories or inquire into their characteristics; what he has to do is to reject altogether the categories that hide the Self. The world should be considered like a dream.

22. Is there no difference between waking and dream?
Waking is long and dream short; other than this there is no difference. Just as waking happenings seem real while awake, so do those in a

dream while dreaming. In dream the mind takes on another body. In both waking and dream states thoughts, names and forms occur simultaneously.

23. Is it any use reading books for those who long for liberation?
All the texts say that in order to gain liberation one should render the mind quiescent; therefore their conclusive teaching is that the mind should be rendered quiescent; once this has been understood there is no need for endless reading. In order to quieten the mind one has only to inquire within oneself what one's Self is; how could this search be done in books? One should know one's Self with one's own eye of wisdom. The Self is within the five sheaths; but books are outside them. Since the Self has to be inquired into by discarding the five sheaths, it is futile to search for it in books. There will come a time when one will have to forget all that one has learned.

24. What is happiness?
Happiness is the very nature of the Self; happiness and the Self are not different. There is no happiness in any object of the world. We imagine through our ignorance that we derive happiness from objects. When the mind goes out, it experiences misery. In truth, when its desires are fulfilled, it returns to its own place and enjoys the happiness that is the Self. Similarly, in the states of sleep, *samadhi* and fainting, and when the object desired is obtained or the object disliked is removed, the mind becomes inward-turned, and enjoys pure Self-Happiness. Thus the mind moves without rest alternately going out of the Self and returning to it. Under the tree the shade is pleasant; out in the open the heat is scorching. A person who has been going about in the sun feels cool when he reaches the shade. Someone who keeps on going from the shade into the sun and then back into the shade is a fool. A wise man stays permanently in the shade. Similarly, the mind of the one who knows the truth does not leave *Brahman*. The mind of the ignorant, on the contrary, revolves in the world, feeling miserable, and for a little time returns to *Brahman* to experience happiness. In fact, what is called the world is only thought. When the world disappears, i.e., when there

is no thought, the mind experiences happiness; and when the world appears, it goes through misery.

25. What is wisdom-insight (*jnana drishti*)?
Remaining quiet is what is called wisdom-insight. To remain quiet is to resolve the mind in the Self. Telepathy, knowing past, present and future happenings and clairvoyance do not constitute wisdom-insight.

26. What is the relation between desirelessness and wisdom?
Desirelessness is wisdom. The two are not different; they are the same. Desirelessness is refraining from turning the mind towards any objects. Wisdom means the appearance of no object. In other words, not seeking what is other than the Self is detachment or desirelessness; not leaving the Self is wisdom.

27. What is the difference between inquiry and meditation?
Inquiry consists in retaining the mind in the Self. Meditation consists in thinking that one's self is *Brahman*, Existence-Consciousness-Bliss.

28. What is liberation?
Inquiring into the nature of one's self that is in bondage, and realsising one's true nature is liberation.

Glossary

Advaita — Non-duality; a school of *Vedanta* philosophy teaching the Oneness of God, soul, and universe, whose chief exponent was *Adi Shankara.*

ahamkara — The ego that considers itself as an 'acting I'.

ajna — Third eye *chakra.* Located between the eyebrows. Intuition and wisdom.

ajnani — One who has not realised the Self; unenlightened.

anahata — (Lit: unstruck sound) Heart *chakra.* Located in the centre of the chest. Unconditional love, compassion and neutrality.

ananda — Bliss. One of the three qualities of the Self: *sat-chit-ananda.*

Arjuna — Main male figure from the *Bhagavad Gita* who receives instruction from Lord *Krishna* about the nature of being and the meaning of life. *Arjuna* represents the human being caught in ignorance.

artha — One of the four 'goals of life'. Considered to be a noble goal as long as it follows the dictates of *Vedic* morality. The concept includes achieving widespread fame, garnering wealth and having an elevated social standing.

artharthi — One who desires material gain (*artha*).

Arunachala — Holy mountain at Tiruvannamalai in South India. Considered to be *Shiva.* Sri Ramana Maharshi called *Arunachala* his *guru.* He arrived there aged sixteen and never left.

Arunachaleswara — Hindu temple dedicated to Lord *Shiva*, located at the foot of *Arunachala*, Tiruvannamalai; home of Lord *Shiva* and his wife Parvati. The inner sanctum is more than two thousand years old.

ashram — In ancient India a Hindu hermitage where sages lived in peace and tranquility amidst nature. Today, the term *ashram* is usually used to refer to an intentional

	community formed primarily for spiritual upliftment of its members, often headed by a religious leader or mystic.
atman	The individual aspect of the Self.
avatar	Incarnation (becoming flesh) of a god, the Divine. The term *avatar* has many similarities with the term 'messiah' in other religions.
Bhagavad Gita	A portion of the *Mahabharata* in which Lord *Krishna*, an incarnation of Lord *Vishnu*, gives spiritual instructions to *Arjuna*.
Bhagavan	God. Respectful title for a realised being.
Bhagavatam	Classical Indian text describing the life of Lord *Shiva*.
bhajan	(Lit: to worship) Song with religious content, which is often dedicated to specific gods.
bhakta	Devotee.
bhakti	Devotion, love. Traditionally, one of the principal approaches to God-realisation.
bhakti marga	The path of devotion.
bhavana	Development, cultivation.
Bodhisattva	One who has gained complete liberation; an enlightened being who is no longer caught in the cycle of birth and death, yet continues to incarnate out of compassion until all sentient beings are awakened.
Brahma	The creator. With *Shiva* (the destroyer) and *Vishnu* (the preserver), one of the main Hindu deities.
brahma bhava	Being in *Brahman*.
Brahman	The impersonal, absolute reality – the Self.
Brahma Sutra	Also known as *Vedanta Sutra*; cryptic statements whose subject matter is *Brahman*.
Buddha	Usually refers to *Gautama Buddha*, the founder of Buddhism, often referred to simply as 'the *Buddha*'. A *buddha* (Sanskrit: awakened) is any being who has become fully awakened.
buddhi	A feminine *Sanskrit* noun derived from the root *budh* – to be awake, to understand, to know.

Chaitanya	Consciousness; or *Chaitanya Mahaprabhu*: a sixteenth century Hindu saint, well-known for his devotion to Lord *Krishna*.
chakra	(Lit: wheel) One of the seven subtle energy centres in the body, located on a line from the perineum to the crown of the head.
Deepam	One of the oldest festivals of light celebrated by Tamil Hindus on the full moon day of the month of Karthikai (Nov/Dec). Houses and streets are lit up with rows of oil lamps. The huge lamp is lit on the peak of the holy mountain, *Arunachala*, Tiruvannamalai.
dharma	Practice or path of Truth.
dhyana/dhyanam	(Lit: meditation) The state of deep meditation. Equivalent term is 'Zen' in Buddhism.
drisha	The world of objects.
dukha	Sorrow.
gunas	The three qualities of all manifestation: *sattva* (purity), *rajas* (activity) and *tamas* (sluggishness).
guru	A teacher in the religious or spiritual sense, commonly used in Hinduism, Buddhism, and Sikhism. The *guru* is seen in these religions as a sacred conduit for wisdom and guidance. In many branches of the aforementioned religions, the importance of finding a true *guru* is given as a prerequisite for attaining Self-realisation.
Iswara	The Lord; the Almighty.
japam	Practice of repitition of the Lord's name or of a *mantra*.
jiva	(Lit: living being) The individual soul, which, until liberation, will continue to incarnate. In essence, it is one with the Universal Soul.
jivanmukta	One who is liberated while still alive.
jivatman	The individual aspect of atman; the 'opposite pole' is *paramatman*, the absolute aspect of *atman*.
jnana	Knowledge of what is real and what is not real. A principal, traditional path to realisation of the final Reality, the Self.

jnana marga	The path of knowledge.
Jnana Vasishta	Teachings of the master and saint *Vasishta,* who is considered the incarnation of *Brahma*; and the title of the book in which this teaching is explained.
jnani	One who has realised the Self.
kamana	Desire, wish.
karma	(Lit: action) Cosmic law of cause and effect, the result of an individual's past action, which is said to invariably return to him at some point in time. Also: the collective storehouse of merit or demerit from all of an individual's past actions.
karma yoga	The *yoga* of action based on the teachings of the *Bhagavad Gita.* Focuses on the adherence to duty while remaining detached from the reward. It states that one can attain salvation (*moksha*) or love of God (*bhakti*) by performing one's duties in an unselfish manner.
kashaya	Hidden desires.
Kenopanishad	One of the older, primary *Upanishads* commented upon by *Shankara.*
Krishna	(Lit: all-attractive) Incarnation of *Vishnu,* who is considered the Supreme God. Usually depicted as a young cowherd playing a flute or as a youthful prince giving philosophical instruction. Represents knowledge and bliss.
leela	The play of God; divine play.
lingam	A symbol of the Divine, in the form of a phallus, for the Hindu god, *Shiva.*
Mahabharata	Great epic of the Bharata people. National epic of India. Consists of 106,000 couplets. Existed in various forms for well over two thousand years. It's most famous text is the *Bhagavad Gita.*
mahatma	(Lit: great soul) Great man or saint.
mala	(Lit: bead) *Japa mala* is a circle of 108 beads, like a rosary, often used as an aid for repetition of a *mantra.*
mananam	Reflection; the second of the three main methods to reach *jnana.*

manipura	(Lit: city of jewels) Navel *chakra*. Located just above the navel. Life force, will and transformation.
manokara	Thinking mind.
manolaya	Absorbed state of the mind, which is temporal in nature.
manonasha	(Lit: extinction of the mind) Destruction of the illusion of a separate I.
mantra	(Lit: tool for the mind) Sacred sound. In the Hindu traditions a sound from the *Vedas*. Repeated either orally or mentally and used as an aid in bringing concentration to the mind. The most well-known *mantra* is the original sound *om*.
manushyatvam	Humanity. Assemblage of all specific qualities that distinguish man from other beings, including those higher values which are essentially human.
marga	A path.
maya	Worldly illusion, mistaking the transient for the real; non-awareness of actuality, appearances masquerading as reality.
mithya	(Lit: unreal) In Hindu thought, the world as we see it is unreal, and is only a projection of God.
moksha	Liberation from *samsara*, the cycle of death and rebirth and all of the suffering and limitations of worldly existence.
mukti	Release. See *moksha*.
muladhara	Base or root *chakra*. Located in the region between the genitals and the anus. Grounding, instinct and survival.
mumukshu	One who desires liberation.
mumukshutvam	The desire to achieve liberation.
nididhyasanam	Final step of the three-step process towards Self-realisation; involves deep meditation and requires *mumukshutvam*.
nitya	Forever, eternal, beyond the influence of time.
om	Cosmic, eternal sound.

omkara	Same as the sacred, mystical syllable *om*.
papa	Sin, crime, evil; negative consequences of bad acts.
parabrahman	The Supreme *Brahman*.
paramatman	Highest, divine *atman*. *Atman* is the Higher Self of human beings; *paramatman* is the Higher Self of God.
Periya Purana	One of the Hindu scriptures speaking about *Shiva*.
prakasha	Radiating beam, clarity, light. Also the ability to see reality clearly.
prakriti	Essential nature, eternal power.
Prakriya	A category of the *Upanishads* which deals with different teaching methods.
pranayama	Breath control.
prarabdha	(Lit: begun, undertaken) One of the three types of *karma*. The fruit of all of our past actions that now has its effect. Destiny or fate.
prasad	A gift of food from the *guru*, usually handed out at the end of *Satsang*, though often also distributed on religious occasions at temples and shrines.
prem	Love.
premananda	Unconditional love and bliss.
puja	Worship. Ritual in which offerings are made and prayers said.
punya	Good *karma* created by good thoughts, words and actions. Generated by giving, kindness and *dharma* practice.
purna	Completeness, fullness.
purusharta	Human effort, individual exertion, ideal.
rajas	One of the three *gunas*. Quality of activity, passion, birth, creativity. The fruit is often pain, even though the immediate effect is pleasure.
reiki	Japanese form of healing using the life force energy by laying hands above the body.
sadguru/satguru	The *guru* who leads one to freedom – Self-realisation.

sadhaka Spiritual seeker.

sadhana Spiritual practice.

sadhu (Lit: right, holy) A pious or righteous man. Traditionally a renunciate, a wanderer with a bare minimum of possessions, who relies on alms for daily needs.

sahaja samadhi Highest state of enlightenment. Effortless and permanent.

sahasrara (Lit: thousand-petaled lotus) Crown *chakra*. Located at the top of the head. Ultimate Self-knowing and understanding.

sakshat sadhana *Sadhana* of the direct path of God-realisation.

samadhi A non-dualistic state of consciousness. The experiencing subject becomes one with the experienced object, the mind becomes still. Direct experience of the Self.

samsara The continuous cycle of birth and death caused by illusion and desire.

sangha The community or gathering of devotees around a *guru*.

sannyasin Renunciate, who, after being initiated by a *guru* or religious superior, is given a spiritual name and takes vows to abandon all ties with conventional society and live with one-pointed attention on God only.

Sanskrit (Lit: refined, consecrated, sanctified) Ancient language of the *Vedas*. In Hinduism and Buddhism it was regarded as 'the language of the gods'. Nowadays used mainly for religious and scientific discourse. Origin of all Indo-Germanic languages.

sastra Sacred scriptures.

sat Truth.

satchitananda Truth – consciousness – bliss. The three qualities of the Absolute, *Brahman*.

satchitananda brahma '*Brahman* is Truth, consciousness and bliss.'

satori (Japanese: enlightenment) Awakening to the profound understanding of the true nature of existence.

Satsang (Lit: abiding in the Truth) The gathering of the *guru* with his students.

sattva Purity, goodness; the highest of the three *gunas*.

sattvic Pure. Anglicised adjective from *sattva*.

sattvika One who is endowed with goodness, one who is pure and still.

satya Truth.

shakti The power of becoming, the energy of creation; as goddess, the female aspect of *Shiva*.

Shankara *Adi Shankara*: Indian sage of the 9th century who is considered the most influential figure of *Advaita Vedanta*.

shishya A pupil or disciple, especially one who has proven himself and has formally been accepted by a *guru*.

Shiva The destroyer. With *Brahma* (the creator) and *Vishnu* (the preserver), one of the main Hindu deities.

shraddha Faith and trust.

shradda shastra Trust in the *Vedic* scriptures; especially that these texts contain higher knowledge which reveals the timeless, 'seen' Truth. In the wider sense: trust in God.

shravanam Listening, hearing.

siddha A person who has achieved a *siddhi*.

siddhi Supernatural power, paranormal ability.

sloka A *Sanskrit* verse.

stitha pragna Person of steady wisdom.

svadhisthana Belly or sacral *chakra*. Located in the lower abdomen, centered between the navel and the genitals. Life energy, creativity and sexuality.

Swami Title for religious attainment and scholarship.

swaroopa ananda The highest state of bliss.

tamas Sluggishness, inactivity, darkness. One of the three *gunas*

tantra Asian body of beliefs and practices which works from the principle that the universe we experience is nothing other than the concrete manifestation of the divine energy. It seeks to ritually appropriate and channel that

	energy within the human microcosm, in creative and emancipatory ways.
turiya	State of pure consciousness similar to *samadhi*.
Upanishad	The concluding portion of the *Vedas* consisting of 108 verses. The *Upanishads* are the texts from which all *Vedanta* philosophy is derived.
Upanishadic rishis	(Lit: *rishi* – seer) Mythological figures who channelled the *Upanishads*.
upasana	(Lit: sitting near) The way or path through which one worships the Divine.
vairagya	Dispassion, detachment, or renunciation from the pains and pleasures in the material world.
vasanas	Emotional and mental tendencies; habits of action, reaction, and desires of the persona or conditional being, which are said to be the product of patterns of living in both this life and past lives.
vasthu	Nature, a surrounding or environment.
Vedanta	A metaphysical philosophy derived from the *Upanishads*.
Vedanta sastra	*Vedic* scriptures.
Vedas	(Lit: knowledge) Four collections of scriptures which were channelled by the *rishis*. The ultimate source of authority for Hindus.
vichara	Search, investigation.
videhamukta	One liberated at the fall of the physical body.
Vishnu	One of the principal Hindu deities worshipped as the protector and preserver of the world.
Vitobha	Representative of Lord *Krishna* and *Vishnu*.
viveka	Discrimination between the permanent and the impermanent.
vrittis	Waves of mental activity.
yoga	(Lit: union) Teaching and practice derived from the ancient *Vedic* philosophy.
yoga sastra	*Yogic* scriptures.
yogi	One who practises *yoga*.

Contact Details

Author's Contact Details

Premananda
Open Sky House
Rheinstr. 54
51371 Hitdorf
(between Cologne and Düsseldorf)
Germany
Phone: +49 2173 4099204
E-mail: office@premanandasatsang.org
Website: www.premanandasatsang.org

Masters' Contact Details

Sri Hans Raj Maharaj
Sacha Dham Ashram
Tapovan Sarai PO
Laxman Jhula, Rishikesh 249192
Tehri Garhwal UT
Phone: +91 135 2433184
E-mail: omguru2001@yahoo.com

Ajja (Puttur Ajja) †
Ananda Kuteera
Village & PO Chikkamudnoor
Kemmai, Puttur 574203 DK Dist.
Karnataka
Phone: +91 8251 237655
E-mail: info@ajja.org.in
Website: www.myajja.org

Ramesh Balsekar
Apartment No. 10 Sindhuli Building
Nawroji Gamadia Road, Off Peddar Road
Mumbai 400 028
Phone: +91 22 23517725
Website: www.rameshbalsekar.com

Sri Brahmam
Bhagavan Sri Ramana Maharshi Asramam
Tadipatri 515 411, Anantapur Dist.
Andrah Pradesh
Phone: +91 8558227234
E-mail: sri@brahmam.net
Website: www.brahmam.net

Swami Dayananda Saraswati
Arsha Vidya Gurukulam
Anaikatti, Coimbatore 641 108
Tamil Nadu
Phone: +91 422 2657001
E-mail: arsha1@vsnl.com
Website: www.arshavidya.in

Ganesan
Ananda Ramana
c/o Sri Ramanasramam PO
Tiruvannamalai 606 603
Tamil Nadu
Phone: +91 4175 237853
E-mail: anandaramana@vsnl.net

D.B. Gangolli †
No contact details

Sri Nannagaru
Sri Nannagaru Ashram
Ramana Maharshi Street No. 2
Rajiv Gandhi Nagar
Chengam Road
Tiruvannamalai 606 603
Phone: +91 4175 235751
Website: www.srinannagaru.com

Swamini Pramananda
Tapasyalayam
Behind Rajarajeshwari Temple
Aham Road, Adiannamalai
Tiruvannamalai 606 604
Tamil Nadu
Phone: +91 4175 235300
swaminipramananda@purnavidya.com
Website: www.purnavidya.org

Radha Ma
Gnaneshwari
Chicken Farm Road
Atiyandhal, Ramanashramam
Tiruvannamalai 606 603
Tamil Nadu
E-mail: radhagiridhar@aol.in
No house visitors please

Samdarshi
House No. 499, P.
Sector 21, Panchkula (Chandigarh)
Phone: +91 871376721
E-mail: samdarshixx@yahoo.com
Website: www.samdarshi.com

Sammasati Dhyan Center
Naggar Road, Budh Ram house
Khakhnal Village (Manali)
VPO Khakhnal 175 143, Kullu Dist.
Himachal Pradesh
Phone: +91 98909 88043

Kiran †
Website: www.kiranji.com

Swami Satchidananda
Anandashram
Anandashram PO
Kanhangad 671 531, Kasaragod Dist.
Kerala
Phone: +91 467 2203036
E-mail: papa@anandashram.org
Website: www.anandashram.org

Ma Souris †
No contact details

Swami Suddhananda
Suddhananda Ashram
Self Knowledge Village
Adiannamalai
Tiruvannamalai 606 604
Tamil Nadu
Phone: +91 4175 233553
E-mail: suddhaji@gmail.com
Website: www.selfknowledge.in

Thuli Baba
Anbin Kudil
253/2 Mettur-Bhavani Main Road
Komboor, Nevinjipettai
Bhavani Taluk 638 311, Erode Dist.
Tamil Nadu
Phone: +91 4256 227655
E-mail: anbinkudil@yahoo.co.in

Sri Ramana Maharshi †
Sri Ramanasramam
Sri Ramanasramam PO
Tiruvannamalai 606 603
Tamil Nadu
Phone: +91 4175 237200
E-mail: ashram@sriramanamaharshi.org
For ordering publications:
bookstall@sriramanamaharshi.org
Website: www.sriramanamaharshi.org

Who am I?